EMPLOYMENT

SECURITY

AND

LABOR

MARKET

FLEXIBILITY

Labor Economics and Policy Series

Editor
John D. Owen
Wayne State University

Series Advisory Board

John T. Addison
University of South Carolina

Morley K. Gunderson
University of Toronto

Günther Schmid
International Institute of Management Science Center, Berlin,
Federal Republic of Germany

Masanori Hashimoto
Ohio State University

Books in this series

EMPLOYMENT

SECURITY

AND

LABOR

MARKET

FLEXIBILITY

An International Perspective

Edited by Kazutoshi Koshiro

Wayne State University Press   Detroit

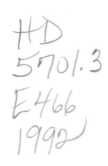

Library of Congress Cataloging-in-Publication Data

Employment security and labor market flexibility : an international
perspective / edited by Kazutoshi Koshiro.
      p.   cm. — (Labor economics and policy series)
   Includes bibliographical references and index.
   ISBN 0-8143-2079-1 (alk. paper)
   1. Labor market—Congresses.   2. Employment (Economic theory)
—Congresses.   3. Job security — Congresses.   4. Full employment
policies—Congresses.
   I. Koshiro, Kazutoshi, 1932–   .
   II. Series
   HD5701.33.E466   1992
   331.12—dc20   91-23307

Designer: Mary Krzewinski

Contents

Acknowledgments

This volume originated from the International Symposium on Employment Security and Labor Market Flexibility in Yokohama, December 9–12, 1986. As an organizer of the symposium, I am grateful for a grant from the Japanese Ministry of Education and for financial support provided by the Labor Problems Research Center, Tokyo. Several graduates of the Faculty of Economics, Yokohama National University, such as Kihachiro Kawashima, Hisashi Nomura, Tatsuo Tamura, Isawo Suzuki, Motoshi Hongyo, Toshio Kawai, and Hirofumi Nakamura also financially supported this symposium. Kayo Adachi, manager of international affairs, Yokohama National University, and her successor, Shunji Wakamatsu, helped to organize it. Without their assistance the symposium would not have materialized. I also appreciate contributions by professors Akira Ono, Humio Otake, Yoko Sano, Yasuo Suwa, Shigeyoshi Tokunaga, Maki Ohmori, Yasuo Kuwahara, Takenori Inoki, Taku Yamamoto, and Tadashi Hanami for their stimulating comments and remarks, which have been incorporated in this book. The final, but not the least, appreciation must be expressed to Professor Alan Griffiths for his generous help in preparing the introduction while he was staying at Yokohama National University as a visiting professor under the Japanese Ministry of Education/British Council scholarship. However, I am solely responsible for the content. I regret the delayed publication of this book, a factor resulting primarily from my appointment as Dean of the Faculty of Economics, YNU, from 1988–90. I do not, however, believe that this delay has detracted from the value of this book.

Kazutoshi Koshiro

Contributors

Richard N. Block
Michigan State University

Oliver Clarke
Social Affairs and Industrial Relations Division, OECD, Paris

Jocelyn F. Gutchess

Masanori Hashimoto
Ohio State University

Kazutoshi Koshiro
Yokohama National University

Yasuhiko Matsuda
Yokohama National University

Asao Mizuno
Chuo University

Tadashi Nakamura
International Labor Organization

John Raisian
Hoover Institution, Stanford University

Atsushi Seike
Keio University

Werner Sengenberger
Institute for Social Research, Munich, and International
Institute for Labour Studies, Geneva

Kazutoshi Koshiro

Introduction

Over the last fifteen years the world's major industrial economies have experienced a period of significant change as new forces converged to challenge prevailing ideas on production and exchange. During this period, most business enterprises began to reconsider their approach to the marketplace and to monitor more rigorously the ways in which they allocated resources. This desire for increased efficiency in both the goods and service industries meant that all the main components of a company's cost structure had to be scrutinized more thoroughly than before with the aim of cost minimization. As a result, it was inevitable that the effective use of both capital and labor resources were to become critical economic issues. These trends had a significant effect on the labor market because, for the average company, wage costs often accounted for a considerable proportion of total costs. Therefore it was logical to assume that ways would have to be found to minimize labor cost pressures by controlling the wage bill while simultaneously making greater efforts to increase labor productivity. To achieve these aims it became important, on both micro and macro levels, to find ways of making the labor market more flexible and to reduce any rigidities that were often seen as endemic to this market.

Kazutoshi Koshiro

Before we scrutinize more closely the various aspects of labor market flexibility and employment stability that constitute the core of this book, it is beneficial to delineate some of the more important factors that have stimulated interest in this area of study over the last decade or so.

First, the oil shocks of the mid and late 1970s provided a common stimulus for most of the industrialized economies to become more cost conscious in order to compensate for high oil prices. This, in turn, led to attempts to improve efficiency not only in the management of raw materials but also in the management of labor. This shift toward cost saving was particularly relevant to Japan since she relied almost exclusively on imported oil and had experienced a rise in labor costs of over 30% after the first oil shock alone. Second, the increasing activities of multinational companies and the internationalization of production brought with it the winds of intense competition. Production of goods and services were no longer the prisoners of national boundaries, but were bound up with the strategies of multinational companies operating outside their country of origin. This sort of competition with its accent on outsourcing in low-cost countries has created serious competitive problems for many major economies and has forced indigenous industries to rethink cost strategies in order to survive. Such strategies have included important attempts to reduce labor costs and to increase labor flexibility.

Third, the major economic downturn of the early 1980s witnessed an acceleration of structural change as many industrialized countries experienced a relative decrease in their manufacturing base and a growth in service industries. The growth of unemployment as a result of the recession coupled with a change in the distribution of those in employment has had fundamental repercussions on the fluidity of the labor market. For example, the growth of unemployment altered the balance of power within the workplace and resulted in the weakening of labor unions while, at the same time, the changing structure of many economies often meant a contraction of the very industries that used to be the bastions of union strength. Structural change has also had important effects on the location of work and the nature of occupations, thus having implications for labor mobility and job type.

Fourth, the rapid change in production technology as evidenced by the growth of robotics combined with the increasing importance of information technology has changed fundamentally the nature of workplace organization. Greater stress has been placed on redesigning factory layouts and on redefining job specifications and job content. It is critical to understand that technological change has affected the service industry as well as manufacturing, so that its effect on the labor market is all pervasive. Finally, it is also worth noting that in most industrialized countries many of the factors noted above have affected, and been affected by, important shifts in ideology. To various degrees the governments of these countries have embraced more enthusiastically the philosophy of the marketplace and its increasing stress on freeing markets from any inherent rigidities. It therefore comes as no surprise that the selling of state assets as witnessed by the privatization movement, in Europe and Japan in particular, have had important effects on the once dominant public sector unions and thus on the labor market of such economies.

From the general points made above it can be seen clearly that nations wishing to experience long-term growth and improved competitiveness need to take a closer look at the efficiency of their labor markets. In this respect, the rapidly changing nature of international competition over the last decade has provided a suitable scenario for taking a more detailed look at the efficiency and flexibility of such markets. However, it should be borne in mind that the labor market cannot be treated in the same way as other markets because it deals directly with human beings who are less likely to obey the immutable laws of the market mechanism. Nevertheless, it is still important to build a framework on which to understand and assess the role of labor flexibility in the competitive process, and it is with this framework in mind that the following chapters have been assembled into one volume. Therefore, the main aim of this volume is to bring together various themes relating to labor market flexibility and employment security in an attempt to clarify some of the underlying problems in this important area.

In the simple classical sense, the labor market is seen, like any other market, as the meeting point of various forces affecting both the demand for, and supply of, labor. Therefore, labor flexibility can be seen as the degree to which the labor market responds to shocks from both demand and supply sides with particular reference to the distribution of the adjustment burden between wage changes on the one side and employment changes on the other. In other words, the question is whether the labor market is cleared mainly through rapid changes in wages or whether wages are relatively rigid, thus placing the burden of adjustment on employment. In any case, the simple market clearing model can work only if there are few rigidities in the labor supply function in particular, but in the real world such rigidities abound because of the complexities of the labor market. Labor flexibility is therefore often seen by many economists in purely economic terms as an essential ingredient for ensuring the workings of a perfect market while others see labor flexibility in its socioeconomic context as the ability of individuals to abandon established ways and adapt to new circumstances.[1]

The aim of this book is to scrutinize and comment on the main issues that affect labor market flexibility and job security in the main industrialized economies of the United States, Japan, and Europe in an attempt to more fully understand the complex forces at work within such labor markets. However, before providing a brief synopsis of the chapters, it is beneficial to bear some important things in mind. First, the whole issue of labor flexibility is multidimensional. From a purely macroeconomic standpoint, the problem revolves around the sensitivity of nominal and real wages to changes in aggregate demand and supply shocks, while on the microeconomic level it concerns the flexibility of relative wages between industries and between occupations. These two aspects may be seen to concentrate on labor markets that are basically external to the company. On the other hand, the concept of labor flexibility has an enterprise-level component that covers both the numerical and functional aspects of corporate labor policy. In this context, numerical flexibility refers to the ability of companies to adjust levels of work or hours in line with changes in the demand for goods and services and involves such aspects as the growth of part-time and temporary working. Functional flexibility, on the other hand, relates to the ability of companies to improve their operating efficiency by reorganizing the methods of production and labor content in order to keep pace with changing technological needs. This aspect covers such areas as multiskilling, decreases in job demarcations, and increased employee involvement. Furthermore, it is worth bearing in mind that functional flexibility may not always be "technology led" as noted above, but may also depend heavily on the ability of companies to vary their product mix in accordance with the changing demand in the product market. In turn, this ability to improve the functional effectiveness of labor as a result of stimuli from the demand side depends on the organizational adaptability and technological know-how of management.

Many of the aspects of labor flexibility and labor adjustments explained above can be aggregated from economic data and tested with a range of statistical techniques in an attempt to obtain a measure of the relative flexibility of labor in different countries. However, it is at this point that pure statistical analysis remains incomplete because it must be understood that statistics reflect the *result* of certain processes that have already occurred and do not automatically say much about the *process* itself. Therefore, there is a need for another dimension within the field of labor flexibility to complement the more aggregative studies. This, of course, provides scope for studies based on the institutional side of the labor market, which cover areas such as the historical aspect of union development and the institutional arrangements for bargaining. Similarly the problems involved with employment stability cover the whole range of disciplines from considerations of cultural norms to the roles of governments and the development of legal frameworks. Finally, it is worth noting that the whole concept of labor flexibility must not necessarily be seen as a one way phenomenon, in other words, that increased flexibility is a priori, a good thing. Rapid labor turnover, increased mobility, weak labor unions, and poorly developed social policies may improve labor flexibility but at the cost of weakening job security. The growth of insecurity in such a labor market may not necessarily create a more efficient labor force nor improve social stability. What is needed is a judicious blend of policies that can improve flexibility without too high a cost in terms of employment security and social stability.

In the context of this brief introduction, it is relevant to note that the various chapters comprising this book have been compiled with the dual aim of providing comparative material on the labor markets of different countries while at the same time retaining a balance between the statistical analysis of labor flexibility and employment adjustments, on the one hand, and the institutional frameworks underlying such labor markets, on the other. The origin of the work emanates from an international symposium on labor flexibility and employment security held in Yokohama in the winter of 1986 in which half the participants took a more aggregative view of the subject area while the other had concentrated on the institutional underpinnings of the labor market. One of the themes that emerged from these comparative studies was the extent to which labor markets have tended to become more similar over the past decade, and, in particular, the degree to which the major labor markets of the world have converged toward the Japanese system of "flexible rigidities" as eloquently described by Ronald Dore. Another strong theme that emerged from these studies was an attempt to provide a critique of the straightforward and simplistic view that sees labor market flexibility as being a good thing, per se, without any apparent costs involved during the process of change.

Before summarizing the findings of the symposium it might be useful to say a few words about recent work that has been done in the field of labor flexibility in order to place this volume in a more meaningful perspective. For example, the straightforward advocacy of labor market flexibility has been criticized in a volume edited by W. Beckerman (1986). This work tends to advocate the search for a more realistic way of achieving economic efficiency and effective economic restructuring, which does not depend on a crude view that labor is merely another factor of production and should be treated as such. In the Beckerman volume, F. H. Hahn and R. M. Solow question the widespread assumption that wage flexibility is, necessarily, a good thing. They remind us of Keynes's view that wage decreases may have a depressing effect on an economy and that a policy of stable wages, with prices gently falling as productivity improves, is the best macroeconomic environment. Another volume that is, in a sense, complementary to our study is that edited by P. T. Chinloy and E. Stromsdorfer (1987). Essentially, this is an international comparison of labor market adjustments resulting from exogenous shocks to the economies of four countries (Canada, Japan, Mexico, and the United States). Although somewhat more mathematically based than our volume, it pays serious attention to the need to understand the different institutional arrangements within labor markets, and the importance of internal labor markets in particular, before making bland comments on the role of labor flexibility in the competitive process.

Finally, three recent books, based on the work of international organizations seem to have come close to our view of the problem of labor market flexibility and employment stability. The book edited by H. Sarfati and C. Kobrin (1988), and based on the work of the International Labour Organization, studies the different forms of labor market flexibility in Western countries from an industrial relations perspective. The work analyzes the different forms of labor flexibility across Western countries and shows a convergence in these counties toward such features as performance related pay, increased skill versatility, and the weakening of employment stability. Many of these themes are echoed in our volume but with some qualitative caveats as shown below. A second work of note is that edited by R. Boyer (1986), which incorporates studies by the European Federation for Economic Research (FERE). The book compares the economic performance of European countries with that of the United States and Japan since the 1960s and relates this to the emergence of new patterns of wage/labor relations and changing regulatory systems. Basically, the book stresses that important modifications are occurring to the system and rules of industrial relations right across national boundaries. These adjustments appear to be in response to changing methods of production, especially at the shop-floor level and the authors believe that this transition is succeeding the previous important shift in the labor scene from "Taylorism" to "Fordism." A third book, edited by Robert Hart (1988), contains both theoretical and empirical studies on international comparisons of labor market adjustments. Its main focus is on the relationship between adjustments in employment and unemployment, on the one hand, and in hours of work wages, on the other. The primary motivation for this book is to assess the much discussed reduction of the workweek to alleviate high unemployment rates in some European countries. The studies contained in this book cover such countries as West Germany, France, Japan, the Netherlands, Norway, the United Kingdom, and the United States.

With these new ideas on the labor market in mind, we now summarize the work of the various contributors to this volume in an attempt to

16

contribute in some positive way to the ever increasing academic literature on the subjects of labor flexibility and employment security.

Chapter Profiles

Chapter 1, written by Tadashi Nakamura, provides an interesting guide to the development of manpower policy in Japan since the Second World War and helps to bring out the Japanese government's pragmatic approach to manpower policy during this period. The difficulties of the immediate postwar era were followed by efforts at indicative planning after 1955 that, in turn, brought labor legislation devised to cover unemployment insurance, employment security, and vocational training. In contrast, Japan reached a rapid growth stage after 1965, and out of the tight labor market came policies designed to improve mobility, job transfer, and lifelong training initiatives. The oil shock of the early 1970s affected Japan severely, and the whole emphasis of manpower policy shifted toward maintaining employment and containing any serious labor displacement that might have occurred. Finally, by the middle of the 1980s, the challenges came from decelerating economic growth coupled with new technological change. Once again manpower policies were designed to meet the new situation with efforts made to solve the problems of labor mismatch and an aging work force by introducing dispatching services and retraining initiatives. Throughout the period, we are given a picture of a pragmatic government committed to the challenges of the time while emphasizing its long-term commitment to employment stability and continuous retraining.

Chapter 2, by Kazutoshi Koshiro, the editor of this volume, studies the flexibility of wages in Japan with particular reference to the relations between bonus payments and profit performance, which has been seen by many Western economists as the key to wage flexibility in Japan. The conclusions of the study tend to confirm the assumption made above, that for the core of Japanese industry both the level of bonuses and the rate of increase of such bonuses are, in fact, sensitive to changes in profits per employee although the magnitude of the response may not be as high as is usually assumed. The study also found that bonuses were more responsive than basic wages to corporate profit and that bonuses may, indeed, be seen as a form of profit-sharing activity. However, the finding that bonus payments have a degree of downward rigidity on a year-by-year basis should serve to warn observers that the bonus system is not purely profit based and that in many ways it is seen by Japanese workers as an expected part of their overall income. This point is borne out by the author's preliminary survey

17

of bonus behavior at the level of the firm where the simple bonus/profit relationship becomes much more complicated. On a macroeconomic level, the chapter also attempts to resolve the dilemma that despite the apparent relative flexibility of the Japanese wage system noted above, it could not prevent the economy experiencing a profit squeeze. Also, real wages in Japan seem to have grown faster than the "warranted" rate of growth (the sum of the growth of national labor productivity and changes in the terms of trade). The author believes that to reconcile these views it is necessary to have a much closer look at factors such as the magnitudes of the elasticity responses, the size distribution of companies, and the complicated relationship between wages, productivity, and resource allocation.

The third chapter, by Masanori Hashimoto and John Raisian, provides an additional insight into their previous important work on labor market flexibility in its international setting. Their chapter is a weave of two main themes. They compare the relative flexibility of compensation and employment over the business cycle in the United States with that of Japan, and they combine this analysis with their ideas on "transaction costs" and "firm-specific" human capital. They conclude that the cyclical rigidity of real compensation and the volatility of employment is greater in the United States than in Japan. In other words, employment adjustments tend to be greater over the cycle in the United States, while real compensation or labor cost adjustments tend to dampen employment variability in Japan. However, they also point out that Japan is not necessarily unique in having wage-type flexibility and that, likewise, the United States is not the only economy with high employment flexibility. For them, Japanese industry is characterized by low "transaction costs,"whereby the costs associated with information exchanges within companies (such as employer/employee haggling or disagreements) are minimized. This, in turn, encourages a form of commitment to "firm-specific" human capital investment by both managers and workers that further helps to decrease transaction costs by "fixing" labor to the enterprise. They therefore see the firm-specific nature of human capital investment in Japan as explaining, to a large degree, the lower cyclical variability of employment and the relatively greater flexibility of wages in that country. The bonus system, therefore, contains a return to this firm-specific human capital investment. The authors end their analysis with a warning that the lower cyclical variability of wages in the United States may have been exaggerated by the distribution of wages over the cycle but that it does not alter their basic conclusions to any significant extent.

The fourth chapter provides a suitable setting for the first half of the book with an interesting analysis by Asao Mizuno of the relative flexibility of Japanese wages. Using coefficient of variation analysis, he explains that between 1974 and 1983 wage flexibility in Japan was relatively more sensitive (and employment less sensitive) to changes in nominal output than in other major economies. He therefore suggests that one of the main reasons for Japanese wage flexibility after 1973 may be the greater economic fluctuations that Japan experienced following the oil crisis. On the question of wage flexibility, Mizuno analyzes both total wages and its components, the regular wage and the special wage (which is basically the bonus payment), in an attempt to disentangle the forces at work in the flexibility process. He finds that total wages are more sensitive to changing labor market conditions in Japan than in European or North American countries. Within Japan, he deduces that the regular wage component is chiefly determined by consumer prices and labor market conditions, while special wages tend to be closely related to changes in profit rate. Finally, the author feels that because there is such a close association between the annual percentage increase in average wages and the movement of nominal economic growth across countries that it may be Japan's response to stimuli such as economic growth and fluctuations rather than some particular feature like the existence of bonuses that help explain Japan's relatively high degree of wage flexibility. The quantitative contribution of special wage payments such as bonuses to the variability of total wages is seen to be as low as 16% or less.

In the next three chapters, the scene shifts somewhat to the employment security aspects of the labor market and looks in detail at the legal and institutional framework on which employment relationships are based. In chapter 5, Richard Block begins to unravel some of the underlying forces that comprise the employment security situation in the United States. He stresses the importance of cultural norms that determine employment relationships. For example, the stress is placed on the legal individuality of the company or corporate body, with employment relationships dominated by strong "property rights" of management. Also, the belief in the primacy of the market and consumer sovereignty coupled with a noninterventionist government tended to further erode the employment security aspect of the labor market so that labor unions found it difficult to obtain formal employment guarantees. Even in the 1980s, when international competition was intense, labor had to accept wage reductions in the *hope* that it would lead to more employment security. In fact, there were no major collective agreements in the United States that would prohibit plant closure as a means of providing job security. In other words, employment security practices existed if employers *allowed* them to exist, as in the case of IBM or Hewlett Packard, and much of this was achieved through labor segmentation. "Core," or permanent, workers were allowed a measure of employment security but workers on the "periphery," such as those on temporary or part-time contracts, had little employment security. Government intervention in this area has been small, and, even in the 1980s, the U.S. government has not felt it necessary to make advance notice of work closure mandatory on a national level. In many ways, the U.S. government has been more active in the labor market in trying to help disadvantaged workers after they have suffered at the hands of the labor market rather than it has been involved before the problems have arisen.

In chapter 6, Werner Sengenberger, in his comparative study of employment security, looks at the important relationship between economic conditions and the labor market and explains the difference between the employment protection legislation of the United States, on the one hand, and Europe and Japan, on the other. He shows how work security was originally established through the development of systems such as job demarcation, seniority rules, and early notice requirements and how these systems of employment security have changed. Since the 1970s, for example, stress has been placed on the development of worker mobility beyond the barrier of jobs or enterprises in order to help maintain employment security. Sengenberger also describes the interrelationships between employment security based on contractual norms and those based on the mutual exchange of information and adjustments made between employer and employee. In statistical terms, he explains how employment adjustment varies with changes in output and shows how the low degree of adjustment in Japan, France, and Italy and the high degree of adjustment in the United States and Canada are linked to the stabilization policies of these countries. Interestingly, he suggests that, since employment stability and productivity are closely related, it could be beneficial for countries to minimize labor turnover and unemployment. Finally, the chapter ends with a discussion of the winners and losers on the employment security scene in terms of various types of labor segmentation. He stresses that the most important institutional prerequisite for such segmentation is the degree of centrality and uniformity in the terms of employment. When terms of employment are more uniform, as in European countries, it is more difficult to adjust to low labor cost strategies but, as he points out, this has not prevented the move toward the "core" and "periphery" models of the labor market. In his chapter, he notes that low wages should not be seen as a substitute for the development of new product strategies by management as a means of maintaining or increasing employment.

Chapter 7, by Yasuhiko Matsuda, provides an illuminating insight into the Japanese attitude toward employment security from a legal perspective. It makes it clear that although an employer has the right to terminate a worker's contract under Article 627 of the Japanese civil code it is also true that other labor laws promulgated after the Second World War make this a difficult article to operate. Employment was also made more secure by the tendency of Japanese employment contracts to follow certain "rules of employment" whereby discharges in violation of these rules are invalid. After the war, the Japanese courts developed a general theory of legal restriction on employers who wanted to discharge employees. The courts felt compelled to take high inflation and insecure employment conditions into consideration when assessing the validity of a dismissal application. Also, employees began using the injunction or provisionary disposition order to temporarily block an employer's attempt to discharge them. Interestingly, the granting of such an order gave the signal to the employer that the court would uphold the employee's plea of illegal discharge. However, since the order could not be enforced unless the employer voluntarily complied with it, there was a tendency for more effective communication between employer and employee to take place.

The chapter also comments on the more recent situation in Japan where the growth of the labor "periphery" has led to the shortening of contracts and the replacement of contracts for an indefinite period with ones for a limited time period. The complication here is to find out whether a series of short-time contracts is equivalent in law to a long-term one that, by definition, gives more employment protection. The Japanese courts once again followed the path of pragmatism and found in favor of temporary workers during downswings and being less lenient during buoyant economic conditions. The picture of discharge in this context seems a far cry from the case of the United States, although, in the future it will be interesting, as Matsuda points out, to look more closely at how the Japanese courts will deal with dismissals for purely business reasons following the appreciation of the yen. It is not difficult to realize that the courts' attitude on discharge and employment protection has also been a reflection of the high value placed on harmonious relations within the Japanese business unit after the Second World War.

Jocelyn Gutchess's work in chapter 8 takes a more detailed view of the various types of employment adjustment methods utilized by major economies, with special attention to the United States and Europe. This chapter is, in essence, an admirable summary of her previous book *Full Employment in Action*, and draws the strong distinction between defensive, containment, and positive strategies toward employment adjustment. Defensive strategies involve methods of preventing layoffs, such as worksharing, redeployment, retraining, buffer techniques, and advance warning systems. On the other hand, containment policies revolve around such variables as job search, early retirement, and employee buyouts, while positive policies are seen to depend on macroeconomic policy and retraining. The crux of the analysis involves the ways in which different countries approach these critical problems, with particular reference to the varying balance of government/private sector initiatives in areas such as advanced warning of job losses, job search activity, and retirement plans, for example. When she discusses the positive adjustment approach, Gutchess points out the varying degree to which governments in Europe and the United States accept responsibility for such a policy. The chapter provides a wealth of detailed case studies relating to employment adjustment and explains that employment security, while incurring some costs to companies, should not be thought of in negative terms only. The *absence* of employment security is also seen as a problem, and the challenge of the future will be to improve policies toward employment security without creating an unacceptable degree of labor inflexibility.

Oliver Clarke, in the penultimate chapter of this book, provides a clear framework on which to compare the nature of labor markets and employment adjustment techniques in the United States, Europe, and Japan. He compares employment relationships in those countries with special reference to concepts such as lifetime employment, payment systems, industrial structure, and internal/external aspects of labor market behavior. He finds that the European model lies somewhere between that of the United States and Japan. For example, he notes that employment adjustment in Europe is not as flexible as in Japan but not as inexpensive to the employers as in the United States. He feels that employment adjustments in the United States are dominated by plant shutdowns, large-scale shifts of corporate resources, limited communication between employer and employee, and a burden of adjustment that is mainly borne by youths and newcomers. In Japan, plant shutdowns and large corporate shifts are not so dominant, communication systems are good, and the burden of adjustment is shared by young and old alike. In Europe, the use of rapid plant shutdowns to adjust employment is less prevalent than the United States and the cost of adjustment is more likely to be shared by the state, as in Japan; communication systems are better than in the United States but not as effective as in Japan; while the burden of adjustment in the past was more similar to that in the United States than to that in Japan. Similar comparisons are made for the speed of labor adjustment and its cost to the economies concerned. Finally, it is important to note that the chapter also contains analyses of the various components of labor flexibility and of the difference between the countries noted above in terms of the numerical and functional flexibility of their labor markets.

The final chapter of this book, written by Atsushi Seike, compares the pattern of employment adjustment in Japan and the United States. In general, he finds that the elasticity of employment with respect to production is lower in Japan than in the United and that the lag between any given production fluctuation and the employment fluctuation associated with it is longer in Japan than in the United States. He suggests that the cause of longer lagged response and smaller employment elasticity in Japan seems to be linked to greater flexibility in the number of hours worked in the Japanese manufacturing industry. He explains that the degree of employment adjustment depends on the costs of such adjustments to the company and that this in turn depends on the nature of employment contracts, the degree of "firm-specific" human capital, and the nature of transaction costs. Since it is difficult to directly quantify these factors, Seike measures these costs indirectly by calculating the degree to which firms can clear all their excess labor rapidly. This employment adjustment ratio, or v, is high if the labor adjustment is smooth and the cost of the adjustment is therefore small. A low v signifies the reverse situation. Briefly, his conclusions are that v is lower in Japan than in the United States, indicating a less complete and more costly employment adjustment in Japan. The low v for Japan is linked to the reallocation of employment between subsidiaries, which is a feature of the Japanese labor adjustment process. However, the picture is clouded by the fact that the rapid layoffs in the United States may need to be subsidized by the state, while the fact that internal labor markets are so deep in Japan may mean that the Japanese look more to retraining to solve the employment dilemma. The latter approach may be expensive but may still be more efficient than paying unemployment benefits to displaced workers. In other words, the Japanese system, intrinsically geared as it is to unemployment prevention, may be better than the system in the United States that is geared to coping with the unemployment created after a period during which companies have adjusted employment too rapidly.

Conclusions

At this stage it is beneficial to summarize some of the most important aspects relating to the subject of labor market flexibility and employment stability, bringing together the ideas represented in this book with other works on the subject. First, it seems that real wage rigidity does vary across national boundaries from low levels of rigidity in Japan to high levels in the European economies such as the United Kingdom and Germany.[2] Also, there appears to be a measure of consensus that the relationship between real wages and employment is a negative one,[3] although it is worth noting that other factors, such as, macroeconomic demand policies and interest rate movements, are also important in influencing employment trends. The chapters by Hashimoto and Raisian, Mizuno, and Seike confirm that, in Japan, wages and real compensation were generally more sensitive than employment to changes in output but that Japan was not necessarily unique in having wage-type flexibility.

Koshiro's study, while showing that bonuses in Japan were flexible, also points to the underlying rigidity of these payments in a downward direction. He stresses that despite the apparent flexibility of wages in the core sector of the economy, real wages at the aggregate level since 1970 still exceed the growth rate of national productivity. This should be further investigated since an Organization for Economic Cooperation and Development (OECD) survey found that, at the industry level, the sensitivity of wages to productivity changes was *greater* in the United States than in Japan. In particular, it was found that in Japan relative wages at this level were more strongly related to *increases* in productivity rather than to *decreases* in productivity. This may mean that industries and sectors in Japan whose productivity falls relatively may not necessarily find that relative wages fall to the same extent.[4] The points noted above indicate that more work needs to be carried out on the relationships between wage flexibility, productivity, and employment on the sectoral as well as the national level.

Although wage flexibility constitutes one of the major themes of this book it is important to mention two other aspects of labor market flexibility that underlie most of the chapters on employment adjustment and job security—numerical flexibility and functional flexibility. Numerical flexibility, or the ability of companies to adjust levels of work or hours in line with changes in the demand for goods and services, is a very important attribute for any economy. The Japanese economy's "core" of regular workers and "periphery" of temporary and part-time workers have been important numerical-flexibility factors, furthering labor adjustment and cost minimization. However, on a statistical level it appears that many other economies have moved rapidly in this direction since the mid-1970s.

Table 1 shows the growth of part-time employment over a range of economies, indicating that labor segmentation has taken place across the board. However, as Sengenberger explains, labor segmentation occurs not only through the use of core and periphery workers but also intercompany wise (i.e., by distancing or subcontracting). Although this phenomenon is on the increase in the United States and Europe it may not become as effective as it has been in Japan, because its efficient working requires a commitment

24

TABLE 1

FULL- AND PART-TIME EMPLOYMENT GROWTH IN SELECTED OECD COUNTRIES[a]

	Average annual percentage growth				Share of part-time employment in total employment 1985 (percent)
	1973/79[b]		1979/85[b]		
	Full-time	Part-time	Full-time	Part-time	
United States	2.4	3.4	1.2	2.4	17.4
Japan	0.5	2.5	0.8	2.1	16.5
Germany	0.6	1.7	1.1	1.1	12.0
France	0.4	2.9	0.6	3.2	11.0
United Kingdom	0.4	1.0	1.2	5.0	21.2
Italy	1.9	1.5	0.4	2.9	5.3
Canada	2.7	4.2	0.8	5.1	15.5
Austria	1.6	4.8	0.2	2.2	8.3
Belgium	0.3	8.0	0.6	2.7	8.6
Denmark	1.7	4.0	0.2	2.2	24.3
Finland	0.3	0.4	1.0	5.1	8.4
Ireland	2.8	4.2	1.1	2.1	6.5
Luxembourg	0.1	0.0	0.4	1.7	7.3
Netherlands	0.4	5.1	1.3	5.9	23.5
Norway	1.0	6.2	0.8	1.9	28.6
Sweden	0.1	6.3	0.4	0.7	24.5
Australia	0.4	8.3	1.1	4.0	18.0
New Zealand	1.5	5.7	0.7	4.0	15.6
Total of European counties above	0.5	2.0	0.1	3.1	13.7
North America	2.4	3.4	1.1	2.6	17.2
Total of above countries	1.1	2.8	0.6	2.7	15.7

Source: OECD Economic Outlook, vol. 41, June 1987, Table 21, p. 32.

[a] The definition of part-time work is not consistent across countries. See OECD *Employment Outlook*, September 1985. Note A of the Technical Annex for details on the definitions and Table 10 for the sources of the data. The U.S. definiton is based on the concept of "usual" activity status. Except for the Netherlands, estimates include the self-employed; agriculture is therefore included. (In *Employment Outlook*, the Japanese data exclude agriculture.)

[b] Due to nonavailability of data or breaks in series, the time periods differ as follows: Australia 1973–77; Denmark, Norway, Ireland all 1975–79; Finland 1976–79; Austria 1979–83; Netherlands 1981–85; other EEC countries average of 1979–81 and 1983–85, except Ireland (1980–81) for the former period.

to information exchange and a degree of production flexibility and attention to inventory economies that is hard to find in other economies.

Functional flexibility, which relates to the ability of companies to improve their operating efficiency by reorganizing production and jobs to meet changing technical needs, has been Japan's strong point. The internal labor market structure of large companies with their high commitment to training has been able to meet the vital needs of changing world demand. Other major economies are, nevertheless, in the process of developing such attributes by introducing multiskilling and attempting to decrease the extent of job demarcation. For example, the United Kingdom, whose labor market has been regarded as particularly rigid, has shown increasing signs of greater functional flexibility.[5] However, the picture is not always clear because even in Japan it is not always possible to rely totally on the internal market to provide the necessary flexibility. This has been shown in particular during the financial services and research oriented boom of the late 1980s when Japanese companies had to rely increasingly on the external market for appropriate skills.

Many of the factors that affect the flexibility issues explained above come from a combination of cultural norms and institutional arrangements explained in many of the chapters of this book. In this sense, labor market movements must reflect, in part, the differences in these particular qualities. The role of government is a typical case in point. The pragmatic rather than ideological nature of the Japanese government's approach is explained by Nakamura and Matsuda while Block and Seike explain the basic difference between a country like the United States, whose government feels more at home in helping workers *after* they have been disadvantaged by unemployment rather than combining with industry to prevent redundancies in the first place. Sengenberger believes that structural change need not always be borne by private industry and that the burden could be "socialized" to some extent by the state as in Japan and in European countries who are more involved in job search and the like. One of the main differences between the labor policies in the major countries lies in their attitude toward human capital, and it is here that effort needs to be placed in the future. Employment adjustment that are too rapid and that rely on the external market to a large extent, as in the United States, may not necessarily be the best in the long run as compared to the slower adjustment and low transaction costs model prevalent in Japan.

One of the most important themes that will need attention over the next decade is the management of change, and, as Clarke and Gutchess point out, it will become even more important for management to accept a much more positive role as an efficient and humane user of labor. The most crucial feature of this change will be the movement from a model where "property rights" are the prerogative of management to a model where both management and labor see their mutual "property rights" converging in the enterprise. Since World War II, Japanese company managers have often reacted to economic recessions by developing the product side of their business to maintain output and employment, whereas European countries and the United States have tended to look for short-term cost decreases by shedding labor. Japanese companies *do* shed labor, as shown so clearly in the work of Koike,[6] but the key lies in the degree to which this is allowed to occur and the weight given to employment security within management circles.

What, then, remains of the question of convergence? Are economies and, in particular, labor markets showing signs of moving toward a common industrial format as a result of world economic pressures? Are Western economies following the Japanese employment "model" or is the reverse occurring? At this level we will not address the vital questions relating to the validity of certain assumptions made by Western observers about the Japanese labor market, but will merely make some more general comments.

The material presented in these chapters appears to point in the direction of partial convergence but with the caveat that it is difficult to see major *qualitative* change occurring in the near future. We have seen that, on a statistical level, labor market segmentation into a "core" and "periphery" model is continuing at a rapid pace in many countries and that job demarcations are becoming more blurred. Similarly, many Western countries seem to be moving toward a Japanese-type system by resorting to more intensive use of subcontracting in order to increase flexibility. It is also obvious that companies such as IBM and Hewlett Packard *are* able to address problems of job security in just as constructive a way as their large Japanese counterparts. The rapid structural change experienced by Japan in recent years has placed great stress on the Japanese "employment retention" model. However the reaction of such firms has been, only in part, to increase redundancies since the main thrust has again been placed on the product market side as firms diversify rapidly into new areas to take advantage of the opportunities provided by the process of change.

Table 2 provides some idea of the nature and speed of diversification in Japanese industry and shows the changes that have taken place in the product range of a number of Japanese companies located in different sectors of the economy. The contraction of mature sectors such as shipbuilding in the heavy machinery industry and even cameras in the precision instruments industry have led firms to diversify into the products based on infrastructure and environmental needs or to the products of new technology such as

27

TABLE 2
DIVERSIFICATION OF BUSINESS ACTIVITIES OUTSIDE OF TRADITIONAL
PRODUCT MARKETS IN SELECTED COMPANIES IN JAPAN IN PERCENTS

Company and Product	1965	1975	1985	1986
Company A (heavy machinery)				
General machinery	80.2	46.7	45.3	46.5
Standard machinery	—	17.5	34.8	26.0
Ships and maritime	—	35.8	19.8	27.5
Mass-production products	17.7	—	—	—
Company B (chemicals and textiles)				
Plastics (including synthetic rubber)	7.4	8.7	31.5	28.1
Textiles	68.3	58.8	27.6	27.1
Housing	0.0	6.2	19.9	23.8
Other chemicals	17.1	23.3	17.5	17.0
Company C (steel)				
Steel products	n.a.	90.7	87.2	87.6[a]
Engineering	n.a.	5.9	9.9	10.3
Chemical and other products	n.a.	0.9	1.6	1.3
Company D (Plant 'Y') (heavy machinery)				
Incinerator and other environmental equipments	8.4	14.1	21.3	37.2
Iron works and bridges	9.2	17.0	25.9	28.8
Turbines and boilers	21.9	27.3	28.1	25.5
Shipbuilding (until 1980) and repairing	60.5	42.8	14.6	6.6
Company E (auto parts)				
Industrial rubber	—	—	40.9	39.3
Oil seals	71.2	58.6	25.5	24.7
Electronics	—	—	12.7	15.4
Company F (precision instruments)				
Cameras	60.8	66.6	49.2	53.7
Semiconductors	0.0	0.0	18.7	15.7
Glasses and lens	7.5	16.2	11.1	11.2

Source: Kazutoshi Koshiro, ed., *A Survey of Corporate Measures to Meet Structural Adjustments*, Tokyo: Koyo Shokugyo Sougo Kenkyujo (Institute of Employment and Occupation) March 1988, p. 19.

[a] This company will reduce the share of steel products in the total amount of sales to 50% by 1995, whereas the remaining half of its sales will be achieved in electronics, information, telecommunication, biochemicals, engineering, and the like.

semiconductors and electronics. Concrete examples of the diversification process can be seen in the case of Japan Steel Corporation, which is shifting its resources toward electronics, high value added goods, and consumer products. Its present goal is the expansion of nonsteel revenues to 50% of total sales by the year 1995. Similarly, Ishikawajima Harima Industries is planning to build theme parks and entertainment complexes, and Japan Tobacco is using some of its biotechnology knowledge in such unlikely areas as the growing of mushrooms to meet increased consumption demand.

Many of these firms have had to lay off labor because of these structural changes, but the worst effects of employment loss have been limited by positive attempts to meet the needs of a changing market. The fact that Japanese firms do not have the same pressures to follow shareholders' wishes to provide short-term returns may also have helped to maintain human capital as intact as possible under such difficult circumstances. To converge on the Japanese labor model, Western companies will have to place just as much effort into developing market strategies as on defensive labor cost minimization strategies.

There are many aspects of labor market flexibility and employment security that will not be amenable to convergence. For example, the use of early retirement to ease labor market adjustment while being more acceptable in European countries may, however, be regarded as close to labor market discrimination in the United States, as pointed out by Gutchess. Also the role of government in the process of change differs widely between the United States, Europe, and Japan, and this may be critical at certain points in economic development. In this respect, one of vital differences between the countries studied in this volume revolves around the subject of information networks. The whole flow of information systems between government and industry, and between various sectors of industry, provides one of the critical differences between Japan, the United States, and European countries. Information is at the base of the Japanese industrial pyramid and it is this fact that often helps to determine the nation's competitive power. However, these information networks are embedded in a large economy that has few natural resources, has a commitment to investment and output growth, and continues to show a "crisis" type of mentality about its future. It will be difficult for Western economies to achieve such a combination of features. True convergence involves a qualitative package of changes as well as mere trends that appear from generalized statistics to be moving in a common direction. For example, we have seen an undoubted trend toward increased use of subcontracting in many Western countries, but this is not the same thing as saying that their use is becoming similar to the Japanese system of subcontracting, where, for many complex reasons, a greater symbiotic-type

Kazutoshi Koshiro

relationship still exists between larger and smaller subcontracting firms than in many other countries.

Finally it should be remembered that global competition is here to stay so that an economy like Japan's will have to modify its past policies to survive the pressures from nations on the pacific "rim" as well as the United States and Europe. This will depend on the judicious blend of macroeconomic policy coupled with overall commitment to change. If these are to be the main ingredients of success, then Japan may still have the edge, and other countries may have to realize that labor flexibility in Japan is imbedded in a *system* geared to change.

Notes

1. For a more extended view of the socioeconomic aspects of labor flexibility see *Labour Market Flexibility; Report by a High Level Group of Experts to the Secretary General* (OECD May 1986) the so called "Dahrendorf Report."
2. Two publications in the *OECD Economic Studies* series that have studied wage rigidity in depth are D. Coe's analysis in Autumn 1985 on "Nominal Wages, the NAIRU and Wage Flexibility" and F. Klau and A. Mittlestadt in the Spring 1986 issue entitled "Labour Market Flexibility." Coe's analysis of short- and long-term real wage rigidity measures the total increase in the unemployment rate that would be necessary to offset the inflationary consequences of a real shock that results in a new real wage. Such shocks could originate from a fall in productivity or changes in the terms of trade. For Klau and Mittlestadt the shocks to the economy originate from the oil crises and they trace the short-run impact of unemployment in restraining nominal wage growth in the periods of inflation following the shocks.
3. For a brief summary of the relationships between real wages and employment see the OECD *Employment Outlook* September 1985 and the OECD 1986 report entitled *Flexibility in the Labour Market; The Current Debate*, pp. 10–13.
4. The relationship between wage changes, value productivity, and employment on a sectorial level is discussed in the OECD 1986 report on labor flexibility (see note 3, above) pp. 30–32.
5. For example, see the survey on multiskilling in the United Kingdom in Michael Cross, *The Costs and Benefits of Multiskilling*, published by the Technical Change Centre, London, 1986. In the work he finds that multiskilling often cuts maintenance costs by between 20% and 30% and increased plant utilization time by between 5% and 17%.
6. See the chapter by Kazuo Koike in Chinloy and Stromsdorfer (1987).

30

References

Beckerman, Wilfred, ed. (1986). *Wage Rigidity and Unemployment*, Baltimore.

Boyer, Robert, ed. (1986). *The Search for Labour Market Flexibility—The European Economics in Transition*, Oxford.

Chinloy, Peter T., and Ernst Stromsdorfer eds. (1987). *Labor Market Adjustments in the Pacific Basin*, Boston.

Dore, Ronald (1986). *Flexible Rigidities: Industrial Policy and Structural Adjustment in the Japanese Economy, 1970–1980*, London.

Hart, Robert, ed., (1988). *Employment, Unemployment, and Labor Utilization*, Winchester, Mass.

OECD (1983). *Economic Outlook 33*, July.

———— (1984). *Employment Outlook*, September.

———— (1985). Manpower and Social Affairs Committee, *Labour Market Flexibility*, Technical Report by the Secretariat, 17 December.

———— (1986). *Flexibility in the Labor Market: The Current Debate*, Paris.

Sarfati, Hedva, and Catherine Kobrin, eds. (1988). *Labour Market Flexibility: A Comparative Anthology*, Aldershot.

Standing, Guy (1986). *Unemployment and Labour Market Flexibility: The United Kingdom*, Geneva.

Tadashi Nakamura

1

Labor Market and Manpower Policy 1945–1985

Introduction

Four decades ago when World War II was over, Japan experienced complete destruction of her industrial base, resulting in a large number of jobless people. This was accompanied by subsistence levels of wages and accelerating inflation, as is regrettably seen in many developing countries today. Fortunately, Japan is now regarded as one of the developed countries, which means that after four decades she has experienced a transitional shift from being a developing country to being a mature, developed country. During this period there were many difficulties, however, employment grew strongly in manufacturing and the unemployment rate stood far below the level of other developed countries. These factors were the result of untiring efforts by employers and workers to adapt to an ever changing environment.

I. Postwar Reconstruction 1945–1954

After the war, the major concern of both occupation forces and domestic policy makers was the restoration of the Japanese economy to its

32

prewar level in order to increase employment opportunities and improve living standards. The Korean War gave Japan the impetus to restore her economy. Retrenchment policies adopted after the Korean cease-fire in 1953 brought Japan its biggest postwar recession. However, these policies eventually proved to be successful as imports declined, the balance of payments improved, and the economy began to show signs of an up-swing by the end of the decade.

Excessive Surplus and Reformation of Administrative Tools

The first half of the decade was devoted to the restructuring of administrative techniques, which included new employment measures. Placement service networks were reorganized, and the incomes of unemployed workers were guaranteed by the unemployment insurance scheme, while temporary job opportunities were provided by public works and unemployment relief works. The Korean War boom created employment opportunities in Japan but, nevertheless, there were still millions of underemployed workers in agriculture, the tertiary sector, and small- and medium-sized enterprises. In the recession that followed the cease-fire, there were many cases of labor unrest caused mainly by plant shutdowns and layoffs. At the end of the decade, the lifetime employment system was gaining ground from the conviction of both workers and unions that employment security in the enterprise was of prime importance for them, while employers found that there would be no industrial peace and long-lasting profit without guaranteeing their employees a significant measure of employment stability.

II. Growth to West European Levels 1955–1964

The second decade was the decade of high economic growth, which continued until the first oil crisis with "Let's try to catch-up to West European level," the widely accepted slogan of the decade. The business world was very active, and investment levels increased in order to achieve mass production and automation, while workers and unions slowly but steadily responded to such increases in capacity in a positive manner as long as their employment was guaranteed and the fruits of the productivity increase were fairly distributed. During this period, the government published many plans for the economy in order to fully mobilize the economic potential of Japan. The best example was the "Income Doubling Plan" of 1960, which, in a timely manner, offered the people a "dream" that their income could be doubled in ten years. The positive attitudes of three parties (management,

33

workers, and the government) created a stimulating environment that helped to bring high economic growth and employment (particularly in manufacturing), so that, by the end of the decade there was a shortage of supply of young workers in the labor market.

Growth of Employment and the Underprivileged

Stimulated by fast industrialization and automation, the need grew for trained workers equipped with skills that could adapt to future technological innovation. The Vocational Training Law was enacted in 1958 to systematize vocational training and to initiate skill tests. Ironically, the steady improvement of the employment situation, in particular for young school graduates, shed light on the problems of the underprivileged. In the first half of the decade, energy sources were being switched dramatically from coal to oil, which created an energy revolution. Because the coal mines were far from industrial regions, and the characteristics of mining work were so different from industrial work, special measures were required to help unemployed coal miners and to promote their re-employment. A special law for this purpose, enacted in 1959, introduced specific counseling, remote area placement service, conversion training with pay, construction of workers' housing in industrial regions, special unemployment relief programs, and subsidies to new employers. This law served, in later days, as a model or basic framework of measures for unemployment caused by structural change. A 1960 revision of the Unemployment Insurance Law extended unemployment benefit payment to cases of vocational training and the relocation of workers. Another law, enacted in the same year, to promoted employment of the handicapped, who remained the most underprivileged group even when the general picture was improving. A requirement to employ a certain number of handicapped in each enterprise—although not legally binding—and job adaptation training with subsidy for that purpose were introduced. However, the biggest underprivileged group of all were the middle aged and older people whose re-employment opportunities were very limited. A 1963 revision of the Employment Security Law provided specific job counseling and training with paid allowances for job seekers of thirty-five years and older.

III. Fast Growth and the First Oil Shock 1965–1974

The high rate of economic growth was maintained until 1974 when the first oil crisis occurred. Personal consumption rose rapidly with sustained demand for durable goods such as color television sets, automobiles, electric refrigerators, and washing machines. Above all, high industrial investment allowed a high level of expansion and modernization to be achieved. Exports, particularly the products of heavy industries, expanded very rapidly thanks to the continued boom in the world economy, partly induced by the Vietnam War, and, as a result of this growth process, Japan was able to increase its international competitiveness. Employment grew very fast, particularly in the tertiary industries during latter half of the decade, (Figure 1), while at the same time unemployment remained at less than 1.5% (Table 1), thus qualifying the period to be called one of "full employment."

The first oil shock in 1973 triggered a rapid rise in consumer prices and resulted in trade union demands for higher wages during the course of the 1974 spring wage negotiations. This resulted in a record-making wage hike of 33%. Soon after the negotiations in 1974, both trade unionists and management became concerned that the negotiated wage rise might have induced a vicious wage-price spiral as had been experienced in many developed countries in the West. However, the statement by the Steel Workers Federation that it would be prepared to adopt a restrained attitude toward wage demands if the government could use its powerful pricing policies to lower the trend of price increases was finally supported by a majority of trade union leaders as well as by employers and the government. Wage negotiations in 1975 were dramatic in that wage increases fell to 13%, reflecting the lower trend of price hikes due to effective government price policies (including freezes on public utility prices). During this period, the Round Table Conference on Labor and Industry provided opportunities for free and informal discussions among top leaders concerning the need to arrive at successful results to wage negotiations.

Manpower Policy

At the start of this decade, it was obvious that the labor market was changing from one of surplus to one of shortage. Shortages would occur in urban areas for young skilled workers whereas labor surpluses would remain for the elderly workers in rural areas. Therefore, some industries would prosper, while others would become depressed. The Ministry of Labor felt it necessary to initiate active manpower policies to cope with these changing situations and to make the labor market more mobile. The Employment Measures Law, enacted in 1965, consolidated the existing measures and added new ones on manpower policy, such as, the formation of the Basic Employment Plan to indicate manpower forecast and to state the policy direction concerned. Also, a comprehensive set of conversion allowances

TABLE 1
DEVELOPMENT OF JAPANESE ECONOMY AND
LABOR LEGISLATION SINCE WORLD WAR II

	Rates in percentages			
Year	Growth of Real GNP[a]	Increase of wages[b]	Unemploy-ment[c]	Major labor legislation
1947				1947 Employment Security Law
				1947 Unemployment Insurance Law
1949				1949 Emergency Unemployment Measures
1955			2.5	
56	6.2	8.7	2.3	
57	7.8	4.4	1.9	
58	6.0	2.5	2.1	
59	11.2	6.6	2.2	1959 Coal Miners Employment Measures
1960	12.5	6.2	1.7	1960 Handicapped Employment Promotion
61	13.5	11.7	1.4	
62	6.4	10.5	1.3	
63	12.5	10.7	1.3	
64	10.6	9.6	1.1	
1965	5.7	9.8	1.2	
66	11.1	10.7	1.3	1966 Employment Measures
67	10.7	12.0	1.3	
68	12.8	13.6	1.2	
69	12.0	15.5	1.1	1969 Vocational Training Law
1970	7.6	19.9	1.1	
71	5.0	14.6	1.2	1971 Employment Promotion of Elderly Workers
72	9.2	16.0	1.4	
73	4.5	21.5	1.3	
74	0.4	27.2	1.4	1974 Employment Insurance
1975	3.9	14.8	1.9	
76	4.6	12.5	2.0	
77	5.3	8.5	2.0	1977 Depressed Industries Employment Measures
78	5.2	6.4	2.2	1978 Depressed Areas Employment Measures
79	5.3	6.0	2.1	
1980	4.0	6.3	2.0	
81	3.3	5.3	2.2	
82	3.2	4.5	2.4	
83	3.7	3.5	2.6	
84	5.1	4.5	2.7	1984 Equal Opportunity Law
1985	4.4	3.6	2.6	1985 Workers Dispatching Law
1986	2.6	3.5	2.8	

Sources: [a] Economic Planning Agency, *Annual Report on National Accounts.*
Discontinued in 1965 because of new SNA. For fiscal year.
[b] Ministry of Labor, *Monthly Labor Statistics.* The average rate of
increase in all industries.
[c] Prime Minister's Office, *Labor Force Survey.*

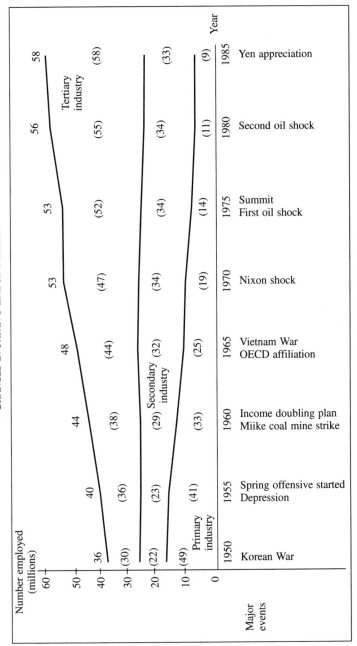

FIGURE 1
CHANGES IN JAPAN'S LABOR MARKET

Note: Figures in parentheses indicate percentage composition of total employment in each year.

were created to facilitate job transfer and to improve employment ratio of the elderly in selected occupations. The enactment of the law was followed in 1969 by the revision of the Vocational Training Law, which established a principle of lifelong training, through the formulation of a Basic Training Plan, and the unification of standards applicable to both public and private training. In 1971, a law to promote employment of elderly persons was enacted in recognition of the fact that their employment would be the biggest social as well as political issue for Japan in the future. Minimum age qualification for this target group was increased from thirty-five to forty-five and it went some way toward meeting the requests from the labor movement for a legal minimum level of retirement age applicable to all enterprises.

IV. Stable Growth 1973–1984

The fourth decade was characterized by stable economic growth. The sudden rise in the price of oil followed by wage increases were the main problems faced by management during the initial phase. As for the wages, a reasonable solution was achieved through the collective bargaining process coupled with a successful price restraint policy by the government. The attitude of unions toward wage negotiation in this decade was to demand wage increases in line with economic reality. In addition, unit energy consumption was reduced dramatically, while the level of employment was reduced through natural attrition or voluntary retirement. Also, new technology, such as, microelectronics and robotics, was actively introduced, all in consultation with the unions concerned. Stagnant employment in older sectors of manufacturing was compensated by the increase in employment in tertiary industries, which absorbed a considerable volume of the increasing female labor force. The result was remarkable improvement of international competitiveness both in terms of price and quality with the consequence that economic growth was stimulated increasingly by the expansion of exports.

Adjustment to Stable Growth

The efforts of employees, particularly in manufacturing, to reduce the size of employment in response to the emergent oil crisis and world recession affected the labor market quite rapidly and to a considerable extent. The number of job-seekers increased, and a sharp rise in the unemployment rate was recorded, with elderly persons, in particular, finding it hard to obtain employment opportunities. Close to the end of 1974, the Unemployment Insurance Law was revised and renamed the Employment Insurance Law. Under this law the duration for which the unemployment allowance was paid was calculated on the basis of the *age* of recipient instead of the previously used length of his insured period.[1] Also, the employment adjustment premium was now to be paid to employers of depressed industries or areas if they trained, dispatched, or suspended their employees with pay without interrupting employment contracts. The major thrust of the premium was to assist the effort of employers to maintain the level of employment, and to smoothly and flexibly adapt it to the changes that followed the so called oil crisis.

In 1976, a revision of the Handicapped Person's Employment Promotion Law laid down legal employment quotas for the handicapped. It also introduced penalties in the form of special contributions to be paid by those employers who failed to satisfy the quota, while, on the other hand, it subsidized employers who met their quota. Also in 1976, a law was enacted to further promote employment of the elderly and to consolidate and strengthen existing measures. A goal "to achieve a general retirement age of at least sixty years old before 1985" was introduced in the fourth Basic Employment Measure Plan with the approval of the Cabinet.

The laws concerning Temporary Measures for Displaced Workers in Specified Depressed Industries (1977) and that of Areas (1978) stabilized employment and promoted re-employment of displaced workers in the industries and areas concerned.

Under the lifetime employment practice, workers in Japan were less resistant to the introduction of new technology during this period. However the introduction of ME, or information technology, provided a somewhat different picture from the past in terms of its scope and speed of application (i.e., for multifarious as well as mass production, for office work as well as production line, and in small as well as big enterprise). Faced with these situations, trade unions stressed more than ever the need for employment guarantees, education and training, industrial safety and health, and prior consultation. Many trade union federations adopted standards or guidelines for use by member unions when they were consulted by, or engaged in negotiation with, employers on the introduction of new technology.

At the national level, in 1984 after two years of discussion, the Round Table Conference on Employment Policy (composed of leading figures from management, unions, universities, and government agencies) reached a consensus on five principles to be applied voluntarily by all parties concerned with the introduction of ME technology.

V. Appreciation of Yen 1985–

Since the G-five agreement in September 1985, the economic environment has changed dramatically with the Yen appreciating very rapidly. Export industries (and the regions where these industries are located) have been severely hit and imports have begun to rise with the NIES (Newly Industrializing Economies) becoming serious competitors to Japan in both domestic and overseas markets. Japanese companies have often transferred production to developed, as well as developing, countries in order to survive. The U.S. balance of payments was slow to recover and so the United States increased the pressure on Japan to open its market in high-tech or agricultural products such as integrated circuits and rice.

The Japanese government endeavored to stimulate domestic demand and to adapt its industrial structure in order to meet some of the U.S. criticisms. Housing, private consumption, and investment showed significant signs of improvement after 1986 and the employment situation also slowly recovered.

Problems in the Labor Market

Mismatch

Unemployment, although lower than in other countries, was still high by Japanese standards and became a sensitive political issue. The appreciation of the Yen, structural change, and the growth of tertiary industry, on the one hand, and the aging population and increased female participation in the labor market, on the other, were the main preoccupations of labor policy. Attempts were made to maintain employment and to alleviate the mismatch between demand and supply that was often aggravated by factors such as age, industry, and regional distribution.

Dispatching Service

As in other developed countries, the number of workers who voluntarily offered their specific knowledge and skill on a part-time or temporary basis was increasing. Some of these workers found employment through manpower supply or placement services, which were, in principle, prohibited by law, and in some cases the workers needed legal protection in terms of working conditions and the application of social security laws. After seven years of study and discussion, including both workers and employers, a bill was presented to the parliament, and approved in 1985, under which dispatching services were authorized for limited categories of work, workers were legally defined as the employees of their respective senders, and workers were thus dispatched to perform work on the basis of a contract between the sender (dispatching service) and the receiver.

The Aged Workers

In 1986, the law involving the employment of the elderly was revised and renamed the Law Concerning the Stabilization of Employment for Elderly People. In addition to existing measures, moral obligation was placed on employers to set the minimum retirement age at sixty years, and measures were instituted to provide employment opportunities for those aged sixty years and older and to authorize activities of the silver centers to offer the aged opportunities for participation in social remunerative activities. These revisions reflected the fact that the retirement age of sixty years had now been generally accepted and that the problems were shifting to those over sixty years old. The act also reconfirmed the fact that employability should depend on health, income/wealth, and the willingness to work.

Hollowing of Production

A high and rapidly appreciating yen induced many serious discussions on the "hollowing" of Japanese production. Business leaders' view was that the process was inevitable both for the survival of the enterprise and for the profitable coexistence and coprosperity of the world. However, it was also realized that due consideration should, at the same time, be paid to employment security and industrial peace within the Japanese employment framework. In view of the possible leveling-off, or reduction, of production and increase in unemployment, trade unions felt threatened by the transfer of production overseas and they asked for guarantees of employment and prior consultation.

The Round Table Conference on Employment Policy was, once again, called to make a in-depth study on the impact of capital out-flows on the level and practice of employment. Its report, presented to the Minister in 1987, suggested that parallel with the efforts of government to achieve high growth through expansion of domestic demand, enterprises were expected to maintain levels of employment and to create new employment where possible. Companies were also asked to provide increased training for their domestic workers and to establish consultation mechanisms in case of transfer of production to overseas.

Equal Opportunities

Although women's participation in the labor market has expanded remarkably over the recent past, the discriminatory treatment of women at

41

work in terms of recruitment, training, and promotion as well as remuneration is still a major problem. After long discussions within the outside parliament, a new law, enacted in 1985, laid down the basic legal framework for promoting equal opportunities for women at work while at the same time slightly reducing the level of protection for working hours and others. At the same time, parliament ratified the U.N. Convention on the Elimination of All Forms of Discrimination against Women.

Conclusion

This brief introduction has aimed to show how Japan's labor policy evolved during the postwar period. The changing course of economic growth created opportunities for the rethinking of labor and manpower policies and in many ways the Japanese labor system accepted such challenges. Structural change after the war acted as a catalyst to improvements in training facilities coupled with government subsidies. During the rapid phase of growth up to the 1960s, the primary need was a consensus between employers and employees on the best way to achieve growth, while at the same time requiring government to provide some guidelines through manpower forecasts. However, during the 1970s, the emergence of the oil shock and then the development of robotics presented serious challenges to labor policy. The Japanese government reacted by adjusting national insurance laws, promoting temporary measures to keep displaced workers, and becoming more closely involved with management, unions, and universities.

The most recent phase, resulting in the effects created by the strong yen coupled with the continuing structural problem, meant that coherent policies concerning older workers and the question of equal opportunities for women had to be tackled. Labor policy in Japan over the last forty years has been orientated toward solving various labor problems as they arose.

Note

1. The formula of calculation was reamended in 1984 in such a way that both the age *and* the insured period of the recipient were taken into account. This was done to meet the needs of the growing number of aged recipients and to avoid an abuse of the formula in their favor.

References

Hosono, Tadashi (1979). *Tenkanki no Koyo Seisaku* (*Employment Policies at the Turning Era*), Tokyo: Nikkan Rodo Tsushin Sha.

Ichino, Shozo (1979). *Koyo Tokei no Mikata* (*How to Use Employment Statistics*), Tokyo: Japan Productivity Center.

Kato, Fumio (1983). "Nihon ni okeru Shizen Shitsugyo Ritsu Kasetsu no Kensho" ("Testing the Natural Rate of Unemployment Hypothesis in Japan"), Bank of Japan, *Kinyu kenkyu shiryo*, no. 11, February.

Kato, Takashi (1985). *Kozo Hendo-ki no Koyo Seisaku* (*Employment Policies at the Era of Structural Changes*), Tokyo: Romu Gyosei Kenkyujo.

Keizai Kikaku Cho, (Economic Planning Agency) (1976). *Keizai Hakusho 1957* (*Economic White Paper on 1957*), Tokyo: Nihon Keizai Hyoron Sha, reprinted.

Koshiro, Kazutoshi (1983a). "Chiiki Rodoshijo no Kozo to Nozomashii Koyo Seisaku" ("The Structure of Local Labor Markets and Desirable Employment Policies"), *Toyo Keizai Kinkei Series*, no. 66, April.

——— (1983b). "Nihon no Koyo Seisaku" ("Japan's Employment Policies"), *Contemporary Economics Quarterly* (*Kikan Gendai Keizai*), no. 56, Winter.

——— (1986). "Small Business and the Labor Market in Japan—the Interrelationship between Large and Small Enterprises since 1970—," *Discussion Paper 86–4 (revised)*, the Center for International Trade Studies, Faculty of Economics, Yokohama National University, November.

Ministry of Labor. *Shitsugyo Taisaku Nenkan* (*Yearbook of Unemployment Measures*), Tokyo: Rodo Horei Kyokai, every year.

——— (1980). *Shitsugyo Taisaku 30 Nenshi* (*30 Years of Unemployment Policies*), Tokyo: Koyo Mondai Kenkyu Kai.

——— (1984). *Labor White Paper 1983*, Tokyo: Ministry of Labor.

Mitsubishi Ginko Chosabu (Research Department of the Mitsubishi Bank) (1981). "Nichibei Keizai Shihyo no Uraomote" ("The Front and Back Sides of the U.S.–Japan Economic Relationship"), *Chosa Tokuho*, no. 22, August.

Mizuno, Asao (1982). "Flow kara mita Nihon no Shitsugyo Kodo" ("Unemployment Behaviour Viewed from its Flows in Japan"), *Contemporay Economics Quarterly* no. 51, Winter.

Nishikawa, Shunsaku (1979). "Tomen no Shitsugyo Mondai to Kongo no Koyo Seisaku," *Contemporary Economics Quarterly*, no. 34, Spring.

Odaka, Konosuke (1982). "Shokugyo Kyoiku wo Kangaeru" ("Revisiting Vocational Education"), *Nihon Rodokyokai Zasshi*, nos. 275 and 276, February and March.

Romu Gyosei Kenkyujo (1982). "Jinzai Haken Jigyo no Jitsujo to Shokuanho Mondai" ("Manpower Dispatching Service and its Problems with Respect to the Employment Stabilization Law"), *Rosei Jiho*, no. 2623, November 26.

Seki, Hideo (1981). *Antei Seicho-ki no Koyo Seisaku* (Employment Policies in the Era of Stable Economic Growth), Tokyo: Romu Gyosei Kenkyujo.

Tadashi Nakamura

Shimada, Haruo (1981). *Rodoshijo Kiko no Kenkyu* (*Studies in the Labor Market Structure*), Tokyo: Economic Institute of EPA, *Kenkyu Series*, No. 37.

Shinozuka, Eiko (1977). "Koyo Hoken Ho no Keizai Koka" ("The Economic Incidence of the Employment Insurance Law"), *Contemporary Economics Quarterly*, no. 28, Autumn.

——— (1982). "Gendai no Shitsugyo to Koyo Seido no Hyoka" ("Contemporary Unemployment and Changes in the Employment System"), *Contemporary Economics Quarterly*, no. 51, Winter.

Shiraishi, Eiji (1982). "Shitsugyo Gainen no Kokusai Hikaku" ("An International Comparison of the Concept of Unemployment"), Ministry of Labor, *Rodo Tokei Chosa Geppo*, March.

Taira, Koji (1983). "Japan's Low Unemployment: Economic Miracle or Statistical Artifact?" *Monthly Labor Review*, July.

Yoshida, Kazuo, and Hiroshi Endo (1982). "Sekiyu Kiki Iko no Shitsugyo Kozo no Henka" ("Changes in the Structure of Unemployment since Oil Crisis"), *Contemporary Economics Quarterly*, no. 51, Winter.

Kazutoshi Koshiro

2

Bonus Payments and Wage Flexibility in Japan

Introduction

European countries have suffered high levels of unemployment over
the last decade and, as a result, there has been growing concern among policymakers and academics alike that labor market rigidities in these countries
have had adverse effects on their economic performance as compared with
that of the United States or Japan, who seem to have experienced more flexible labor markets. The OECD (1983; 1984; 1985) has recently concentrated
its attention on this problem from a practical policymaker's viewpoint. Also,
Sachs (1979); Hashimoto (1979); Branson and Rotemberg (1980); Gordon
(1982); Weitzman (1983; 1984; 1985) Grubb, Jackman, and Layard (1983);
and Kahn (1984) have studied the problem from a more academic standpoint. Most of the studies written by Western scholars seem to support the
view that the Japanese labor market exhibits more flexibility than labor markets in Western countries and that this has contributed to the maintenance
of low unemployment as well as decreased rate of inflation in Japan over
the last decade.[1]

Kazutoshi Koshiro

On the whole, Japanese scholars have been rather critical of such views of Japan's labor market but at the same time are, themselves, split into two conflicting groups. One group admits that the Japanese labor market is flexible, while the other group denies it. Ono (1985), Mizuno (1985a), and Shinpo (1985) belong to the former group, although they differ in their reasons for supporting the view, while Muramatsu (1985), Ohtake (1986), and Brunello and Ohtake (1987) belong to the latter group.

In between these two groups, Tachibanaki (1987) states that "Although it is true that the real wage flexibility is considerably high in Japan, it has not helped to increase the number of employment. The role of wages as an adjusting factor has been quite limited." In addition to these studies, Taira (1983) has raised serious doubts about the statistical comparability of the unemployment rate in Japan with that of the United States because of the technical and cultural differences between the two countries.[2] Taira (1985) is also critical of the social unfairness of a Japanese employment system that segregates the majority of workers from a privileged minority. He argues that without this segmentation of the labor market, wage and employment flexibility could not be maintained.

Based on these previous studies, the present author would like to elaborate on the definition of and the method of measurement of wage flexibility with special reference to the Hashimoto, Gordon, Sachs, and Mizuno studies. This study underlines the importance of the distinction between the flexibility of *negotiated* wage rates and bonuses on the one hand, and wage flexibility at the macroeconomic level on the other. Using the techniques of empirical analysis this study attempts to show that wage determination under collective bargaining by "enterprise unions" in Japan is flexible enough to reflect the changing profitability of individual companies or industries. However, the flexibility, or sensitivity of wages to fluctuation in profits, differs from industry to industry and even from firm to firm. Furthermore, it is shown that basic earnings, which are decided by collective bargaining in major enterprises, are also very sensitive to changed profits as are bonuses. However, in both cases the degree of sensitivity is not necessarily as large as usually imagined by the Western scholars.

Behind the fairly flexible wage determination system in Japan is a fundamental socioeconomic factor, that is, the consciousness among Japanese workers of the scarcity of good job opportunities.[3] This tends to affect the basic framework of collective bargaining, particularly in the export-oriented industries. This consciousness, unlike the class consciousness of blue-collar workers in the West, tends to restrain the upward shift of the labor supply function because workers are sensitive to any sign of serious economic difficulty affecting the enterprise that is expected to provide

46

them with a significant degree of employment security (so-called "lifetime employment").

After describing briefly the wage-setting institutions in Japan, this chapter addresses four main themes. The first is an examination of the sensitivity of negotiated bonus payments to changed profitability by type of industry. Second, the sensitivity of negotiated basic earnings by industry is looked at from two aspects; (1) the elasticity of the average wage level with respect to the amount of current profit per employee and (2) the elasticity of the average amount of increased wages, again with respect to profit. These results are then compared with those for bonus payments. Third, the flexibility of wages at the aggregate economy level is examined from a somewhat different perspective and compared with that of other major OECD countries. Fourth, a brief comment is made on the need for further studies to examine other important aspects of labor market flexibility in Japan.

I. Wage-Setting Institutions in Japan

Some previous studies, including those of Sachs (1979) and Gordon (1982), have quite properly paid considerable attention to the international differences of wage-setting institutions among major OECD countries. However, even these studies did not make clear the distinction between flexibility (or rigidity) of *negotiated* wages at the firm or industry level and wages at the wider *macroeconomic* level.

Because of the prevalence of enterprise-wide collective bargaining, Japan's wage-setting institutions possess several advantages for the researcher. First, wage rates and bonus payments are negotiated mostly at the enterprise level, which makes it possible to scrutinize the responsiveness of wages and bonus payments to the changed profitability of each individual company. Second, main wage negotiations in Japan occur once a year in the springtime (called the spring offensive or "Shunto") and involves almost ten million organized workers. This makes it possible for the parties concerned to adjust contract wages to changed economic conditions both at the macro- and microeconomic levels. Third, in addition to the negotiation of basic wages, a lump sum cash payment, often equivalent to about five months basic wage is paid (around half in summer and the remaining half at the year's end) through the process of negotiations in major firms. It is widely believed that such bonus payments can, and should, reflect business fluctuations more closely than basic wage.

47

In Japan, union density has been continuously declining since 1970 when organized labor constituted 35.4% of total employees. By 1987, the ratio had fallen to 27.6%, with most union members being concentrated in large private-sector firms and in public-sector employment. The spillover of negotiated wage increases from the major sector of economy to small- and medium-sized firms is also clearly detectable, but the wage gap between large and small firms still remains significant (Sano, Koike, and Ishida 1969, pp. 122–134; Sano, Ishida, and Inoue 1971, pp. 61–96; Koshiro 1986, pp. 42–43). Wage differentials between large and small firms reflecting the duality of labor markets have long been the subject of serious discussions, although such differentials did decrease considerably in the 1960s due to the emergence of labor shortages. Some argue that the official statistics on wage differentials by size of firms exaggerate the picture and that *actual* wage differentials adjusted for skill differences and worker-career profiles are only half the official estimates (Koike 1983, pp. 90–104). However, the fact that the majority of workers in Japan are employed in the unorganized sector compels us to address another aspect of the problem; that is, how flexible (or rigid) are wages and bonuses for the *whole* economy and not only for the relatively privileged unionized sector.[4]

A third aspect to be taken into account with regard to the institutional aspect of wage-setting is the question of the minimum wage. Japan established a fairly effective system of legally binding prefecture-wide minimum wage rate structure by industry in 1959, but since 1978 each prefectural wage board has set the local across-the-board minimum wage rate for *all* industries. Rates range from the highest figure of 497 yen per hour in Tokyo to the lowest level of 416 yen in the Kyushu and Tohoku areas. In 1987, the national average minimum hourly wage rate stood at 460 yen, which was equivalent to about 40% of the average hourly earnings of all industries. The corresponding figures in the United States were 42% in 1981, and in France 84.4% in 1984.[5] If the minimum wage rate is set too high compared with the marginal productivity of the lowest grade of labor, it discourages employers from employing more workers and thus increases unemployment. The prefecture-wide system of minimum wages can therefore reflect labor market conditions in each locality and tends to be more flexible than a nationally based minimum wage system. The relatively low ratio of minimum wages to average wages, combined with a prefecturally determined minimum wage system, has provided Japan with a relatively high degree of wage flexibility.

II. Flexibility of Bonus Payments

Bonus Payments as a Source of Wage Flexibility

Hashimoto (1979), Gordon (1982), Weitzman (1984), and OECD (1984) emphasized the importance of bonus payments as a major source of wage flexibility in Japan. For example, the OECD makes the following comment: "The Japanese economy combines its long tenure with some flexibility in worker remuneration through the system of bonus payments. . . . Is the Japanese economy somehow more efficient at allocating labour than other OECD economies? If so, how does this come about? . . . In Japan, . . . , where tenure is less easily broken, especially in large firms, these costs of adjustment to demand and supply shocks are shared more evenly among employers and employees as for example through the use of bonus payments."[6]

Hashimoto has suggested that the system of bonus payments can be understood as a system of sharing the increased return from human-capital investment. In this sense, the Japanese bonus system can be regarded as a form of profit sharing.[7] In order to support his arguments, Hashimoto presents industrial comparisons of cyclical sensitivity and the bonus-earnings ratio (RB).[8] From his work he was able to conclude that there was a meaningful correlation between these two sets of coefficients, thus providing evidence of the flexibility of bonus payments in response to business fluctuation.

The RB seemed to increase in prosperous periods and decrease in periods of recession. However, this analysis does not directly prove the degree of sensitivity of bonus payments to *profit* fluctuation nor is it necessarily evidence that bonus payments are the essential source of flexibility because other parts of earnings, such as, basic wage and overtime payments, may also be sensitive to business fluctuations.[9] Therefore, it is better to measure more directly the sensitivity of bonus payments to changed profitability in comparison with that of other components of earnings, particularly the basic wage. Also, such sensitivity may change from time to time and from industry to industry, so that it is essential to monitor these aspects also.

Sensitivity of Negotiated Bonus Payments to Changes in Profits by Industry

Bonus payments constitute about a quarter of the average total earnings of all Japanese workers.[10] If we take bonus payments to employees of large firms only, the proportion rises up to about 30%. If this part of earnings fluctuates according to changes in the corporate profit of each firm, then it is reasonable to expect that total earnings would also be very responsive to economic changes. Therefore, we must first examine the extent to which bonus payments are responsive to corporate profitability, and then extend our analysis to include the flexibility of basic wages.

Every year the Ministry of Labor publishes the results of negotiated bonus payments for around 288 major Japanese firms whose authorized capital is more than two billion yen. These firms also have stocks that are listed on the First Class Stock Exchange, employ more than 1,000 employees, and are unionized. In other words, these companies represent the key sector of Japanese economy and the labor unions organized in these enterprises represent the most influential part of organized labor covering some 2.4 million workers. Furthermore, the Ministry of Labor publishes the results of negotiated wage increase for the same group of companies every year so that it is possible to measure the sensitivity of both negotiated basic wages and bonus payments to changed profitability for the same group of companies over time.

If the system of bonus payments is a kind of profit sharing as insisted by Hashimoto and Weitzman, a desirable level of bonus payments (B_t) should be explained by a variable that represents the state of corporate profit (π). Based on the partial adjustment model developed by Nerlove (1956), it is possible to measure the responsiveness of actual bonus payments (B_{it}) to changes in corporate profit by using the following regression, equation (1), which links the elasticity of bonus payments to corporate profit.[11]

$$B_{it} = \alpha + \beta(\frac{\pi}{L})_{it} + \gamma B_{i,t-1} + e_t, \tag{1}$$

where Bit is the average annual amount of bonus payments, π is the average annual amount of "ordinary profit,"[12] L is the average number of employees, i indicates each industry, and e is the residuals.

Table 1 shows the results of regression analyses based on equation (1), linking the negotiated bonus payments of the major firms to their profitability. The results are satisfactory except for four industries, that is, the iron and steel industry, the automobile industry, private railways, and electric power industries. For these industries, the *lagged* value of ordinary profit per employee $(\pi/L)_{t-1}$ was applied, which tended to improve the stability of regression coefficients for the iron and steel and the automobile industries, but not for the remaining two industries. Therefore, the simplest form of the regression equation using a single explanatory variable $(\pi/L)_{it}$ was applied to the last two industries as seen in table 2.

50

TABLE 1

NEGOTIATED BONUS PAYMENTS[a] OF MAJOR FIRMS AND
THEIR SENSITIVITY TO ORDINARY PROFITS[b], 1973–1984

Industry	Parameter[c]			$\bar{R}^2$	DW[d]	Durbin[e] h statistics
	α	β	γ			
Total private industries	178.847 (4.77)	0.0583299 (2.14)	0.742012 (9.59)	0.9721	2.84	−1.51
Textile	118.822 (6.73)	0.0874838 (10.27)	0.814064 (25.67)	0.9897	2.99	−1.725*
Paper and pulp	168.51 (2.27)	0.0926294 (3.51)	0.721312 (6.37)	0.8849	2.92	−1.732*
Chemicals	217.55 (4.05)	0.0835492 (3.999)	0.66733 (9.13)	0.9454	2.33	−0.591
Iron and steel	159.13 (2.86)	0.0360491 (1.90)	0.814127 (12.07)	0.9294	1.97	0.053
Machinery	177.958 (4.95)	0.118556 (2.95)	0.642678 (7.10)	0.9740	2.65	−1.186
Electrical machinery and appliances	197.094 (5.02)	0.0639352 (2.78)	0.693466 (7.87)	0.9805	2.63	−1.146
Automobile	125.529 (6.10)	0.0263659 (1.22)	0.867893 (14.53)	0.9926	2.60	−1.062
Shipbuilding	69.8916 (0.71)	0.13675 (2.11)	0.863234 (6.95)	0.818	1.96	0.077
Private railways	162.356 (4.74)	0.057495 (0.65)	0.841673 (14.24)	0.9734	2.75	−1.327
Electric power	155.239 (2.72)	0.00221383 (0.34)	0.872815 (10.36)	0.9531	1.77	0.417

[a] Bonus payments are annual averages in units of 1,000 yen.
[b] "Ordinary profit" per employee is the average annual in 1,000 yen.
[c] t-value in parentheses.
[d] Durbin-Watson ratio.
[e] The * mark indicates that the Durbin h statistics is larger than 1.65 and, therefore serial correlation exists at the significance level of 5%.

TABLE 2

NEGOTIATED BONUS PAYMENTS OF MAJOR FIRMS AND THEIR SENSITIVITY TO
ORDINARY PROFIT IN THE SELECTED INDUSTRIES, 1973–1984

| Industry | Parameter[c] | | | $\bar{R}^2$ | DW[c] | Durbin h statistics[d] |
	α	β	γ			
Iron and steel[a]	169.726 (4.97)	0.0563375 (4.55)	0.777949 (17.55)	0.9700	2.27	0.468
Automobile[a]	123.626 (6.96)	0.0408785 (2.26)	0.842237 (18.38)	0.9945	2.59	1.035
Private railways[b]	504.108 (4.49)	0.920746 (3.08)	—	0.4358	0.561*	—
Electric power[b]	711.198 (10.75)	0.049783 (3.19)	—	0.4551	1.614	—

[a] The parameters for the iron and steel and the automobile industries are measured by the following regression equation with lags for the ordinary profit per employee:

$$B_{it} = \alpha + \beta(\pi/L)_{i,t-1} + \gamma B_{i,t-1}.$$

[b] The parameters for the private railways and the electric power industries are measured by the regression equation as follows:

$$B_{it} = \alpha + \beta(\pi/L)_{it}.$$

[c] The * mark indicates the existence of serial correlation at the significance level of 1%.

[d] If Durbin h statistics are larger than 1.65, then serial correlation exists at the significance level of 5%.

Since the purpose of this analysis is to calculate the degree of elasticity of bonus payments to changes in the average per capita ordinary profit (π/L), it would be logical to think that a logarithmic variant of the equation should be used. But that is not technically feasible in this case because π sometimes shows negative value. Therefore, we must measure the elasticity at the mean value of each variable, using the observed parameter β in equation (1).[13] Table 3 (column 1) shows that, contrary to the view prevailing among Western writers concerning the high flexibility of bonus payments in Japan, the *short-run* profit elasticity of negotiated bonus payments in the all private industries category is fairly small (0.1001). The elasticity is highest in the machinery industry, which is one of the most volatile industries, and is lowest in the iron and steel industry. The low elasticity value in the iron

TABLE 3

A COMPARISON OF PROFIT ELASTICITY OF
BONUS PAYMENTS AND OF BASIC WAGES

Industry	Profit elasticity			
	Bonus payment negotiated at major firms[a]		Basic wages negotiated at major firms[d]	
	Short-run	Long-run	Short-run	Long-run
Total private industries	0.1001	0.3879	0.0472	0.3024
Textile	0.0641	0.3448	0.0954[e]	0.1143[e]
Paper and pulp	0.1207	0.4333	n.a.[i]	n.a.[i]
Chemical	0.1456	0.4378	0.0379	0.2652
Iron and steel	0.0636[b]	0.2864[b]	0.0206	0.3778
Machinery	0.1935	0.5414	0.0588	0.1924
Electric	0.1164	0.3797	0.0400	0.2024
Automobile	0.0859[b]	0.5446[b]	0.0986[f]	0.4130[f]
Shipbuilding	0.1038	0.7593	0.0181	0.2428
Private railways	n.a.[h]	(0.3863)[c]	0.0122	0.1320
Electric power	n.a.[h]	(0.1929)[c]	— [g]	— [g]

[a] The observation period is 1973–1984. Observed by ordinary profit per employee of the same fiscal year (π/L) unless otherwise mentioned.

[b] Observed by the lagged ordinary profit per employee $(\pi/L)_{t-1}$.

[c] Observed without B_{t-1} because of unsatisfactory statistical results if B_{t-1} is included as one of the independent variables.

[d] The observation period is 1973–85 unless otherwise mentioned.

[e] The observation period is 1975–85.

[f] The observation period is 1974–85.

[g] Not available because the coefficient of (π/L) is unstable.

[h] Not available because of the reason stated in note c.

[i] Data are not available.

and steel industry may be attributed to the specific role this industry plays in wage determination.

The five major companies in the iron and steel industry have become pattern setters for wage negotiation during the spring offensive almost every year since 1959. The industry has been the most essential industry throughout the industrial development of Japan, particularly during the four decades after World War II. Continuous investment in modern equipment since the 1950s transformed this industry into one of the most efficient and competitive in the world by the middle of the 1960s. It also became the core of the export industries, which made it possible for the labor and management of this industry to take a leadership role during the spring wage negotiations, especially since the late 1950s. Reflecting its strategic position in Japanese industrial relations, the iron and steel industry seems to have decided their

Kazutoshi Koshiro

wages and bonus payments not only on the narrow base of its own profitability but also on broader criteria, taking into account the macroeconomic interest of the national economy as a whole (Sano 1969).

It is also worth noting from table 1 that in the two public utilities industries (private railways and electric power) a different pattern seems to have developed between bonus and profits. Bonus payments in these two industries cannot be explained satisfactorily by equation (1). Fares charged by these two industries are under strict public control, which, in turn, influences their profit rates. Bonus payments in these utilities are also sensitive to changed profitability but not to the same extent as in the other industries.

From the estimated parameters based on equation (1) (which are shown in tables 1 and 2), we can also calculate the *long-run* profit elasticity[14] of bonus payments, shown in column 2 of table 3.

Here again, the iron and steel industry has the lowest elasticity value (0.2864), while the highest value is experienced by the shipbuilding industry, which has suffered greatly since the oil crisis in 1973. On average, the long-run elasticity of bonus payments to profits is a little less than 0.4, which is quite high compared to the short-run elasticity.

Column 4 of table 1 also indicates that bonus payments in major firms seem to have considerable downward rigidity. For example, the parameter γ for total private industries shows that, on average, bonus payments in any given year were set at 74.2% of the bonus payments of the previous year. Table 4 also shows that the yearly lagged bonus payments elasticity (i.e., the elasticity of bonus payments in one period B_t to the previous period

TABLE 4
THE YEARLY-LAGGED-BONUS-PAYMENTS-ELASTICITY BY INDUSTRY

Industry	The yearly-lagged-bonus-payments-elasticity
Total private industries	0.687
Textile	0.742
Paper and pulp	0.658
Chemical	0.615
Iron and steel	0.722
Machinery	0.596
Electric machinery and appliances	0.640
Automobile	0.773
Shipbuilding	0.803
Private railways	0.778
Electric power	0.815

Note: Elasticity at the mean value of the observation period (tables 1 and 2).

54

B_{t-1} for total private industries is 0.687, which is considerably higher than the profit elasticity of 0.1001 shown in table 3). The downward rigidity of bonus payments expressed in terms of the yearly lagged bonus payments elasticity is highest in the electric power industry (0.815) and lowest in the machinery industry (0.596).

If it were possible, it would be desirable to show a similar analysis concerning small- and medium-sized firms.[15] The Ministry of Labor does publish the results of negotiated bonus payments in the organized small- and medium-sized firms, but information on ordinary profit per employee is not available for this sector. Unfortunately, therefore, we can not extend our analyses to this sector.

Sensitivity of Negotiated Bonus Payments to Changes in Profits by Firm

Another useful area for further study would be an investigation of the responsiveness of bonus payments to corporate profit on the basis of the individual firm rather than the industry. Brunello and Ohtake (1987) studied forty-six companies in three industries (banks, textiles, and electric machinery) and, using the Granger test, concluded that bonus payments were responsive to profits only in the case of firms in the banking sector. They conclude that "the positive relation between profits and bonuses found by Freeman and Weitzman in macroeconomic data may be the result of misspecification." However, the present author has reached somewhat different conclusions as a result of analyzing data on two hundred individual companies in seven separate industries (iron and steel, automobile, electric machinery, textile, electric power, and private railways). In this new study, which is to be published in 1991, the author found that bonus payments were quite sensitive to changes in profits per employee in some companies, but not in others. Furthermore, the quantitative relationship between bonus payments and corporate profits is not necessarily simple. In some cases, the positive relationship, as expected from equation (1), is detectable in some firms, but not in others. Results even vary within the same industry. In many cases, unions prefer to negotiate bonus payments not in terms of the absolute amount but in terms of a ratio, for example the number of months of basic monthly pay that should be paid as bonuses. As a result, the bonus ratio can also be responsive to profits in some cases but not in others. For example, Toyota has paid the same ratio of bonus payments (6.1 months basic wage equivalent a year) for more than twenty years. In such a case, the amount of bonus payments may be responsive to corporate profit while the bonus ratio may not. Moreover, the explanatory variables relating to

55

profit vary case by case. In some cases, ordinary profit per employee serves as the most effective explanatory variable while in other cases variables, such as the rate of change of ordinary profit, the ration of ordinary profits to the total amount of sales or to the total amount of capital used, are more appropriate. Similarly, the other type of explanatory variable representing the rigidity of bonus payments differs by company or industry. In some cases, the average amount of bonus payments in total private industries is more suitable than the yearly lagged bonus payments based on the firm.

In short, the relationship between bonus payments and corporate profitability at the enterprise level is much more complicated than hitherto assumed and needs much further research.

We can conclude this section by summarizing some of the major findings of our analyses. First of all, bonus payments do seem, on average, to be sensitive to changes in corporate profits. However, the degree of bonus flexibility as measured by the elasticity of bonus payments to profits in the short run is not as large as usually assumed by Western observers. Second, on the other hand, bonus payments have a considerable degree of downward rigidity in the sense that they are largely determined by the amount of bonus payments paid in the previous year. This is not as strange as it may seem because, historically speaking, bonus payments in Japan originated mostly from a cost-of-living allowance given to workers to compensate them for high inflation during the postwar period. They were originally lump sum compensation twice a year to meet unexpected inflation. This concept is still accepted as meaningful by employers and employees. Finally, data based on the relationship between bonus payments and changes in profits on the level of the firm is much more complicated and deserves further research.

III. Flexibility of Basic Wages

Sensitivity of the Negotiated Level of Basic Wages to Changes in Profits

As noted earlier in this study, Mizuno insists that the major source of wage flexibility in Japan rests on the flexibility of regular earnings rather than that of bonus payments. Whether his judgment is defensible or not is the subject of this section. In order to examine this point, we need to study the responsiveness of the *negotiated* wage levels to corporate profits and to compare the results with the sensitivity of bonus payments to corporate profitability.

56

Every year the Ministry of Labor publishes, together with the levels of basic wage before the negotiation, the results of any negotiated wage increases using the same 288 major firms as that for bonus payments. Therefore, it is possible to compare the profit elasticity of negotiated basic wage levels of these firms with that of bonus payments. Table 5 presents the results of regression analyses of the changes in the negotiated basic wages levels right after wage increase ($W = W_0 + \Delta W$, where W_0 denotes the wage level prior to wage increase) by industry.

The results of the regression analysis is not as satisfactory as in the case of bonus payments except in a few industries (total private industries, chemical, and automobile) because the t-values are too low. In particular, the β value in the private railways is completely unstable, and in the case of the electric power industry, it has a negative sign. However, in order to compare the sensitivity of bonus payments to profits with that of the sensitivity of basic wage levels to profits, the observed β parameters were used to calculate the profit elasticity of basic wage levels of each industry in columns 3 and 4 of table 3.

The short-run profit elasticity of the basic wage level for total private industries is only 0.0472 at the mean value, which is considerably lower than that for bonus payments. The long-run profit elasticity is 0.3024, which is fairly close to that of bonus payments.[16] Judging from these findings, the negotiated levels of regular wages are less flexible than the levels of bonus payments.

So far, we have compared the responsiveness of bonus payments to profits with that of basic wage in terms of the *level* of each payment after it had been increased through negotiation every year. It was found that the short-run profit elasticity of bonus payments (B) was an average 0.1001, whereas that of basic wage (W) was 0.0472. In the long-run, profit elasticity of bonus payments was 0.3879, whereas that of basic wages was 0.3024. In both cases, bonuses were more responsive to corporate profits than basic wage.

The next task is to examine the degree of responsiveness of the *variation* of increased bonus payments (ΔB) and the *variation* of increased basic wages (ΔW) with respect to corporate profits. In this case, the problem is how to specify theoretically meaningful functions for these new dependent variables. Unlike the levels of both bonus payments (B) and basic wages (W), those two variables (ΔB and ΔW) seem to be more affected not only by changes in corporate profits but also by other macroeconomic and institutional factors not included in the earlier equations.

TABLE 5

NEGOTIATED BASIC WAGE LEVELS OF MAJOR FIRMS AND
THEIR SENSITIVITY TO ORDINARY PROFIT, 1973–1985

Industry	Parameter[a]			$\bar{R}^2$	DW	Durbin h statistics[d]
	α	β[b]	γ			
Total private industries	341.54 (7.90)	0.0701 (2.10)	0.8438 (22.46)	0.994	2.52	−0.94
Chemicals	353.67 (6.83)	0.0542 (2.21)	0.8570 (24.79)	0.992	2.57	−1.036
Iron and steel	205.22 (2.92)	0.0469 (1.75)	0.9454 (27.31)	0.985	2.41	−0.745
Machinery	381.97 (5.90)	0.0922 (1.44)	0.8445 (14.24)	0.991	2.68	−1.255
Electrical machinery	406.59 (5.36)	0.0541 (1.32)	0.8023 (12.43)	0.981	2.72	−1.335
Automobile	385.73 (8.59)	0.099 (3.19)	0.7613 (15.39)	0.995	0.57	2.62*
Shipbuilding	251.21 (4.11)	0.0653 (1.59)	0.9254 (36.71)	0.991	2.04	−0.07
Private railways	310.08 (5.23)	0.0759 (0.51)	0.9073 (24.45)	0.989	2.37	−0.673
Electric power	378.02 (6.57)	−0.0034 (−0.45)	0.8998 (28.06)	0.9921	2.34	−0.617
Textile[c]	240.64 (2.42)	0.0475 (1.21)	0.9166 (14.65)	0.9849	1.96	0.07

[a] The regression equation is as follows:

$$W_t = \alpha + \beta(\pi/L)_{t-1} + \gamma W_{t-1},$$

where W_t denotes the average basic wage after the wage increase every spring and $(\pi/L)_{t-1}$ is the average amount of ordinary profit per employee in the previous fiscal year (ending in March of the same year as wage increase). For the purpose of comparing with the profit elasticity of bonus payments, W_t here represents the annual amount.

[b] The data source for (π/L) is the Bank of Japan, *Shuyo Kigyo Keiei Bunseki*, (Financial Analysis of Major Firms) Tokyo: the Bank of Japan, 1985.

[c] The observation period for the textile industry is limited to 1975–1985.

[d] The mark * indicates the existence of serial correlation at the significance level of 5%.

Sensitivity of Negotiated Wage Increase to Corporate Profit

As a direct result of intensive interest in the Phillips curve relationship during the 1960s various kinds of wage functions concerning not only the macroeconomic wage changes but also negotiated wages have been developed.[17] One such wage relationship was formulated by the Ministry of Labor right after the first oil crisis. In this wage function, changes in the negotiated wage increase achieved by major firms (ΔW) are related to the following three variables: the ratio of job offers to job seekers (UY), the rate of increase of consumer prices (PC), and ordinary profit per employee (π/L). However, a similar type of wage function developed by the author using another explanatory variable (a dummy variable representing the industrial relations situation) was able to explain more fully the negotiated wage increase between 1973 and 1985 (table 6).

The dummy variable represents special industrial relations situations in both 1974 and 1982. 1974 was the year of economic and social disturbance caused by the first oil crisis in 1973. To pacify social unrest, some additional wage increases seemed to be necessary. On the other hand, 1982 was the year when major enterprise unions of such private industries as the iron and steel, automobile, electric machinery, shipbuilding, machinery, textile, chemical, pharmaceutical, private railways, and electric power organized a united council called *Zenmin Rokyo* (All Private Sector Trade Unions Council) in December. At the time of the spring offensive of that year, the formation of the council had been expected and the employers seemed to favor this trend because of the more business-minded nature of the new organization. Therefore, it is conceivable that the wage increase in 1982 was higher than the expected level simply because of these economic factors alone. This hypothesis is supported by the quantitative analyses presented in table 6. On average, the profit elasticity of negotiated basic wage increase (ΔW) at the mean value of the observation period was 0.23 for all private industries.

For comparison with this figure we need to measure the elasticity of the changes in bonus payments (ΔB) with respect to ordinary profits per employee. Here we define ΔB as the difference between B_t and B_{t-1}, and B_t is measured using equation (1). Therefore, ΔB can be specified as follows:

$$\Delta B = \alpha + \beta(\frac{\pi}{L})_t - (1 - \gamma)B_{t-1} + e_t. \tag{2}$$

Table 7 gives the result of the regression analysis based on equation (2) for several industries in Japan between 1973 and 1984. The elasticity of changes in bonus payments (ΔB) with respect to ordinary profits per

TABLE 6
REGRESSION EQUATIONS TO EXPLAIN NEGOTIATED AMOUNT OF WAGE INCREASE (ΔW)]^a Scaps[by Industry] 1973–1985

Industry	Constant	PCs	UYs	$(\pi/L)_{t-1}$[b]	DMY (1974 and 1982 = 1 others = 0)	$\bar{R}^2$	DW[c]	SEE	Profit elasticity of wage increase
Total private industry	548.05 (0.40)	693.15 (10.3)	5299.44 (4.93)	2073.39 (3.42)	3564.48 (3.02)	0.956	3.07+	1100.6	0.229
Major five steel companies	4910.19 (9.05)	775.03 (15.9)	—	1020.23 (2.64)	3742.75 (3.12)	0.9609	2.69+	1034	0.0858
Major eight private railways	3776.19 (2.93)	721.28 (8.12)	2905.22 (2.08)	5656.31 (2.62)	3126.05 (2.03)	0.9223	3.12+	1391.4	0.1548
Automobile	976.81 (0.58)	606.01 (8.21)	4324.09 (4.22)	2233.35 (3.54)	3029.25 (2.72)	0.9330	2.46*	1046	0.3262
Electrical machinery	1669.74 (1.03)	613.43 (6.68)	5064.31 (3.62)	1611.54 (2.44)	2977.88 (1.92)	0.9077	2.80+	1436	0.1805
Chemical and pharmaceutical	1870.47 (1.28)	740.37 (9.62)	5118.23 (3.92)	1537.49 (2.91)	3342.09 (2.36)	0.9451	3.20+	1335	0.1787
Machinery and metal trades	1097.28 (0.67)	651.24 (8.80)	6079.93 (4.93)	1876.28 (2.42)	2847.36 (2.06)	0.9445	2.57+	1240	0.1866
Electric power	2925.21 (3.70)	789.70 (17.10)	4006.38 (5.54)	496.27 (4.73)	3671.50 (4.73)	0.9807	2.22*	731	0.1168

a The original data for wage increase (ΔW) are from the Ministry of Labor. This survey covers major 288 companies in the private sector, similar to bonus payments.

b The data for ordinary profit per employee (π/L) are taken from the Data Bank (NEEDS) of the *Nihon Keizai Shinbunsha* (newspaper). The subscript $(t - 1)$ represents the data at the end of the previous fiscal year preceding the spring wage negotiation.

c The mark * indicates that the serial correlation does not exist; whereas the mark + shows that the Durbin-Watson ratio is too high to decide the non-existence of serial correlation.

TABLE 7
THE ELASTICITY OF CHANGES IN BONUS PAYMENTS (ΔB)
WITH RESPECT TO CORPORATE PROFIT BY INDUSTRY, 1973–1984

Industry	Variable and parameter			$\bar{R}^2$	DW^c	Elasticity of ΔB to (π/L)
	Constant term	(π/L)	B_{t-1}^b			
Total private industries	178.87 (4.77)	0.0583 (2.14)	−0.2579 (−3.33)	0.4778	2.84+	1.3482
Textiles	118.90 (6.67)	0.0875 (10.18)	−0.1861 (−5.82)	0.9077	2.99+	0.7266
Chemical	217.58 (4.05)	0.0836 (4.00)	−0.3328 (−4.55)	0.6687	2.33*	1.8698
Paper and pulp	168.48 (2.27)	0.0926 (3.50)	−0.2786 (−2.46)	0.5108	2.92+	1.3664
Iron and steel	169.67 (4.97)	0.0564^a (4.55)	−0.2220 (−5.01)	0.7765	2.27*	0.8831
Machinery	177.93 (4.95)	0.1186 (2.95)	−0.3573 (−3.95)	0.5721	2.65+	2.6489
Electrical machinery	183.37 (5.76)	0.0567 (2.99)	−0.2744 (−3.79)	0.5488	2.46*	1.3364
Shipbuilding	69.71 (0.71)	0.1368 (2.11)	−0.1365 (−1.10)	0.2615	1.96*	1.4766
Automobile	123.65 (6.98)	0.0408^a (2.26)	−0.1575 (−3.45)	0.5421	2.59+	1.0483
Private railways	161.90 (4.69)	0.0594 (0.66)	−0.1587 (−2.66)	0.4072	2.77+	0.3304
Electric power	155.56 (2.73)	0.0023 (0.35)	−0.1279 (−1.52)	0.1093	1.77*	0.1349

^{a} Measured by $(\pi/L)_{t-1}$ instead of $(\pi/L)_t$.
^{b} The sign of the parameter of B_{t-1} should be minus because

$$B_t - B_{t-1} = \alpha + \beta(\pi/L)_t + \gamma B_{t-1} - B_{t-1}$$

$$\Delta B = \alpha + \beta(\pi/L)_t - (1-\gamma)B_{t-1},$$

where $0 < \gamma < 1$ and $0 < (1-\gamma) < 1$.

^{c} The mark * indicates that the serial correlation does not exist; whereas the mark + shows that the Durbin-Watson ratio is too high to decide the nonexistence of serial correlation.

employee was 1.35 for the total private industries, which was much higher than the corresponding elasticity for basic wages (0.23). In this respect, the above analysis reconfirms the previous analysis that bonus payments are more responsive to corporate profits than basic wages. The elasticity of changes in bonus payments (ΔB) to corporate profits varies from the highest figure of 2.65 in the machinery industry to the lowest figure of 0.13 in the electric power industry. Meanwhile, the value of the elasticity of basic wage increase (ΔW) to corporate profits is highest in the automobile industry (0.33) and lowest (0.086) in the iron and steel industry. In spite of the variation in the value of elasticity by industry, it is clear that the elasticity value for the change in bonuses (ΔB) is larger than that for the change in basic wages (ΔW) for each industry.

IV. Wage Changes at the Aggregate Economy

Wage Rigidity and Profit Squeeze

The assumption that bonus payments are flexible also appears to pre-suppose some degree of wage flexibility at the aggregate economy level. If real wages are less rigid at the aggregate level then less profit squeeze will be experienced. Also if the views developed by Hashimoto and Gordon are correct, Japan should therefore be classified in a group of countries possessing a high degree of wage flexibility and a low degree of profit squeeze. For example, if we apply the definition of wage rigidity developed by the OECD (1983), Japan seems to be classified under a group of countries that has the least degree of both wage rigidity and profit squeeze.

> Decline in capital returns has in part been associated with a rise in the share of labour in value added reflecting more than proportionate increase in non-wage labour costs and sluggish adjustments of real wage incomes to reduced (terms-of-trade adjusted) productivity growth. The degree of real wage rigidity depends upon the elasticity of nominal wages with respect to inflation and employment. In a situation where unemployment and inflation are both rising, the degree of real wage rigidity will be high if:
> i) nominal wages react little to the rise in unemployment (low cyclical responsiveness); and
> ii) nominal wages respond strongly to the acceleration of inflation (strong inflation momentum).

62

A high degree of real wage rigidity in a cyclical downturn will not only produce a strong fall in the rate of return on capital but, by adding to inflation and reinforcing inflationary expectations, may also contribute to higher real long-term interest rates. In consequence, pure profit rates will be strongly squeezed.[18]

Based on these judgments, the OECO used a simple and practical measure of real wage rigidity and defined the degree of real wage rigidity as the "elasticity of money wage with respect to inflation minus elasticity of money wages with respect the rise in unemployment."[19]

According to this measure, Japan is ranked as the country with the least degree of wage rigidity among twelve OECO countries, and, if we accept this conclusion, then Japan must also be relatively free from profit squeezes. However, several studies have pointed out that, contrary to this view, Japan *has* suffered from profit squeezes. For example, Sachs (1979) pointed out that Japan was one of four countries (France, Germany, Italy, and Japan) that suffered from a profit squeeze throughout the periods 1969–73 and 1973–75.[20] Therefore, Sachs's findings seem to contradict arguments that stress the flexibility of wages in Japan. Sachs's data was, however, concerned with the aggregate economy up to 1975, and these findings may not be so valid for the subsequent period since the rate of wage increases has slowed down considerably since 1975.

Sachs's idea of the warranted rate of real wage growth is based on equation (3) as follows:[21]

$$g\left(\frac{W}{P_c}\right) = g\left(\frac{V}{L}\right) + g\left(\frac{P_v}{P_c}\right) \tag{3}$$

where W denotes nominal wage rate, P_c represents consumer prices, P_v is the Gross National Product (GNP) deflator, V is real GNP, L stands for the number of employed persons, and g is the growth rate.

In order to maintain the relative share of factors constant, the rate of growth of real wage, $g(W/P_c)$, should be equal to the sum of two elements on the right-hand side of equation (3). If real wage increases faster than the sum of the growth rate of national labor productivity, $g(V/L)$, and of the relative prices, $g(P_v/P_c)$, then capital's share will be squeezed. Table 8 shows the warranted rate of real wage growth in major four countries.

These figures reveal several interesting points. First, Japan is the only country where the growth rate of real wages exceeded warranted real wages (WRW), not only in the period between 1970 and 1984 but also in the period between 1975 and 1984. Therefore, the degree of profit squeeze seems most serious in Japan while the other three countries have managed

Kazutoshi Koshiro

TABLE 8
RATES OF GROWTH OF THE WARRANTED REAL WAGE AND ITS COMPONENTS
AND OF ACTUAL REAL WAGES FOR THE MANUFACTURING INDUSTRY,
BY COUNTRY, FOR THE PERIODS 1970–1984 AND 1975–1984

Country and period		Average annual growth rate (%)				
		Actual real wages		Warranted real wages		
		$(W/P_v)^a$	$(W/P_c)^b$	National labor productivity (V/L)	Terms of trade (P_v/P_c)	Total
Japan	1970–84	5.04	3.26	3.84	−1.70	2.14
	1975–84	3.58	1.72	3.48	−1.78	1.70
U.S.A.	1970–84	0.72	0.38	0.92	−0.50	0.42
	1975–84	0.81	0.23	1.15	−0.83	0.32
U.K.	1970–84	1.77	1.97	1.97	0.15	2.12
	1975–84	1.98	1.52	2.03	0.01	2.04
West	1970–84	1.79	1.64	2.57	−0.13	2.44
Germany	1975–84	1.17	0.70	2.44	−0.37	2.07

Source: OECD, *Main Economic Indicators*; for U.K., Bank of Japan,
     International Comparative Statistics gives gross domestic product
     (GDP) in market prices.
[a] $g(W/P_v)$ should be compared with $g(V/L)$.
[b] $g(W/P_c)$ should be compared with the total growth rate of warranted real
 wages.

to keep the growth rate of real wages below the growth rate of national labor productivity, throughout the two periods. In this sense, these three countries were freed from a profit squeeze after 1970. Second, in each country, the elasticity of real wages with respect to national labor productivity declined considerably in the second period (between 1975 and 1984), so that labor's share diminished in comparison with the first period, but Japan's real wages still exceeded national labor productivity. Even if we take into account the terms of trade, Japan's situation is still the worst of the four countries studied. It should be noted here that Japan has been seriously affected by the deterioration of the terms of trade since the oil crises, and, with the exception of one year (1979), Japan's terms of trade has been falling continuously since 1970. The United States and West Germany were less affected by the oil crises than Japan, while the picture emerging from the United Kingdom is the best of all (table 9).

64

TABLE 9
CHANGES IN THE TERMS OF TRADE^a IN
SELECTED COUNTRIES (IN %), 1970–1984

	Japan	U.S.A.	U.K.	West Germany
1970–71	−1.50	0.68	−0.21	2.19
1971–72	−0.30	0.89	1.54	0.11
1972–73	−0.61	−0.43	−1.15	−0.92
1973–74	−2.60	−1.15	−0.57	−0.62
1974–75	−2.82	0.44	2.30	0.75
1975–76	−3.47	−0.66	−0.74	−1.24
1976–77	−2.36	−0.41	−1.82	0.14
1977–78	−0.36	−0.34	1.93	1.12
1978–79	0.48	−2.33	0.94	0.43
1979–80	−4.26	−4.29	1.17	−0.63
1980–81	−2.10	−0.50	−0.20	−1.96
1981–82	−0.95	0.02	−1.12	−0.67
1982–83	−1.40	0.69	0.54	−0.03
1983–84	−1.60	0.38	−0.58	−0.48
Average annual growth rate				
1970–84	−1.70	−0.50	0.15	0.13
1975–84	−1.78	−0.83	0.01	0.37

Source: The same as table 8.
^a As measured by the ratio of GNP deflator index to consumer price index
  (P_v/P_c). For the United Kingdom GDP deflator is used.

Judging from these findings, we can conclude that Japan is the only country among the major four economies that is still suffered from profit squeezes at the level of aggregate economy.[22] How far these conclusions are compatible with the earlier findings (that negotiated wages and bonus payments in major firms are responsive to changed profitability), is the question to be tackled in the following sections.

Wage Responsiveness to Changed Profitability in Small- and Medium-Sized Firms

Labor markets in Japan are segmented into at least five groups as can be seen in Figure 1: (a) major companies (as defined by the NEEDS Data Bank) employing about 4 million employees, most of whom are organized into enterprise unions (besides these, another 2 million employees are estimated to be employed by major banks, life insurance companies, newspapers, and other companies not listed on the major stock exchanges);

65

Kazutoshi Koshiro

FIGURE 1
LABOR MARKET SEGMENTATION IN JAPAN

Total number of employees: 43 million as of 1985*

(a) Major private companies (mostly organized): 4 million, plus their equivalent 2 million, totalling 6 million (14%)

(b) Public sector (mostly organized) 5 million (12%)

(c) Organized small- and medium-sized firms: 1.5 million (3%)

Subsidiaries | Independent

(d) Unorganized small- and medium-sized firms: 22.7 million (53%)

Subsidiaries | Independent

(e) Very small firms fewer than 30 employees, mostly unorganized: 7.8 million (18%)

* Prior to the privatization of NTT, Tobacco Monopoly, and Japan National Railways. Employees of these three public corporations are included in the category (b) here.

(b) about 5 million public employees in the central and local governments as well as national and local public enterprises, most of whom are organized; (c) about 1.5 million organized workers in small- and medium-sized firms; (d) about 23 million unorganized workers in small- and medium-sized firms; and (e) about 8 million workers employed by very small firms employing less than 30, almost none of whom are organized.

In Sections II and III, we analyzed the negotiated wages and bonus payments among the core groups included under category (a). The wage levels and bonus payments negotiated in this group are expected to spill over directly to groups (b) and (c) and indirectly to the (d) and (e) categories. However, we have not yet assessed the extent to which wages (inclusive of bonus payments) in the (c), (d), and (e) groups are sensitive to changes in profitability.

Mizuno (1985a) found that the growth rates of wages, including bonus payments as well as overtime premiums, were quite sensitive to business cycle activity in small- and medium-sized firms throughout the period 1960–83.[23] However, he does not explicitly show the elasticity of wages with respect to profit rates. If we utilize the data for firms employing more than thirty employees *en bloc*, the changes in the growth rates of nominal cash earnings (inclusive of bonus payments and overtime premiums) from 1966 to 1984 can be explained as follows:

$$\dot{W} = -7.0727 + 7.8046 \text{ UYF} + 0.7136 \text{ PCF} + 107.9 \left(\tfrac{R}{S}\right)_{t-1}, \quad (4)$$

$$(-3.90) \quad (4.48) \quad (7.79) \quad (2.64)$$

$$\bar{R}^2 = 0.9358, \quad DW = 2.22,$$

where UYF is the ratio of job offers against job seekers in the fiscal year; PCF is the consumer price index in the fiscal year and $(R/S)_{t-1}$ is the ratio of operating profit over the amount of sales in the previous fiscal year. The elasticity of the rate of increase of cash earnings with respect to the operating profit ration against sales (R/S) is 0.5917 at the mean values of the observation period.[24] This elasticity is much larger than that of negotiated wage increases in large firms (ΔW) shown in table 6. A precise comparison between the two values is not possible because of the difference in the nature of the dependent variable and the different method of measurement. In particular, the dependent variable in equation (4) includes basic wage, bonus payments, and overtime premiums. Therefore, a considerable part of greater elasticity observed above (0.5917) can be attributable not necessarily to greater responsiveness of basic wage in smaller firms but to the inclusion of both bonus payments and overtime premiums in the calculation. Nevertheless, wage changes in smaller companies are perhaps more sensitive to changed profitability than in large firms.

Causes of Profit Squeeze at the Aggregate Economy in Japan

At this stage it would be beneficial to attempt to reconcile the apparent contradiction between the seemingly flexible wages and bonus payments negotiated within major firms together with the flexible cash earnings in small- and medium-sized firms, on the one hand, and the profit squeeze experienced at the aggregate level of the economy, on the other hand.[25] One or a combination of the following reasons is conceivable:

First, the degree of elasticity of nominal basic wages and bonus payments with respect to changed profitability in major firms is not large enough to prevent a profit squeeze. Wages and bonus payments seem to have a strong downward rigidity, which is supported by their high elasticity with respect to the levels of the previous year.

Second, among small- and medium-sized firms, the magnitude of the elasticity of total cash earnings with respect to profit rates may not be large enough.

Third, earnings differentials among different sizes of firms might be smaller than differentials of labor productivity because wages and bonus payments negotiated in the core sector of the economy may have a strong "spillover effect" on to the remaining sectors.

Fourth, aggregate labor productivity may be dampened largely because of low labor productivity in agriculture, the wholesale and retail trades, and services as well as the lower productivity of small firms across all industries. On the other hand, workers employed by major firms tend to be better paid than the rest of workers in the Japanese economy reflecting their higher labor productivity.

It should be added that Ohtake (1986), using comprehensive quantitative analysis based upon Chow's method of disequilibrium analysis, has denied the flexibility of real wages in Japanese firms employing more than thirty workers. He contends that real wages in Japan adjust to the equilibrium level with long time-lags of five or six years, while labor input can be adjusted almost completely within only one year. Although these findings seem to contradict previous studies in this field, they need to be integrated into the findings of this paper.

At the moment, it seems that the third and fourth factors noted above may have contributed most to the considerable degree of profit squeeze (and therefore contributed to "wage rigidity" at the level of the aggregate economy) in Japan. Also it should not be forgotten that profits have also been squeezed by a continuous deterioration of the terms of trade.

Thus, if we take all these elements into consideration, we may conclude that the measurement of the responsiveness of wages or bonus payments to changes in profits alone will not provide a decisive answer to the question of what determines wage flexibility at the macroeconomic level. Hence the problems of wage flexibility need to be scrutinized from a broader perspective, taking into account such factors as the differences of labor productivity between different sectors of economy as well as the impact of industrial and employment structures.

V. Conclusion

Wages in Japan are usually assumed to be more flexible than in other advanced countries because of the strategic role played by bonus payments. This study has attempted to quantify the responsiveness of both bonuses and basic wages to corporate profits in Japan.

According to many labor economists in the West, trade unions are often deemed to be responsible for decreasing wage flexibility and so the present study took as its base a group of about 290 large firms who comprise the "core" group of organized workers in Japanese industry. The analysis was made easier by the fact that official statistics are available for this group overtime, thus enabling an in-depth study to be undertaken. The argument follows that if wages and bonus payments for this group are flexibly determined, then it might further follow that wages in all sectors of the economy are also flexible since the rest of Japanese economy is less organized and free from the pressure of collective bargaining.

First, it was observed that bonus payments in major large firms were indeed responsive to changed profitability. In particular the elasticity of bonus payments to ordinary profits per employee was higher than the elasticity of the basic wage payment to such profit.

However, the *magnitude* of the elasticity values for basic wages and bonus payments with respect to ordinary profit per employee were not necessarily as large as usually imagined by Western commentators. The short-run elasticity of bonus payments with respect to ordinary profit per employee was only 0.1 on average, while that for basic wage levels was only 0.0472. On the other hand, the elasticity of negotiated amount of basic wage *increase* (ΔW) in major firms, with respect to ordinary profit per employee, was higher at 0.229. Also, the elasticity of the negotiated amount of *increased* bonus payments (ΔB) to profit was 1.3482 and was high by any standards. Also some tentative information was presented that showed that the sensitivity of bonus payments to corporate profitability on the level of the firms is a complex matter that needs further research.

In spite of such wage flexibility in the core sector of the economy, real wages at the aggregate level in Japan since 1970 exceeded the growth rate of national labor productivity. This was the case even in the period from 1975 to 1984 when unions endeavored to restrain wage increases in order to maintain employment opportunities. This phenomenon was partly due to the deteriorating terms of trade, which was far more serious in Japan than in other Western countries.

In order to reconcile the seeming contradiction between the flexibility of basic wages and bonuses in the major sector of the economy, on the one hand, with the rigidity of real wages at the aggregate level, on the other, two factors should be taken into account. First, the magnitude of profit elasticity of basic wages and bonus payments in the key sector of the economy may not have been large enough to avoid profit squeeze. Second, the magnitude of profit elasticity of nominal cash earnings among small- and medium-sized firms may not be large enough to maintain wage flexibility for the whole economy, although the magnitude itself is more than double that of large firms. However, with respect to the points noted above, the real problem for researchers is that we cannot be sure what constitutes a "desirable" profit elasticity of bonus payments or basic wages that would be sufficient to solve the unemployment problem.

A third, and final, reason for the contradiction noted above may have to do with the earnings and productivity differential between large and small firms. In Japan, earnings differentials between different sizes of firms may be smaller than differentials of labor productivity for at least two reasons. First, wages and bonus payments negotiated in the core sector of the economy may have a strong "spillover effect" on the remaining sectors, so that earnings in the latter sectors may exceed their marginal labor productivity. Second, aggregate labor productivity might be lowered mostly because of the low levels of labor productivity in the remaining sectors. Workers employed in Japan's major firms are better paid than the rest of the workforce because these companies occupy a strategic position in the economy possessing higher capital/labor ratio, easier access to financial resources, and higher quality of labor. This, in turn, would increase the marginal labor productivity of these workers. On the other hand, the labor productivity of workers employed in the remaining sectors, particularly in agriculture, the service sector, and many small firms across industries tends to be lower than that of workers in the major large firms.

Finally, it should be emphasized that wage or bonus flexibility by themselves may be a necessary but are not a sufficient condition to maintain economic efficiency. Resource allocation by industry or by size of firms and the resulting productivity differentials are crucial factors to bear in mind when assessing the efficiency of any economic system.

Notes

1. Sachs (1979) may be the exception. He stressed that real wage increases in Japan between 1969 and 1978 exceeded the limit of "warranted real wage" and resulted in a sizable "profit squeeze."
2. Stimulated by Taira's criticism, some Japanese experts on this subject thoroughly re-examined the unemployment statistics in Japan in comparison with that of the United States. However, Shiraishi (1984), Nagayama (1984), and Tomita (1984) presented counterevidences to reject Taira's view. See also Sorrentino (1984).
3. For more details about this concept, see Koshiro (1983a; 1983c).
4. Wage determination in the public sector is another area of study not covered here. In some countries, the public sector may become a source of wage distortion from a macroeconomic stabilization point of view due to the influence of strong unions in this sector. Fortunately in Japan, the principle of pay comparability between the private and the public sectors has been firmly established since the 1950s. However, even in this framework, public employee unions have played an influential role in wage setting on a few occasions up to the early 1970s but they have lost their bargaining power since around 1975. In particular, the privatization of three public corporations (Japan National Railways, Nippon Telephone and Telegram, and Japan Tobacco Monopoly) between 1985 and 1987 contributed to a decrease in the bargaining power of public employees. For more details of wage determination in the public sector, see Koshiro (1983b, 1985b).
5. Local minimum wage rates are published in the Japan Productivity Center, *Katsuyo Rodo Tokei (Handbook of Labor Statistics) 1988*, p. 70; the average hourly earnings in all industries for 1987 is obtainable from the Ministry of Labor, *Monthly Labor Statistics* covering the establishments employing more than thirty employees; for the United States, U.S. Department of Labor, Employment Standards Administration, *Minimum Wage and Maximum Hours Standards under the Fair Labor Standards Act, 1381*. For France, Ministère du Travail, *Evolution du Salaire Minimum Interprofessionel de Croissance (SMIC)*. The average hourly earnings in the United States and France are for the manufacturing industry.
6. OECD (1984), p. 67.
7. See also Gordon (1982), p. 17.
8. Cyclical sensitivity is measured by regression analysis relating indexes of industrial production to gross national product (GNP), while the bonus earnings ratio (RB) is likewise determined by regression analysis relating indexes of bonus earning ratio to GNP.
9. Mizuno (1985a) criticizes Hashimoto, Gordon, and Kahn on the following two points. First, the proportion of special payments (bonus payments plus additional payments due to wage increases, which are usually paid a few months after the agreed wage increase) to regular earnings (basic wages plus overtime

71

premiums), which is almost equivalent to Hashimoto's RB, is limited to at most 26.1%. Second, the extent of the contribution of bonus payments to the variance of total earnings is limited to only 9% at most during the period between 1960 and 1983 and to 16.4% between 1974 and 1983. He insists that the major source of wage flexibility in Japan rests on the flexibility of regular earnings, which constitute three quarters of total earnings. But Mizuno himself does not compare the sensitivity of basic wages and bonus payments to changed profitability.

10. According to the Ministry of Labor, *Monthly Labor Statistics Survey*, the average *monthly* total cash earnings of all workers in establishments employing more than thirty in all industries including the service industry in 1985 was 317,100 yen of which 223,400 yen (70.5%) was straight-time basic wages, 13,200 yen (4.2%) was overtime payments, and 80,500 yen (25.4%) was bonus payments. JPC, *Katsuyo Rodo Tokei* (Handbook of Labor Statistics), Tokyo: Japan Productivity Center. (1987), p. 59.

11. Theoretically, this equation can be derived as follows. The desirable level of bonus payments in year t (B_t^*) can be measured by:

$$B_t^* = a + b(\frac{\pi}{L})_t + \epsilon_t, \qquad (i)$$

where ϵ_t is the random disturbance whose average is zero and whose covariance matrix is $\sigma_t^2 I$, where I represents a unit matrix. Each observed value of B_t is not the desirable value B_t^* but a partially adjusted value with the adjustment speed λ as follows:

$$B_t - B_{t-1} = \lambda(B_t^* - B_{t-1}). \qquad (ii)$$

Substituting (i) into equation (ii), we obtain

$$B_t = (1 - \lambda)B_{t-1} + \lambda[a + b\left(\frac{\pi}{L}\right)_t + \epsilon_t], \qquad (iii)$$

$$B_t = \lambda \cdot a + \lambda \cdot b\left(\frac{\pi}{L}\right)_t + (1 - \lambda)B_{t-1} + \lambda\epsilon_t. \qquad (iv)$$

Comparing equation (iv) with equation (1) in the text

$$\alpha = \lambda a, \qquad \beta = \lambda b, \qquad \gamma = (1 - \lambda), \qquad \text{and } e_t = \lambda\epsilon_t.$$

In equation (i), it is assumed that ϵ_t has no serial-correlation so that e_t in equation (1) is expected to have no serial correlation either.

However, in the following observations, some of the Durbin-Watson ratios (DW) are too low or too high, which shows the existence of serial correlation. Therefore, for these biased parameters, further elaboration of the model would be required to get rid of the biases. However, in this preliminary research the observations will be presented for the time being without such elaboration.

For these econometric problems, the author is grateful for comments by Mr. Hitoshi Hayami of Keio University at the Tokyo Workshop of Labor Market Study Committee, Institute of Statistical Studies (Tokei Kenkyu Kai) in July 1986.

12. "Ordinary profit" is a standard concept used in Japanese official accounting. It includes the sum of ordinary operating income (net of depreciation and taxes) *plus* nonoperating income *minus* nonoperating expenses. Basically speaking this concept correspond to "net income after tax."

13. The elasticity (η) can be measured as follows:

$$\eta = \beta \cdot \frac{\overline{(\pi/L)}}{\bar{B}},$$

where the bars indicate the mean value of each variable in the observation period.

14. The long-run profit elasticity (η^*) is measured as follows:

$$\eta^* = \frac{\beta}{(1-\gamma)} \cdot \frac{\overline{(\pi/L)}}{\bar{B}},$$

where β and γ are the parameters obtained by estimating equation (1) for each industry.

15. Mizuno (1985a, pp. 66–67) finds out, through the analysis of the coefficient of variance of bonus payments, that the flexibility of total earnings including bonus payments does not differ significantly among the different sizes of firms.

16. The statistical results of the regression equations in table 5 are not necessarily satisfactory. If we limit the observation period to 1975–85, the results improve for total private industries as follows:

$$W = 364.05 + 0.06869 \ (\pi/L)_{-1} + 0.83428 \ W_{-1},$$
$$\quad \quad (6.58) \quad \ \ (2.47) \quad \quad \quad \quad \ \ (19.33)$$
$$\bar{R}^2 = 0.9966, \quad \ DW = 2.84, \quad \ \ SEE = 22.32;$$

where the short-run profit elasticity of wage level is 0.0459 and the long-run elasticity is 0.2771.

17. To cite only a few pioneering works, see Watanabe (1966), Sano (1969), Ono (1973), Ministry of Labor (1975), and Koshiro (1983a).

18. OECD (1983) p. 48.

19. Ibid.

20. Sachs (1979) p. 284. His arguments are based on the simple algebra concerning the relationship between the rate of growth of real wage (w/p_c) and the national labor productivity (V/L) as well as the terms of trade (P_v/P_c) as equation (3) in the text. If factor shares are to remain constant, the algebra should stand. If the actual growth rate of real wages exceeds the rate of growth of the warranted real wages, $g(W/P_c)$, then the capital (nonlabor) share is to be squeezed.

21. For simplicity, here we ignore the indirect tax rate.
22. This situation may have changed since the appreciation of yen after the autumn of 1985. In both 1986 and 1987, the rate of wage increases was dampened by the adverse effects of the strong yen, which forced down exports. Furthermore, management succeeded in further restraining wage increases in the spring of 1988 when corporate profits recovered strikingly. At the same time, the terms of trade (the ratio of the export price to the import price) has improved by 40% since 1985.
23. Mizuno (1985a) p. 68. He also points out that "specially-paid wages" (most of which are bonus payments) are quite sensitive to changed profitability even among very small firms employing only five to twenty-nine employees.
24. The elasticity η of the rate of increase of cash earnings $(\dot{W})$ with respect to the operating profit ratio against the amount of sales $(R/S)_{t-1}$ is measured as follows:

$$\eta. = \frac{d\dot{w}/\bar{w}}{d(R/S)/(\overline{R/S})} = 107.9\frac{0.0636582}{12 \cdot 2286} = 0.5617,$$

where $\bar{w}$ and $(\overline{R/S})$ denote the mean value of each variable, respectively, during the observation period.
25. Mizuno (1985) also contends that labor's share in Japan has expanded in recent years sacrificing employment and nonlabor income (p. 65).

References

Branson, William H., and Julio J. Rotemberg (1980). "International Adjustment with Wage Rigidity," *EER*, 13:309–32.

Brunello, Giorgio, and Fumio Ohtake (1987). "The Relation between Bonuses, Wages, Profits and Employment in Japan: A Reconsideration based on Microeconomic Data," *Ohsaka Daigaku Keizaigaku*, 37 (No. 1, June).

Gordon, Robert J. (1982). "Why U.S. Wage and Employment Behaviour Differs from that in Britain and Japan," *EJ*, 92:13–44.

Grubb, Dennis, Rilchard Jackman, and Richard Layard (1983). "Wage Rigidity and Unemployment in OECD Countries," *EER*, 21:11–39.

Freeman, Richard B., and Martin L. Weitzman (1986). "Bonuses and Employment in Japan," National Bureau of Economic Research, Inc., Working Paper, No. 1878, April.

Hart, Robert (1988). *Employment, Unemployment, and Labor Utilization*, Winchester, Mass.

Hashimoto, Masanori (1979). "Bonus Payments, On-the-Job Training, and Lifetime Employment in Japan," *JPE*, 87(5):1086–1104.

74

Kahn, G. A. (1984). "International Differences in Wage Behavior: Real, Nominal, or Exaggerated?" *AER*, 74(2):155–59.

Koike, Kazuo (1981). *Chusho Kigyo on Jukuren(Skill in Small Firms)*, Tokyo.

——— (1983). "Workers in Small Firms and Women in Industry," in *Contemporary Industrial Relations in Japan*, edited by T. Shirai, Madison, Wis., pp. 89–115.

Koshiro, Kazutoshi (1983a). "Development of Collective Bargaining in Postwar Japan" in *Contemporary Industrial Relations in Japan*, edited by T. Shirai, Madison, Wis., pp. 205–57.

——— (1983b). "Labor Relations in Public Enterprises" in *Contemporary Industrial Relations in Japan*, edited by T. Shirai, Madison, Wis., pp. 259–93.

——— (1983c). *Nihon no Roshikankei (Industrial Relations in Japan)*, Tokyo.

——— (1985a). "Job Security: Redundancy Arrangements and Practices in Japan," Discussion Paper Series 85-3, the Center for International Trade Studies, Yokohama National University, January.

——— 1985b). "Labor Relations in Public Service and the Impact of Union Activity on Public Administration's Actual Organization and Functioning," Discussion Paper 85-2, the Center for International Trade Studies, Yokohama National University, March; also Faculty of Economics, Yokohama National University, *Economia*, 86 (September): 26–70.

——— (1986). "Small Business and the Labor Market in Japan—the Interrelationship between Large and Small Enterprises since 1970—," Discussion Paper 86-4, the Center for International Trade Studies. Faculty of Economics, Yokohama National University, November.

Ministry of Labor (MOL) (1973). *Labor White Paper for 1973*.

——— (1975). *Labor White Paper for 1975*.

——— (1983). *Labor White Paper for 1983*, Tokyo.

Mizuno, Asao (1985a). "Chingin Shinshuku-sei to Koyo Hendo" ("Wage Flexibility and Employment Changes,") in *Gendai Nihon no KeizaiSystem (The Economic System of Modern Japan)*, edited by T. Nakamura, S. Nishikawa, and Y. Kosai, Tokyo.

——— (1985b). "An Empirical Analysis of Wage Flexibility and Employment Fluctuations in Japan," *Pacific Economic Papers*, no. 124, July.

Moll, Verena (1986). "The Japanese Bonus-System: Its Workings and Adaptations in the Business Cycle," *Economia*, no. 90, September.

Muramatsu, Kuramitsu (1983). *Nihon no Rodoshijo Bunseki (Analyzing the Japanese Labor Market)*, Tokyo.

——— (1985). "Koyo Kansu kara mita Chingin no Koyo he no Eikyo—Tenbo" ("The Impact upon Employment of Wages Viewed from Employment Functions—An Overview"), *Academia*, 87 (July): 1–25.

Nagayama, Sadanori (1984). "Nihon no Shitsugyo wa Hikusugiru no ka?" ("Is Unemployment in Japan too Low?"), *Nihon Rodokyokai Zasshi*, March.

Nerlove, M. (1956). "Estimates of the Elasticities of Supply of Selected Agricultural Commodities," *Journal of Farm Economics*, 38.

Kazutoshi Koshiro

OECD (1983). *Economic Outlook* no. 33, July.

———— (1984). *Employment Outlook,* September.

———— (1985). Manpower and Social Affairs Committee, *Labor Market Flexibility,* Technical Report by the Secretariat, 17 December.

Ohtake, Fumio (1986). "Jisshutsu Chingin no Shinshuku-sei ni tsuite" ("On the Flexibility of Real Wages"), unpublished mimeo, January.

Ono, Akira (1973). *Sengo Nihon no Chingin Kettei (Wage Determination in Postwar Japan),* Tokyo.

———— (1985). "Saikin no Teikeizai Seicho to Kongo no Rodoshijo" ("Low Economic Growth in Recent Years and the Future of Labor Markets") in *Senshin Kogyokoku no Koyo to Shitsugyo (Employment and Unemployment in Advanced Industrialized Countries),* edited by R. Minami and A. Mizuno, Tokyo.

Sachs, Jeffrey D. (1979). "Wages, Profits, and Macroeconomic Adjustment: A Comparative Study," *Brooking Papers on Economic Activity,* 2:269–332.

Sano, Yoko (1969). *Chingin Kettei no Keiryo Bunseki (Econometric Analyses of Wage Determination),* Tokyo.

Sano, Yoko, H. Ishida, and S. Inoue, eds. (1971). *Chusho Kigyo no Chingin Kettei (Wage Determination in Small- and Medium-Sized Firms),* Tokyo.

Sano, Yoko, K. Koike, and H. Ishida, eds. (1969). *Chingin Kosho no Kodo Kagaku (Behavioral Science of Wage Negotiation),* Tokyo.

Sasajima, Toshio (1984). *Nichi-Bei-Ohu no Koyo to Shitsugyo (Employment and Unemployment in Japan, the U.S.A., and European Countries),* Tokyo.

Shinpo, Shoji (1985). *Bunseki Nihon Keizai (Analyzing Japanese Economy),* Tokyo.

Shiraishi, Eiji (1984). "Shitsugyo Gainen no Kokusai Hikaku" ("An International Comparison of the Concept of Unemployment"), Ministry of Labor, *Rodo Tokei Chosa Geppo,* March.

Sorrentino, C. (1984). "Japan's Low Unemployment," U.S. Department of Labor, *MLR,* March.

Tachibanaki, Toshiaki (1987). "Labour Market Flexibility in Japan in Comparison with Europe and the U.S.," *European Economic Review* 31.

Taira, Koji (1983). "Japan's Low Unemployment," U.S. Department of Labor, *MLR,* July.

———— (1985). "Japan's Lifetime Employment Revisited," Faculty Working Paper no. 1137, College of Commerce and Business Administration, University of Illinois, April.

Tomita, Yasunobu (1984). "Waga Kuni no Shitsugyo Tokei ni kansuru Kosatsu" ("Reflections on the Statistics of Unemployment in Japan") in *Gendai no Shitsugyo (Contemporary Unemployment),* edited by K. Koike, pp. 117–142, Tokyo.

Tsuru, Shigeto (1961). "'Barometer' to Shukei Gainen" ("'Barometer' and the Aggregated Concepts") in *Kindai Keizaigaku Ronshu (Readings in Modern Economics),* edited by S. Tsuru, Tokyo.

Watanabe, Tsunehiko (1966). "Chingin, Kakaku no Kankei to sono Seisakuteki Igi" ("The Relationship between Wages and Prices and Its Policy Implications") in *Nihon no Bukka* (*Prices in Japan*), edited by H. Kumagai and T. Watanabe, Tokyo.

Weitzman, Martin L. (1983). "Some Macroeconomic Implications of Alternative Compensation System," *Economic Journal*, 93, December.

—— (1984). *The Share Economy*, Cambridge.

—— (1985). "The Simple Macroeconomics of Profit Sharing," *American Economic Review*, December.

Masanori Hashimoto and John Raisian

3

Aspects of Labor Market Flexibility in Japan and the United States

I. Introduction

Recently, much attention has been directed in the United States at Japanese-type industrial relations as a potential explanation for that nation's high rates of output and productivity growth.[1] Indeed, Japan has surpassed the United States in the rates of growth in output and output per hour—especially in manufacturing, where Japanese productivity is now higher than that in the United States.

Permanent employment and related practices are thought by some to be a unique Japanese phenomenon, responsible for high productivity growth in Japan. There is even a suspicion that the U.S. style industrial relations have become detrimental to high productivity growth. Available evidence, some of which we developed and reported in our previous papers, does indicate that tenure levels are higher, employer-employee attachments stronger, and unemployment rates lower in Japan than in the United States (see, for example, Hashimoto and Raisian 1985). In other words, job mobility is lower in Japan. It should be noted, however, that job mobility may improve employer-employee matches, thereby increasing productivity. If so,

78

mobility may not be a negative factor in the United States, to be discouraged in response to the apparent success of Japanese employment practices.

Our focus here is on how the two countries adjust employment, hours of work, and wages over the business cycle. Differences in these adjustments have a direct bearing, in our view, on the much lower unemployment rates in Japan than in the United States.[2] By and large, our findings agree with a commonly held view: namely,in the United States, wages are relatively rigid over the business cycle with employment fluctuating a great deal; but in Japan, employment tends to remain stable, while wages are quite flexible.

II. Hypothesis and Evidence

To gain perspective on the data, it is desirable to have a conceptual framework. In explaining cross-country differences in labor markets, we hesitate to appeal to culture and tradition. Rather, we seek explanations based on the principles of efficient resource allocation.

In this research, there is good reason for minimizing our reliance on culture and traditions. Namely, some of these labor market differences appear to have emerged rather recently. For example, (1) Japanese labor turnover appears to have been quite substantial in the early 1900s and through the early 1950s (Taira 1970, Chapter 6; Shimada 1983, p. 7) and (2) the United States appears to have experienced a drastic decline in the responsiveness of wages to economic conditions after the end of World War II (Gordon 1982). The cultural explanation, which would suggest unchanging persistence over time, seems unsatisfactory, taken by itself.

We argue that, because of low transaction costs, Japanese workers invest in firm-specific human capital to a greater extent than a typical U.S. worker. By transaction costs, we mean costs that Robinson Crusoe would not have incurred until he met Friday. They are the costs associated with exchanging goods and information. In employment relationships, an employer and an employee must constantly communicate about their firm's economic conditions and the employee's reservation wages. For information to be used effectively, the parties must be willing to accept its accuracy. Mistrust reduces the value of the match, as the parties insist on further verifications. Haggling and postcontractual opportunistic behavior reflect high transaction costs.

Various features of Japanese industrial relations point to the low transaction costs that characterize Japanese employment relationships. For example, the employment relationship in Japan is said to be something more than a mere trade of labor and wages. It is well known, for example, that Japanese workers tend to identify with their employers. The employer-employee relationship in Japan is "accompanied by the feeling that the employee's families are subordinated to, and dependent on, the employer for protection" (Hanami 1979 p. 47). Also, the famous joint consultation approach to decision making in Japanese businesses would seem to be impossible unless transaction costs are low.

Wage flexibility in Japan is another manifestation of low transaction costs there. Wage flexibility, in turn, encourages investments in human capital by reducing the dissipation of wealth caused by costly transactions, haggling, and other moral hazard behaviors in the postinvestment phase of employment relationships. This argument is the subject of analysis in Hashimoto and Yu (1980), and the associated wage contract model is sketched in Appendix I. This model serves as an analytical framework within which we attempt to organize the empirical findings reported in this paper (see also Hashimoto and Raisian 1986b). We take the transaction-cost differences to be exogenous, though in the future we hope to address factors that may illuminate this phenomenon. What we do show is that observed labor market differences between Japan and the United States are consistent with the differential transaction cost hypothesis—an important first step, in our judgement.

The presence of firm-specific human capital makes labor a quasi-fixed factor (Becker 1962; Oi 1962; and Hart 1984). On this point, refer to table 1, which offers the following relevant observations:

1. The importance of wages and salaries in total compensation cost is much lower in Japan than in the United States, ranging between 75% to a little over 80% for the United States, but only around 60% for Japan.

2. Clearly, bonuses are responsible for the above phenomenon. If bonuses are added to wages and salaries in row 3, the two countries look very similar.

3. Some have argued that in the United States nonwage benefits are larger than in Japan, giving U.S. labor more quasi-fixity. The sum of rows 4 and 5 shows that the two countries are quite similar in nonwage benefits, thereby refuting such an argument.

Hashimoto (1979) argued that Japanese bonus payments largely represent returns on investments in firm-specific human capital, a form of profit-sharing arrangement made possible by low transaction costs. Based on this argument, we view the information contained in table 1 as indicative of the greater importance of firm-specific human capital in Japan than in the United States.

Table 2 offers additional evidence from earnings profiles in the manufacturing industries. Instead of considering just the slopes of earnings

80

TABLE 1

STRUCTURE OF COMPENSATION COSTS FOR PRODUCTION
WORKERS IN U.S. AND JAPANESE MANUFACTURING INDUSTRIES

	United States			Japan		
	1966	1972	1977	1965	1971	1978
(1) Wages and salaries	82.4%	79.0%	74.8%	64.6%	61.2%	56.7%
(2) Bonuses	0.6	0.5	0.4	18.2	21.3	20.3
(3) (1) + (2)	83.0	79.5	75.2	82.8	82.5	77.0
(4) Nonmonetary benefits	11.4	14.4	17.3	12.3	12.3	16.1
Pay for leave time	5.6	6.2	6.9	3.2	3.2	4.7
Pay in kind	—	—	—	4.2	4.1	4.0
Benefits	5.8	8.2	10.4	4.9	5.0	7.4
(5) Legally required insurance	5.5	6.2	7.4	4.8	5.2	6.9
(6) Total	100	100	100	100	100	100

Source: U.S. Bureau of Labor Statistics, *Handbook of Labor Statistics*, 1985,
    table 134.

Notes: Figures don't always add up to the indicated totals because of
    rounding. Wages and salaries include basic time and piece rates, plus
    overtime premiums and shift differentials. Bonuses include all bonuses
    and premiums not paid monthly. Pay for leave time includes pay for
    vacation, holidays, and personal leave. Sick leave pay is included in
    benefits. Pay in kind includes the cost to the employer of goods and
    services provided free or at reduced costs, such as food or housing, or
    cash allowances paid in lieu of pay in kind. Benefits include private
    benefit plans.

profiles, we attempt to quantify investment amounts by using a modified
Mincers (1974) technique to estimate the amount of human capital formation
on the job in manufacturing industries. Because of space limitations, we
refer the reader to Hashimoto and Raisian (1986a) for technical details of
this procedure. In that article, we estimate the magnitudes of investments
for the entire private economy rather than just for manufacturing, as we do
here.

In table 2, the overtaking year refers to the year in which the earnings
of those who undertake investments catch up with the earnings of those
who do not invest at all (cf. figure 1). According to the table, the value of
the peak year (year of employment when earnings reach their peak) and the
peak earnings, both are greater in larger firms.

Looking at investments measured in years in this table, it is evident
that Japanese workers invest more than American workers, and workers
in larger firms invest more in both countries. This general conclusion also
holds if you look at investments in monetary units. These are estimates of

81

TABLE 2
EARNINGS PROFILES AND ON-THE-JOB INVESTMENTS IN HUMAN
CAPITAL: MALE WORKERS IN MANUFACTURING INDUSTRIES

	Firm Size				
	(1) Small	(2) Medium	(3) Large	(4) (2)/(1)	(5) (3)/(1)
Japan (1980)					
Overtaking year	5	6	7	1.2	1.4
Peak year	13	21	30	1.6	2.3
Monthly earnings in overtaking year (1000 yen)	194.93	213.85	223.83	1.1	1.1
Monthly earnings in peak year (1000 yen)	278.10	358.01	480.05	1.3	1.7
Estimated investments in:					
1000 Yen	7,269	12,350	22,271	1.7	3.1
Dollars*	20,191	34,306	61,864		
Time (years)	2.6	3.7	5.5	1.4	2.1
Unites States (1979)					
Overtaking year	5	5	5	1.0	1.0
Peak year	25	28	31	1.1	1.2
Weekly earnings in overtaking year ($)	268.91	288.27	312.84	1.1	1.2
Monthly earnings in peak year ($)	360.12	376.45	418.43	1.0	1.2
Estimated investments in:					
Dollars	25,807	24,615	28.838	0.9	1.1
Time (years)	1.7	1.5	1.6	0.9	0.9

Sources: From regression estimates using the *Basic Survey of Wage Structure*
(Chingin Kozo Kihon Tokei Chosa 1980) and the U.S. *Current
Population Survey* (1979). Regression coefficients are available upon
request.
* Converted at the most conservative exchange rate of 360 yen to a dollar. The
internal rate of return is forced to be equal among the firm-size groups, 13%
for Japan and 17% for the Unites States, to select the overtaking year. See
the text for details.

total investments—the sum of specific and general investments. Assuming
that the ratio of firm-specific capital to total capital is not sufficiently nega-
tively correlated with the total amount of capital, the evidence supports our
assertion that there is more human capital invested in the Japanese than the
U.S. workers.[3]

These two tables indicate that workers have higher degrees of fixity in Japan than in the United States. In addition, the general set of

FIGURE 1
ON-THE-JOB INVESTMENTS IN HUMAN CAPITAL

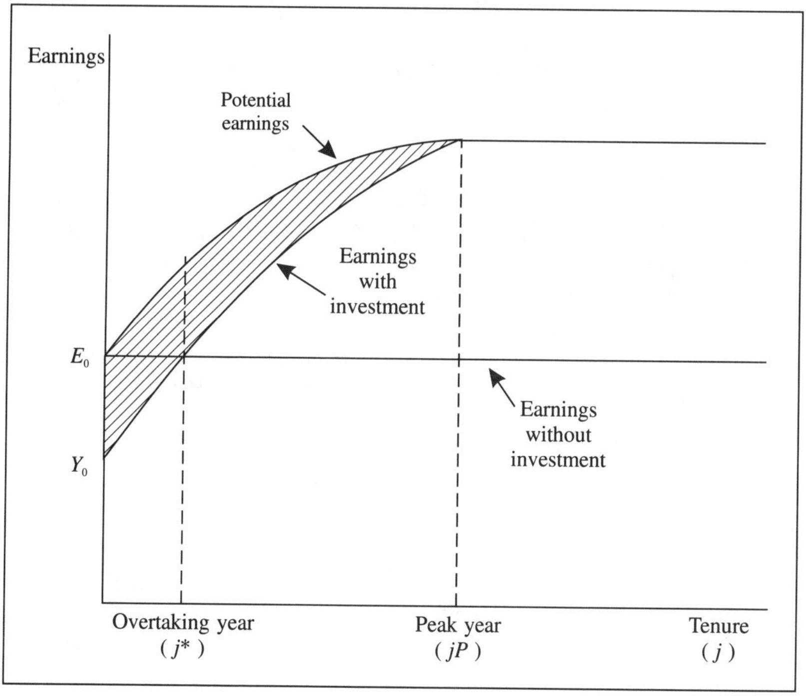

circumstances we have investigated for the two countries—the relative importance of firm tenure in determining the shape of earnings profiles, the duration of employment tenure, the prevalence of bonus payments in Japan, but not in the United States—represent evidence, in our view, consistent with the fixity argument.

III. Japan-U.S. Labor Market Differences in an International Perspective

Are Japan and the United States uniquely different from other developed countries in how their labor markets adjust to fluctuations in demand? To shed light on this question, we begin with some cross-country comparisons.

Tables 3 and 4 present estimates of variabilities for selected labor market variables for the manufacturing industries of eleven countries. The underlying data are adjusted by the U.S. Bureau of Labor Statistics (BLS) in an attempt to present series with improved comparability across countries (see *Handbook of Labor Statistics*, U.S. Bureau of Labor Statistics, Bulletin 2217, 1985, Washington D.C., 1985, pp. 414–16).

Table 3 presents output-normalized variabilities for four labor market variables pertaining to manufacturing industries. These magnitudes are obtained by calculating the ratios of two standard deviations, the numerator being the standard deviation of year-to-year changes in the logarithm of the variable in question (e.g., employment), and the denominator being the standard deviation of year-to-year changes in the logarithm of real output. The ratio is an index of the variability in the chosen variable standardized for influences of variability in output. The compensation measures pertain to all workers in the manufacturing industry and include items of compensation other than hourly earnings.[4]

Among the eleven countries, the United States is at the lowest end of the spectrum for variabilities in hours of work (0.19) and compensation (0.40 for nominal and 0.25 for real), while Japan is at the lowest end in employment variability (0.46). Note that the U.S. employment variability is quite similar to that of other Western countries, ranging between 0.51 for Italy and 0.94 for Denmark. In the United States, employment exhibits the greatest variability of the four labor-force measures—by nearly a three-to-one margin over real compensation, and over a three-to-one margin over hours worked. In Japan, both employment and real compensation exhibit a similar extent of variation—0.46 and 0.50, respectively—and both variabilities are more than twice that of hours (0.21). These comparisons leave one with the impression that compensation variability dampens employment variability in Japan, at least relative to the United States. This apparent trade-off between employment and compensation variabilities is less apparent, however, when other countries are included in the comparisons.

Table 4 contains information on the relation between movements in labor market magnitudes and output. The procedure used to generate this information is straightforward. Suppose we describe a variable in question as follows:

$$\ln Y = a + bT + c \ln Z + e, \tag{1}$$

where $\ln Y$ is the logarithm of the chosen variable; T is time; $\ln Z$ is the logarithm of real output; a, b, and c are regression coefficients; and e is an

TABLE 3

INTERNATIONAL COMPARISONS OF OUTPUT-NORMALIZED VARIABILITES IN
LABOR MARKET MAGNITUDES FOR MANUFACTURING INDUSTRIES: 1950–1983

	U.S.	Japan	Germany	U.K.	Canada	Denmark	France	Italy	Netherlands	Norway	Sweden
Employment	0.67	0.46	0.66	0.71	0.66	0.94	0.59	0.51	0.63	0.68	0.64
Weekly hours	0.19	0.21	0.33	0.30	0.30	0.43	0.40	0.42	0.29	0.32	0.26
Nominal hourly compensation	0.40	0.77	0.60	1.30	0.69	1.05	1.43	1.20	0.98	1.03	1.01
Real hourly compensation	0.25	0.50	0.54	0.54	0.34	0.80	0.79	0.79	0.82	0.84	0.82

Source: Calculated from relevant series, *Handbook of Labor Statistics*, 1985, U.S. Bureau of Labor
　Statistics.

Note: These magnitudes are the ratios of the standard deviation of year-to-year changes in the
　logarithm of the specified variables to the standard deviation of year-to-year changes in the
　logarithm of real output.

TABLE 4
REGRESSIONS OF PERCENTAGE CHANGES IN LABOR MARKET VARIABLES ON PERCENTAGE CHANGES IN OUTPUT BY COUNTRY: MANUFACTURING, 1950–1983

Equation	Coefficient	U.S.	Japan	Germany	U.K.	Canada	Denmark	France	Italy	Netherlands	Norway	Sweden
Employment	Output	0.5802	0.3329	0.5723	0.4660	0.5617	0.7086	0.4733	0.1484	0.4389	0.4377	0.4385
		(9.6)	(5.7)	(9.5)	(4.9)	(9.1)	(6.4)	(7.4)	(1.7)	(5.3)	(4.7)	(5.2)
	Constant	-0.0118	-0.0081	-0.0220	-0.0167	0.0143	-0.0262	-0.0211	0.0003	-0.0227	-0.0092	-0.0145
		(2.9)	(1.0)	(4.9)	(3.8)	(3.6)	(4.4)	(5.5)	(0.0)	(4.4)	(2.3)	(3.5)
	R-square	0.75	0.51	0.75	0.43	0.73	0.57	0.64	0.08	0.48	0.41	0.46
Weekly hours	Output	0.1606	0.1241	0.1484	0.1834	0.1072	-0.0250	0.2408	0.2419	0.0412	0.0153	0.0129
		(9.1)	(4.0)	(2.8)	(4.3)	(2.1)	(0.3)	(4.2)	(3.9)	(0.8)	(0.3)	(0.3)
	Constant	-0.0053	-0.0161	-0.0176	-0.0078	-0.0073	-0.0074	-0.0177	-0.0224	-0.0093	-0.0079	0.0103
		(4.5)	(3.8)	(4.5)	(4.0)	(2.3)	(1.8)	(5.2)	(4.7)	(2.9)	(3.2)	(4.5)
	R-square	0.73	0.34	0.20	0.37	0.13	0.003	0.36	0.32	0.02	0.002	0.003
Nominal compensation	Output	-0.1241	0.0743	0.0519	-0.7984	-0.2450	-0.2946	-0.5319	-0.4900	0.0769	-0.2944	-0.2459
		(1.8)	(0.5)	(0.5)	(4.3)	(2.1)	(1.6)	(2.2)	(2.5)	(0.4)	(1.7)	(1.4)
	Constant	0.0659	0.1019	0.0867	0.1134	0.0857	0.1110	0.1387	0.1533	0.0950	0.1038	0.1065
		(14.3)	(5.4)	(10.8)	(13.4)	(11.6)	(11.4)	(9.8)	(10.2)	(8.6)	(13.6)	(12.4)
	R-square	0.10	0.01	0.01	0.38	0.13	0.08	0.14	0.17	0.01	0.08	0.06
Real compensation	Output	0.0362	0.1175	0.2365	-0.0822	0.0215	0.1112	0.1371	0.0395	0.3084	0.2005	0.2365
		(0.8)	(1.4)	(2.7)	(0.9)	(0.3)	(0.8)	(1.0)	(0.3)	(2.2)	(1.4)	(1.7)
	Constant	0.0180	0.0393	0.0446	0.0324	0.0286	0.0315	0.0393	0.0466	0.0363	0.0289	0.0293
		(6.0)	(3.3)	(6.9)	(7.4)	(7.3)	(4.1)	(4.7)	(4.3)	(4.3)	(4.6)	(4.2)
	R-square	0.02	0.06	0.19	0.02	0.004	0.02	0.03	0.003	0.14	0.06	0.08
Output per hour	Output	0.2448	0.5493	0.2831	0.3469	0.3729	0.3022	0.2759	0.5136	0.5194	0.5509	0.5510
		(4.9)	(9.1)	(5.1)	(4.0)	(6.6)	(2.3)	(3.3)	(6.9)	(5.3)	(5.8)	(5.9)
	Constant	0.0176	0.0237	0.0394	0.0246	0.0199	0.0342	0.0391	0.0248	0.0318	0.0170	0.0248
		(5.3)	(2.9)	(9.6)	(6.1)	(5.5)	(4.8)	(7.8)	(4.4)	(5.3)	(4.1)	(5.4)
	R-square	0.44	0.73	0.46	0.34	0.59	0.14	0.26	0.61	0.48	0.52	0.53

Source: U.S. Bureau of Labor Statistics, *Handbook of Labor Statistics*, 1985.

Note: Magnitudes in parentheses are absolute t-values. All variables are transformed into year-to-year changes of the natural logarithm of the various magnitudes.

error term. We estimate this relationship in the first difference form using the least squares method as follows:

$$d \ln Y = b + c \; d \; \ln Z + de \qquad (2)$$

where d denotes a first-difference operator. In the above equation, the output coefficient, c, indicates the percentage change in the chosen variable associated with a 1% change in output. A positive value of c signifies a procyclical movement in the chosen variable. The constant term, b, is the estimated percentage growth in the chosen variable when output does not change.

In table 4, the statistical significance of some of the relevant coefficients is low, and as a result, these findings are best viewed as being explorative rather than confirmatory. Taking these estimates at face value, the United States exhibits greater procyclical movements in employment and hours of work for a given percentage change in output than Japan. Consequently, output per hour, a measure of productivity, exhibits greater cyclical movement in Japan than in the United States (see the above identity). In fact, except for Denmark, the United States appears to have the highest cyclical sensitivity to employment of all the countries, although West Germany and Canada are close behind.[5] Japan exhibits greater procyclical movement in real compensation than the United States; nominal compensation exhibits countercyclical movements in the United States and procyclical movements in Japan.

It is noteworthy that real compensation variability in Japan is by no means the largest, as West Germany, the Netherlands, Norway, Sweden, and France exceed Japan. Interestingly, none of these countries have overlapping three-year wage contracts like those of the United States or Canada.[6] Except for Canada and the United Kingdom, which show a countercyclical coefficient, the United States exhibits the lowest procyclical variability in real compensation. The finding for the United Kingdom is puzzling. In Britain, labor contracts often do not have fixed duration and are subject to renegotiation at the request of one of the parties (Sachs 1979, p. 303). One would have predicted high cyclical compensation sensitivity there.

The theory also suggests that workers with higher degrees of fixity experience less cyclical employment variability, but greater variability in hours of work and wages. More generally, the variability in wages and hours taken together should be greater in Japan than in the United States for a given range of demand changes. The sum of the output coefficients in the hours of work and compensation equations indeed is more than 20% greater for Japan than for the United States.

Masanori Hashimoto and John Raisian

Finally, labor productivity, measured by output per hour, fluctuates more in Japan than in the United States. In table 4, the output coefficients for employment (E), weekly hours of work (h), and output per hour (Z/H) should sum to unity [$1 = d \ln(Z/H)/d \ln Z + d \ln E/d \ln Z + d \ln h/d \ln Z$, where $H = E \times h$]. So, this finding simply mirrors the findings of larger coefficients for employment and hours in the United States than in Japan.

What have we learned from the international comparisons? Perhaps it is not surprising that the countries examined do not line up systematically. We do find that Japan is not unique in having flexible wages, that compensation in the United States shows the lowest cyclical variability of the countries examined, and that some countries have employment volatility that is as high as, or higher than, that in the United States. No clear pattern of trade-offs among the cyclical variabilities of various variables emerges, however.

Comparing the United States with Japan, table 4 indicates that in both countries employment and hours worked exhibit more pronounced movements over business cycles than nominal or real compensation. But in Japan, although employment and hours of work fluctuate more than compensation, real compensation does exhibit considerable variability over the business cycle, much more so than in the United States. The sum total of the output coefficients for hours of work and real compensation is greater for Japan than for the United States—more than 20%. Moreover, there is a larger relative difference between this sum total and the output sensitivity of employment in the United States than in Japan—the ratio of this sum to the output coefficient for employment is 0.34 for the United States, but 0.72 for Japan. This discrepancy is clearly due to the greater cyclical rigidity of real compensation and to the greater volatility of employment in the United States than in Japan.

Focusing on the United States, table 5 reports regression coefficients of the logarithm of various labor force magnitudes on a time trend and the overall civilian unemployment rate. A percentage point rise in the unemployment rate is associated with statistically significant declines in employment, as attested to by the negative coefficients. Weekly hours, overtime hours, and real earnings also exhibit significant procyclical sensitivity. Observed cyclical sensitivity in real earnings appears to be due to the sensitivity in overtime earnings, as the regression for straight-time earnings obtains insignificant unemployment coefficient. This is evidence for the rigidity in straight-time wages in the United States economy.

In table 6, we can examine how employment and hours of work in the United States adjust over the business cycle. Reductions in hours of

TABLE 5
TREND AND CYCLICAL SENSITIVITY IN U.S. EMPLOYMENT,
HOURS OF WORK, AND EARNINGS: 1958–1983
(t-values in parentheses)

	Private nonagr. industries		Manufacturing industries	
	Trend	Cycle	Trend	Cycle
Total employment	0.0231	−0.0198	0.0100	−0.0351
	(12.7)	(−12.2)	(4.4)	(−17.2)
Production workers:				
Employment	0.0216	−0.0216	0.0068	−0.0425
	(11.6)	(−13.1)	(2.8)	(−19.7)
Weekly hours	−0.0032	−0.0035	0.0020	−0.0084
	(−2.9)	(−3.6)	(0.9)	(4.4)
Overtime hours	—	—	0.0314	−0.1037
			(1.7)	(6.4)
Real earnings	0.0087	−0.0087	0.0089	−0.0068
	(2.4)	(2.7)	(2.7)	(−2.3)
Straight-time earn.	—	—	0.0081	−0.0041
			(2.7)	(1.6)

Sources: U.S. Bureau of Labor Statistics, *Employer Surveys* as reported in
   Handbook of Labor Statistics, 1985, (assorted tables on pp. 172–206).
Notes: The magnitudes are regression coefficients in the regression of the
   logarithm of the relevant variable on a time trend and the civilian
   unemployment rate. The regression for nominal earnings obtained
   insignificant coefficients, which are not reported.

work may take place on a given job, but many workers who lose regular full-time jobs also end up working on part-time jobs. This is clear from table 6. Although both full-time workers and workers who are working part time for voluntary reasons exhibit procyclical employment, those workers working part time for economic reasons show countercyclical movements in employment. In other words, employment of part-time workers for economic reasons increases during recessions. The spill-over from full-time jobs to part-time jobs is evident in the category, "Usually Full Time."

Turning to Japan, cyclical variability in bonus dominates variabilities in employment, hours of work, and base wages. This is clear in table 7.

Not only are the output coefficients large in bonus regressions but they are all statistically significant. In contrast, the output coefficients for base earnings are statistically significant only for real earnings, and their magnitudes are small by comparison. These findings agree with the findings of Koshiro (1986) and of Freeman and Weitzman (1986) that the bonus varies more than other components of Japanese earnings.

Masanori Hashimoto and John Raisian

TABLE 6

TREND AND CYCLICAL SENSITIVITY IN EMPLOYMENT
FOR U.S. WAGE AND SALARY WORKERS: 1958–1983
(t-values in parentheses)

	All workers		Workers in manufacturing	
	Trend	Cycle	Trend	Cycle
Total	0.0232	−0.0131	0.0119	−0.0330
	(16.1)	(−10.2)	(3.7)	(−11.6)
Full-time workers	0.0215	−0.0913	0.0135	−0.0417
	(15.8)	(−16.0)	(4.5)	(−15.8)
Part-time workers:				
For voluntary reasons	0.0385	−0.0142	0.0259	−0.0438
	(7.6)	(−3.1)	(2.5)	(−4.8)
For economic reasons				
All workers	0.0150	0.1121	−0.0343	0.1724
	(1.2)	(10.4)	(1.0)	(5.5)
Usually full time	−0.0114	0.1203	−0.0433	0.1719
	(0.5)	(5.6)	(−1.1)	(4.7)
Usually part time	0.0337	0.1045	−0.0106	0.1743
	(2.2)	(7.8)	(0.4)	(6.8)

Source: U.S. Bureau of the Census, Current Population Survey, as reported in
   Handbook of Labor Statistics, 1985, (assorted tables on pp. 40–63).
Notes: The magnitudes are regression coefficients in the regression of the
   relevant variable on a time trend and the civilian unemployment rate.

Since bonuses and base earnings differ greatly by education and worker status, we convert these estimates to monetary equivalents, reported in brackets in table 7. According to these estimates, both bonus and base earnings are more cyclically sensitive for nonproduction (skilled) than for production (less skilled) workers. This finding is consistent with our hypothesis, implying that workers with more firm-specific human capital experience greater wage flexibility. For nonproduction workers, except for those with low education, the cyclical sensitivity for bonus increases with education, as predicted. The pattern-breaking finding for low-education workers may have something to do with the fact that many of these workers are older, and therefore, more senior, than others.

As expected, cyclical sensitivity of base earnings increases uniformly with education levels for nonproduction workers. For production workers, the opposite pattern is observed; those with low education exhibit more cyclical sensitivities than those with high education not only in base earnings but also in bonuses. We think that production workers in the high-education

TABLE 7
OUTPUT SENSITIVITIES OF LABOR MARKET VARIABLES FOR MALE WORKERS IN
JAPANESE MANUFACTURING BY WORKER STATUS AND EDUCATION: 1965–1983*

	Production workers Education groups			Nonproduction workers Education groups				
	All	Low	High	All	Low	Middle	High	College
Employment	0.5220	—	—	0.4285	—	—	—	—
	(5.57)			(3.69)				
Hours	0.1710	0.1712	0.1411	0.1608	0.1948	0.1518	0.1383	0.1063
	(1.9)	(2.0)	(1.5)	(2.4)	(2.7)	(2.0)	(2.0)	(1.3)
Ratio: Emp/Hrs	3.05	—	—	2.66	—	—	—	—
Nominal earnings:								
Bonus	1.2048	1.2583	1.0720	1.1144	1.2610	1.1318	0.9533	1.0591
	(2.3)	(2.5)	(2.1)	(2.3)	(2.4)	(2.4)	(2.3)	(2.1)
	[42.1]	[44.5]	[36.9]	[65.4]	[67.2]	[60.2]	[62.9]	[71.8]
Base	0.3448	0.3572	0.3103	0.3055	0.1188	0.3586	0.3116	0.4404
	(0.7)	(0.8)	(0.6)	(0.6)	(0.2)	(0.8)	(0.8)	(0.9)
	[41.9]	[44.6]	[36.3]	[49.7]	[18.9]	[55.1]	[55.5]	[76.9]
Real earnings:								
Bonus	1.1900	1.2436	1.0572	1.1000	1.2463	1.1171	0.9386	1.0443
	(5.0)	(5.4)	(4.0)	(4.8)	(3.5)	(6.1)	(4.8)	(4.6)
	[16.9]	[17.9]	[14.8]	[26.6]	[27.4]	[24.3]	[27.0]	[29.4]
Base	0.3878	0.4002	0.3534	0.3486	0.1619	0.4017	0.3546	0.4835
	(1.9)	(2.0)	(1.7)	(1.5)	(0.5)	(1.9)	(2.5)	(2.3)
	[19.5]	[20.6]	[17.3]	[23.6]	[10.7]	[25.5]	[27.3]	[35.3]
Means (1965–1983) for bonus-earnings ratios								
Bonus/base	0.27	0.26	0.28	0.35	0.32	0.33	0.37	0.38

Sources: Maigetsu Kinro Tokei Chosa (Monthly Labor Survey) for employ-
ment, and Chingin Kozo Kihon Tokei Chosa (Basic Survey of Wage
Structure) for others, as reported in Japan Yearbook of Labor
Statistics, various years. The output data are from U.S. Bureau of
Labor Statistics, Handbook of Labor Statistics, 1985.
* For employment, the data are for 1959–1983.
Notes: Figures in parentheses are t-values, and those in brackets are monetary
equivalents of the output-sensitivity coefficients (in 1000 yen),
calculated at the mean values of respective earnings during 1965
through 1983. For the educational categories, low means lower
secondary, high for production workers means upper secondary school
and over, middle, high and college for nonproduction workers refer,
respectively, to upper secondary, junior college, and university.

category include workers who lost out in a bid for promotion to white-collar jobs.

According to the last row of table 7, the ratio of bonus to base earnings is greater for nonproduction than for production workers, holding education constant, and for workers with higher educational attainment within each class of workers. This pattern is consistent with the assumptions that bonus earnings contain returns to firm-specific human capital and that nonproduction workers and workers with higher levels of education invest more in firm-specific human capital (see Hashimoto 1979). Both employment and hours of work exhibit procyclical movements.

Nor surprisingly, production workers exhibit larger cyclical sensitivities of employment and hours of work than nonproduction workers. Also, hours of work appears to vary less over the cycle the higher the level of education, partly because overtime hours are more likely to be reported for less skilled workers.

The third row of table 7 shows that the ratio of the cyclical sensitivity of employment relative to that of hours of work is greater for production than for nonproduction workers. This pattern is sensible since nonproduction workers are likely to have more firm-specific capital invested in them than production workers.

Let us now turn to table 8. In this table, we investigate the effects of the "structural changes" experienced by the Japanese economy in the 1970s on the output coefficients of various magnitudes.

In the regime of high rates of economic growth such as prevailed in Japan starting in the late 1950s and lasting throughout the 1960s, changes in demand are likely to be viewed as reflecting long-run, or permanent, changes. In the 1970s and 1980s, however, the rate of growth slowed substantially, and demand changes came to be viewed as short-run business-cycle phenomena—at least to a greater extent that in previous years. In our view, the emergence of cyclical labor markets in Japan is symbolized in the Employment Insurance Law enacted in 1975.[7]

In table 8, we separate the years into pre- and post-1974 (or post-oil shock) periods using the dummy variable technique. Note first, that the estimated coefficients indicate that the output sensitivity of employment is greater for production than for nonproduction workers in both pre- and post-1974 periods. (See the coefficients for output, Z, and for the interaction variable, $D \times Z$.) Note also that days of work exhibit considerably greater output sensitivity for production than nonproduction workers. It seems that workers do get "laid off" in Japan, though they continue to be classified as employed persons.

Of more interest is how output sensitivities changed after 1974, as indicated by the coefficients for the interaction variable. These coefficients

TABLE 8

CYCLICAL SENSITIVITY OF MALE LABOR INPUTS AND EARNINGS
IN JAPANESE MANUFACTURING INDUSTRIES: 1959–1983
(t-values in parentheses)

	Regression coefficients				
	Intercept	Output (Z)	Dummy (D)	$D \times Z$	R^2
	Production workers				
Employment	−0.0790	0.9325	0.0534	−0.7758	0.74
	(−4.1)	(7.7)	(1.7)	(−2.4)	
Days per month	−0.0174	0.7699	−0.0015	0.1908	0.56
	(−3.9)	(2.3)	(−0.2)	(2.8)	
Hours per month	−0.0428	0.2601	0.0123	0.2365	0.76
	(−6.8)	(5.5)	(1.3)	(2.5)	
Contract earnings	−0.2930	−0.0288	−0.1071	−0.0281	0.001
	(−1.1)	(−0.1)	(−1.6)	(−0.05)	
Bonus earnings	−0.4872	0.6376	−0.1081	−0.5446	0.22
	(−1.3)	(1.6)	(−1.2)	(−0.7)	
	Nonproduction workers				
Employment	−0.0309	0.7796	0.0313	−0.7501	0.62
	(−1.3)	(5.4)	(0.8)	(−1.9)	
Days per month	−0.0219	0.1154	0.0068	0.0737	0.28
	(−3.3)	(2.3)	(0.7)	(0.7)	
Hours per month	−0.0353	0.2232	0.0148	0.1081	0.68
	(−6.1)	(5.2)	(1.7)	(1.2)	
Contract earnings	−0.3340	0.3816	−0.0336	−0.4301	0.73
	(−4.8)	(5.4)	(−2.0)	(−3.2)	
Bonus earnings	−0.5907	1.0966	−0.0428	−0.7037	0.67
	(−4.0)	(7.3)	(−1.2)	(−2.5)	

Sources: Maigetsu Kinro Tokei Chosa as reported in *Japan Yearbook of Labor
Statistics*, various years. The output data are from U.S. Bureau of
Labor Statistics, *Handbook of Labor Statistics*, 1985.
Notes: All variables except for the dummy variable are in first difference
of logarithms. The dummy variable is unity for the post-1974 years.
Contract and bonus earnings are in real terms (using the consumer
price index), and their regressions include a time trend. All variables
are for regular workers in firms with thirty or more employees.

indicate that after 1974, (1) output sensitivity for employment decreased for production and nonproduction workers alike, but that the statistical significance is higher for production workers and (2) both days of work and hours of work increased in output sensitivity for both types of workers, though the significance level is higher, again, for production than for nonproduction workers.

The findings of reduced output sensitivity of employment, along with increased sensitivities of hours and days of work after 1974, make sense if one accepts the importance of firm-specific human capital in Japan. In other words, before 1974, changes in output reflected permanent changes, and as a result, they were accompanied by greater employment response but smaller response in hours and days of work than after 1974, when output changes increasingly became a reflection of temporary changes.

Interestingly, output sensitivities of earnings are significant only for nonproduction workers, suggesting that for white-collar workers, wage flexibility is a prevailing mode of adjustment in addition to flexibility in labor input. Earnings, both contract and bonus, became less output sensitive after 1974, suggesting that wages became less flexible for nonproduction workers after 1974. We have no explanation for this finding.

IV. The U.S. Wage Rigidity May Be Overstated

Available evidence of wage rigidity relies on aggregate data. These data underestimate the degree of wage flexibility for individual workers, however. One reason is that low-wage workers are more likely to lose their jobs during recessions than high-wage workers. As a result, they become less represented in the aggregate wage and employment statistics during recessions as compared to prosperous times.[8] Any procyclical fluctuations in the wages of those who remain employed throughout a cyclical disturbance become obscured in the aggregate data by the exit of low-wage workers during bad times and their entry during good times.[9] This bias will effectively exaggerate the wage rigidity in the United States relative to Japan, as there is more cyclical employment turnover in the United States than in Japan.

This bias is more serious for the United States than for Japan, as cyclical labor turnover is much greater in the United States, thereby causing an exaggeration of the difference between Japan and the United States in wage rigidity. The data on individual workers provide more reliable evidence about the underlying pressures on wages over the course of cyclical activity.

To examine this point, we drew samples from the U.S. Panel Study of Income Dynamics (PSID) for the period 1967–79, and compared individual wage flexibility with an aggregate measure based on the samples.[10] The technical details are reported in the Appendix II. Our findings clearly suggest that the use of aggregate data causes substantial overstatement of the wage rigidity phenomenon, at least for the United States. For each of the samples, and for both nominal and real wage measures, the individual variability exceeds the aggregate counterpart by a significant margin. (These results are not reported here to save space. See Hashimoto and Raisian 1987 for detail.)

Does this bias invalidate the common belief that U.S. wages are more rigid than Japanese wages? To answer this question, Table 9 reports U.S.–Japan comparisons of wage flexibility. The U.S. magnitudes are based on individual worker wages, whereas the Japanese magnitudes rely on aggregate wage data. By comparing the Japanese results based on aggregate data with the U.S. results based on individual data, one obviously is bending backward to narrow any Japan–U.S. difference in wage rigidity. Quite clearly, Japanese wages remain more flexible than U.S. wages in this comparison in table 9.

TABLE 9

CYCLICAL WAGE FLEXIBILITY FOR MALE WORKERS
IN U.S. AND JAPANESE MANUFACTURING

	United States	
	[Nominal wages]	[Real wages]
Overall sample	0.019	0.019
Job maintainers	0.014	0.014
Reported wage rate	0.014	0.015

	Japan	
	[Nominal wages]	[Real wages]
Base earnings	0.097	0.043
Bonus earnings	0.102	0.050
Total earnings	0.100	0.051

Sources: The U.S. results are calculated from the *Panel Studies of Income Dynamics,* the Japanese results are calculated from *Chingin Kozo Kihon Tokei Chosa* (Basic Survey of Wage Structure).

Notes: The figures represent the variability in trend-adjusted wages attributable to cyclical disturbances. The U.S. magnitudes are averages of individual wage variability, and the Japanese magnitudes, variability in average aggregate earnings.

V. Summary

Labor markets in Japan and the United States differ in the use of lay-offs, employment duration, the shape of earnings profiles, and the method of adjustments to demand fluctuations. Our view is that these differences reflect the difference between the two countries in the extent of investment in firm-specific human capital. The latter difference is caused, in turn, by lower transaction costs in Japan than in the United States. Our findings by and large offer support for our hypothesis. Thus, cyclical wage flexibility is much more, and employment variability much less, pronounced in Japan than in the United States. In contrast, employment variability is the distinguishing feature of the U.S. labor market.

Japan is not alone in having flexible wages, however. We find that West Germany, the Netherlands, Norway, Sweden, and France have more output sensitivity in real compensation than Japan. To help evaluate our hypothesis more thoroughly, a detailed study of the reasons for the observed country differences in the extent of wage flexibility will be essential.

Appendix I
A Wage Contract Model by Hashimoto and Yu

The purpose of this appendix is to discuss the wage contract model that emerges from the analysis of Hashimoto and Yu (1980). For the purpose at hand, we start with a worker in the midstream of his contact having completed his investments. The sharing ration and the amount of human capital investment have been determined optimally by maximizing the joint wealth of the parties. Maximization of joint wealth is optimal because the model assumes the absence of transaction costs at the time of contracting. Transaction costs are positive, however, once the investment is completed, and this fact potentially causes wealth loss from suboptimal separations. As long as transaction costs are not prohibitively high, however, the parties have a mechanism for reducing such loss, namely, elements of wage flexibility built into a wage contract.

Wage flexibility is achieved by the parties agreeing to use mutually acceptable indicators of productivities, one for the worker's alternative value and the other for the worker's inside value. The wage contract is given by:

$$W = H + bZ_y + a(m + aZ_v - bZ_y)h,$$

where H is the amount of general human capital; Z_y and Z_v are, respectively, the indicators of worker's alternative and inside productivity values; m is the specificity of a unit of the human capital, h, created in the firm; and a and b $(0 < a, b < 1)$ indicate the accuracy of the respective indicators.

In the above contract, the degree of wage flexibility depends on how good the indicators are. As the quality of the indicators improves, the parameters, a and b, approach unity. If the indicators are perfect, both a and b are unity, and the wage contract will reflect fully the true values of productivities, a case of perfect wage flexibility. If they are totally useless, both a and b are zero, and the wage contract implies completely rigid wages. The quality of the indicators, in turn, is related to transaction costs. Were transaction costs zero, the parties would not mistrust each other, and as a result, they would not have to rely on the indicators. In this cases, both a and b would be unity and Z_v and Z_y would be replaced by their true values in the wage contract, and a completely flexible wage would prevail even in long-term contracts. We assume that as transaction costs increase, the parties must settle on lower and lower quality indicators. It can be shown that flexible wages reduce potential wealth loss from inefficient separations (Hashimoto and Yu 1980).

Some authors have proposed that wage flexibility occurs mainly in response to changing alternative values of the worker (see, for example, Hall and Lilien 1979; McDonald and Solow 1981). It seems plausible, however, that the information about the prices of the product the firm sells is less costly to obtain than alternative values of workers. If so, this situation is better characterized by a being larger than b. In this case, the effect of a recession on the values of worker marginal product may be assessed at a lower cost than the effect on the alternative values, and, as a result, wage reduction is plausible even in the face of unknown or unchanging alternative values.

Appendix II
Correction for the Aggregation Bias in the U.S. Data

This paper applies our earlier method (Hashimoto and Raisian 1987) to the PSID samples of manufacturing workers. In addition to the overall PSID sample, we consider two additional samples. The sample of job-maintainers consists of those who remained employed throughout the years under consideration. This sample enables us to control for influences of unemployment and job changes on measured cyclical wage variability. The reported-wage sample consists of those with reported wage rates. The PSID distinguishes between the average hourly wage series and a reported wage rate series. In the early part of a calendar year, heads of households are asked about their earnings for the previous calendar year and their current straight-time hourly wage rate, if appropriate. Whereas the sample period for the average hourly wage series is 1967–79, reported wage rates are available for the period 1970–80.

Using these samples, we estimated the following two regressions:

$$\ln W_t = a_1 + b_1 t + v_t, \qquad \text{and} \qquad (a)$$
$$\ln W_t = a_2 + b_2 t + c_2 u_t + e_t, \qquad (b)$$

where $\ln W_t$ is the natural logarithm of the chosen wage magnitude for time period t, u_t is the overall unemployment rate at time t, the a's are constant terms, the b's are trend coefficients, c is a cyclical coefficient, and v and e are disturbance terms. These regressions are estimated for each individual separately as well as for average hourly wages in the three samples. Average hourly wages are calculated by the standard BLS procedure—total annual earnings of all persons in the sample divided by total hours worked of all persons in the sample.

The trend-adjusted standard errors of the estimate are decomposed into two components: one that is attributable to overall cyclical disturbances with the other being a random component, as follows:

$$s_v = s_u + s'_e, \qquad \text{where} \qquad (c)$$
$$s'_e = s_e \left(\frac{n-3}{n-2} \right)^{0.5} \qquad (d)$$

and s_e is the standard error of the estimate for regression (b). This standard error is renormalized to form s'_e, so that the two standard errors are deflated by the same number of degrees of freedom. This renormalization ensures that $s_v > s'_e$ and $s_u = s_v - s'_e > 0$.

Trend-adjusted standard errors attributable to cyclical disturbances, s_u, are computed for each of the aggregate series as well as for each of the individual series. Averages of the s_u's are then computed across individuals for each of the samples and reported in table 9.

Notes

1. We are grateful to Professors Fumio Ohtake, Akira Ono, Yoko Sano, and the participants at the Symposium for helpful discussions, and to Professor Kazutoshi Koshiro for having organized the successful symposium. We thank Barbara Brugman for helpful comments as well as for editorial help.

2. In fact, Japanese unemployment rates are lower than those of most other developed countries as well. According to statistics developed by the U.S. Bureau of Labor Statistics that are compiled to minimize definitional differences in labor force concepts, unemployment rates averaged 2.3% in Japan during the period 1978–83 compared to 7.7% in the United States, 4.4% in West Germany, and 0.9% in the United Kingdom.

3. One limitation here is that we ignore differences in pensions and other compensation in examining the profiles, because of data limitations. Pensions may be important, but it is worth recalling that in table 1 compensations other than wages and salaries are similar in the two countries.

4. The U.S. Bureau of Labor Statistics computes compensation measures by adjusting regularly published earnings statistics for items of compensation not included in earnings. Adjustment factors are obtained from labor cost surveys, surveys of manufactures, or reports on social security and fringe benefit systems. The bureau tries to include the same items of compensation for every country. See U.S. *Handbook of Labor Statistics*, 1985, pp. 414–16.

5. The finding for Denmark is reminiscent of much higher multiple spells of unemployment in that country than in the United States as reported in a study by the OECD. That study cites two possible reasons for this difference: (1) Danish data are from administrative data, and include all short spells of unemployment, whereas the U.S. data are based on labor force survey, but more importantly, (2) the Danish unemployment insurance program is not experience-rated and thereby encourages unemployment. Also, an unemployed person who becomes ill for more than three weeks is transferred from unemployment to sickness benefits. If, after recovery, the individual moves back to unemployment benefits, the one period of joblessness is recorded as two spells of unemployment. In addition, during the period under study, an unemployed worker was immediately eligible for benefits. Hence, very short periods on layoffs are recorded as spells of unemployment (OECD, 1985, p. 100).

6. The normal length of contracts in France, West Germany, and the United Kingdom is about one year. The Netherlands have a mixtured of one-, two-, and three-year contracts, but their relative importance is unknown to us. See related discussions in Sachs (1979, Appendix B) and Braun (1976).

7. The previous legislation, the Unemployment Insurance Law, which existed since 1947, was changed drastically in 1974. The revised law shifted the emphasis from unemployment compensation to the subsidizing of payrolls and prevention of layoffs and workforce reductions through additional taxes on employer payrolls. The new law enables employers to avoid dismissals by granting subsidies

to cover partial wage payments to workers put on work furloughs extending for one-third of the month or longer. Qualifying firms can receive grants for six months, and extensions for as long as nine months have been granted.

8. The results reported here apply to manufacturing industries, whereas those reported in Hashimoto and Raisian (1987) are based on all private industries. At least two other researchers have considered the aggregation bias. As we were working on this project, we came across papers by Stockman (1983) and Bils (1985) that deal with the same issue.

9. Another reason that aggregate data underestimate the degree of wage flexibility is that contractions in labor demand are not evenly dispersed throughout the economy during a recessionary period. Given the existence of skill specificity, mobility costs, and implicit contracts, the pressure by the market to reduce wages is not even throughout the economy. Instead, it is concentrated in those sectors that are most affected by the overall contraction. Consequently, computation of overall wage aggregates could easily underestimate the degree of individual wage flexibility where demand contractions are pronounced.

10. There are 21,261 observations in our PSID sample and 3,688 separate household heads.

References

Becker, Gary S. (1962). "Investment in Human Capital: A Theoretical Analysis," *Journal of Political Economy* 70 (Supplement): 9–49.

Bils, Mark (1985). "Real Wages over the Business Cycle: Evidence from Panel Data," *Journal of Political Economy* 93:666–89.

Braun, Anne Romanis (1976). "Indexation of Wages and Salaries in Developed Economies," *IMF Staff Papers* 23:226–71.

Freeman, Richard B., and Martin L. Weitzman (1986). "Bonuses and Employment in Japan," NBER working paper No. 1878.

Gordon, Robert J. (1982). "Why U.S. Wage and Employment Behavior Differs From That in Britain and Japan," *Economic Journal* 92 (March): 13–44.

Hall, Robert E., and David M. Lilien (1979). "Efficient Wage Bargains Under Uncertain Demand," *American Economic Review* 69:868–79.

Hanami, Tadashi (1979). *Labor Relations in Japan Today*, Tokyo: Kodansha International.

Hart, Robert A. (1984). *The Economics of Non-Wage Labor Costs*, London: George Allen & Unwin.

Hashimoto, Masanori (1975). "Wage Reduction, Unemployment and Specific Human Capital," *Economic Inquiry* 13:485–504.

——— (1979). "Bonus Payments, On-the-Job Training and Lifetime Employment in Japan," *Journal of Political Economy* 87:1086–1104.

—— (1981). "Firm-Specific Human Capital as a Shared Investment," *American Economic Review* 71:475–82.

Hashimoto, Masanori, and John Raisian (1985). "Employment Tenure and Earnings Profiles in Japan and the United States," *American Economic Review* 75:721–35.

—— (1986a). "Productivity of Japanese and U.S. Workers in Firms of Varying Size," *Conference on Income and Wealth*, National Bureau of Economic Research, under editorial review.

—— (1986b). "Employment, Hours of Work, and Wage Adjustments in Japan and the United States," a paper presented at the Conference on Employment, Unemployment, and Hours of Work, West Berlin, September 1986.

—— (1987). "Wage Flexibility in the United States and Japan," in *Labor Market Adjustments in the Pacific Basin*, edited by Peter Chinloy and Ernst Stromsdorfer, Boston: Kluwer-Nijhof Publishing.

Hashimoto, Masanori, and Ben T. Yu (1980). "Specific Capital, Employment Contracts and Wage Rigidity," *The Bell Journal of Economics* 11:536–49.

Koshiro, Kazutoshi (1986). "Labor Market Flexibility in Japan—With Special Reference to Wage Flexibility," Working Paper, Yokohama National University.

McDonald, I. M., and Robert R. M. Solow (1981). "Wage Bargaining and Employment," *American Economic Review* 71:896–908.

Mincer, Jacob (1974). *Schooling, Experience, and Earnings*, New York: National Bureau of Economic Research.

OECD (1985). *Employment Outlook*.

Oi, Walter (1962). "Labor as a Quasi-Fixed Factor," *Journal of Political Economy* 70:538–55.

Raisian, John (1979). "Cyclic Patterns in Weeks and Wages," *Economic Inquiry* 17:475–95.

—— (1983). "Contracts, Job Experience and Cyclical Labor Adjustments," *Journal of Labor Economics* 1 (April): 152–70.

Rosen, Sherwin (1968). "Short-Run Employment Variation in Class I Railroad in the U.S., 1947–1963," *Econometrica* 36: 511–29.

—— (1985). "Implicit Contracts: A Survey," *Journal of Economic Literature* 23:1144–75.

Sachs, Jeffrey D. (1979). "Wages, Profits, and Macroeconomic Adjustments: A Comparative Study," *Brookings Papers on Economic Activity* 2:269–332.

Shimada, Haruo (1983). "New Challenges for Japanese Labor Management Relations in the Era of Global Structural Change," *Japan Labor Bulletin* 22:5–8.

Stockman, Alan (1983). "Aggregation Bias and the Cyclical Behavior of Real Wages," unpublished manuscript, University of Rochester.

Taira, Koji (1970). *Economic Development and the Labor Market in Japan*, New York: Columbia University Press.

Asao Mizuno

4

Japanese Wage Flexibility: An International Perspective

Introduction

Like other industrialized countries, Japan experienced drastic changes in various aspects of its labor market in the decade after the first oil crisis in 1973. The crisis resulted in a continuous decline in the economic growth rate, employment in manufacturing ceased to expand, and the unemployment rate rose from 1.28% in 1973 to 2.77% in 1986—the highest level since the end of the Second World War. At the same time, the lower rate of economic growth decreased the ratio of job openings to applicants and moderated the rise in real wages and real disposable income. One of the results of this process was to encourage a number of married women to enter the labor market to supplement the family income.

Nevertheless, Japan's remarkably low unemployment rate relative to other industrialized countries remains a puzzling feature of the Japanese postwar economy. In the light of the debate on the macroeconomic performance of the labor market, one of the main reasons for Japan's low unemployment rate may be ascribed to its highly flexible wages, in both nominal and real terms, over the cycle. Wage flexibility, or strictly speaking, the large

102

decline in the growth rate of real wages during economic recession, may, other things being equal, lead to the stability of employment and prevent the unemployment rate from rising. However, a national labor market is a heterogeneous entity, and the seemingly stabilizing impact of wage flexibility on employment behavior often differs among subsections of the labor market. If wages in one sector of the economy are flexible and wages in another are rigid, the unemployment generated by the latter sector can be absorbed into the former, thus keeping the overall unemployment rate constant.

In order to examine wage flexibility in Japan in response to the economic changes mentioned above, and to give an indirect insight into why the Japanese unemployment rate is relatively low, this study is divided into four sections. The first section describes one of the important institutional aspects of the Japanese labor market, namely, the existence of bonus payments, and explains some analytical methods that can be used to test the relationships between wage flexibility and bonus payments. Section II focuses on the responsiveness of employment and wage changes to fluctuations in total output, and here we emphasize that the larger variability of the nominal rate of economic growth could be responsible for the more flexible wage situation in Japan in comparison with other industrialized countries. Section III estimates the Phillips-type wage function and looks for the main factors that may contribute to Japanese wage flexibility. International comparisons suggests the different importance of changing labor-market conditions in determining the changes in wages and therefore, this aspect is investigated. Finally, analytical results disaggregated by size of firm are presented in this section. Our contention here is that, contrary to the view expressed in earlier works, our statistical evidence does not regard the existence of bonus payments as an essential factor in making the Japanese overall wages relatively flexible. The final section summarizes the main findings and offers some concluding remarks.

I. Analytical Framework

1. The Macroeconomic Relationship between Changes in Wages, Employment, and Nominal GNP

According to the formulation developed by Gordon (1982), the macroeconomic relationship between output, wages, and labor input is expressed, in the simplest form, as

$$Yn = (W \times E \times H) + K, \tag{1}$$

where Yn is nominal gross national product (GNP), W is compensation per man-hour, E is the number of employees, H is hours worked, and K is nonlabor income. If μ is defined as the share of labor income in nominal GNP, then equation (1) may be written in terms of percentage change as

$$\dot{Y}n = \mu(\dot{W} + \dot{E} + \dot{H}) + (1 - \mu)\dot{K}. \tag{2}$$

Assuming $\dot{H}$ and $\dot{K}$ are constant, this equation suggests the existence of a trade-off between $\dot{W}$ and $\dot{E}$ for given $\dot{Y}n$. In other words, a given percentage change in nominal GNP yields a combination of a larger (or smaller) increase in wages with a smaller (or larger) increase in employment. When there is such a trade-off between wages and employment, does the existence of a long-term attachment between employer and employees lead to high stability of employment for a given percentage change in nominal rate of economic growth over time, or does the implicit contract to pay a stable wage to workers lead to wage stability? Alternatively, does high wage flexibility bring about stable employment? Although the precise answers to these questions will depend on what other types of employment adjustments are available to employers (Hall 1980; Blandy and Richardson 1982, 1984; Koshiro 1986), it is highly probably that Japan's flexible wage system is associated with stable employment performance.

Since an increase in nominal GNP is accompanied by an increase in employment under normal economic conditions, $\dot{W}/\dot{Y}n < 1$ would be true. However, there will be some exceptional cases where $\dot{W}/\dot{Y}n > 1$ is true. For example, even if the economy experienced a sudden and drastic decline in total output in a given year, employers might concede a wage increase in excess of $\dot{Y}n$, to be met from nonlabor income, with the object of maintaining stable or peaceful industrial relations, as long as output had increased considerably in the previous year or there was a firm prospect of economic recovery. This suggests that if the change in wages in any year were geared directly to the contemporaneous change in nominal GNP, wage changes over time would be more variable, so that the "installment" nature of the wage system (Hall 1980) would be weakened or lost. If the values of $\dot{W}/\dot{Y}n$ (the elasticity of wage changes with respect to $\dot{Y}n$) are near to unity over time and similar to all countries under consideration, this means that one of the reasons for the internationally greater variability of the changes in nominal wages should be ascribed to the larger fluctuation of growth rates of nominal GNP.

An important qualifying factor in the above argument is the share of labor income in nominal GNP (μ), because the relationship between $\dot{Y}n$ and $\dot{W}$, or $\dot{E}$, will be weakened or neutralized through the behavior of μ. In other words, in an economy where labor's share is low, wages and employment can be more flexible for a given percentage change in nominal GNP. In analyzing the time series or making international comparisons of wage flexibility, proper account must be taken of the level of, and changes in, labor's share.

2. The Two-Tier Labor Market Model and the Wage Changes

On the other hand, a national labor market is stratified into many sub-sidiary markets with very different patterns of behavior, and some attention must be paid to this fact. According to the two-tier labor-market model developed by Okun (1973), the labor market is composed of two classes of firms: class A firms are interested in promoting a long-term attachment between employer and employee and provide a wage premium to pursue this objective, while class B firms are not interested in long-term attachment and pay wages depending on the short-term contribution of employees to the production of marginal revenue. And so, Okun states that

> wage rates are likely to be more sensitive to easing and tightening of the labor market in class B than in class A firms. The arrangements designed to promote job attachment in class A put wage decisions into a longer-run context, insulating them from cyclical fluctuation. (p. 239)

It follows that, although the coexistence of small firms (corresponding to class B firms) with large firms (class A firms), and the resultant wide wage differentials between them is an important factor in the greater flexibility of Japanese wages in general, the major interest here is to identify the primary determinants of wage change from an international perspective according to the type of wage and the size of firm.

To trace the origin of Japanese wage flexibility and give it substantial meaning, it is necessary to examine the possible factors that determine the wage changes. The estimated equation is comparatively simple, and is specified as follows:

$$\dot{W}i,j = a_0 + a_1 \text{PRO} + a_2 \dot{P}c_t + a_3 \frac{O}{A} + a_4 \text{STR}, \tag{3}$$

where PRO is the ratio of net profit to sales for enterprises with share capital of 100 million yen and over in all industries and is a proxy for business achievements, which are very important in regulating wage changes; $\dot{P}c_t$ stands for annual percentage change in the consumer price index with a time lag, t; O/A stands for the ratio of job openings to applicants, which is commonly adopted as an index representing labor market conditions; and STR stands for the ratio of union members involved in industrial disputes to total union members. The variable STR is selected to ascertain the union impact on wage changes. Also, i represents the type of wage payment (W_1 = the total cash earnings including overtime premiums and bonus payments divided by total actually worked hours; W_2 = the regular monthly wage divided by contracted hours of work; and W_3 = the average monthly *special* wages, which are a sum of bonus payments and retroactive wage increase) and j is the firm size as measured by the number of regular employees (1 = 500 and more, 2 = 100–499, 3 = 30–99, and 4 = 5–29 regular employees).

At this stage it may be appropriate to make some comments in relation to the wage function seen above. As equation (3) shows, the independent variables are not disaggregated by firm size (j), simply because relevant data are not available. In interpreting the estimated results of this type of wage-change function, therefore, discussions should be based on the statistical level of significance or the magnitude of the estimated coefficients. In addition to this, there exists a more complicated problem of the causality between the changes in money wage and the changes in consumer prices (Boehm 1984). However, without going deeper into this specific problem, and by making allowances for the fact that regular wages are usually raised once a year (mostly in April) while special wages (mostly bonus payments) are paid to workers twice a year (early summer and winter) in Japan, we expect that the length of the lag distribution (t) on the variable $\dot{P}c$ will vary among the types of wage payments, so that changes in consumer prices would result in wage changes. The variable $\dot{P}c_0$ stands for changes in consumer prices with no time lag, $\dot{P}c_{-1}$ and $\dot{P}c_{-2}$ show lags of one quarter and two quarters, respectively, prior to wage changes.

Using equation (3) it appears that changes in the regular wage, $\dot{W}_2$, will depend mainly on the movement of the consumer price index and changing labor market conditions, while the special wages ($\dot{W}_3$) may strongly respond to an index of the business achievements, so that the Japanese bonus-payment system may be seen as a kind of profit-sharing (Gordon 1982). In smaller firms the relationship between special wages and PRO tends to be close, but employers in large firms place much emphasis on preserving stable industrial relations, so that a change in special wages may not be directly connected with changes in profits. On the other hand, if special wages change in response to movements in the consumer price index, they cannot be called bonuses in the literal sense. Therefore, one of the important purposes of the present paper is to ascertain the nature of special wages, which are often believed to be a major source of Japan's comparatively high wage flexibility.

3. The Bonus Payments as One of the Institutional Background of the Japanese Labor Market

In an article investigating the movements of wages and employment over time in three major industrialized countries, Gordon (1982), using quarterly data, found that, when expressed in terms of the standard deviation of the relevant percentage changes of wages and employment, the United States had a more rigid wage system (in nominal terms), combined with a less stable employment pattern than is the case in either Japan or Britain. In explaining the greater flexibility of nominal wages and the greater stability of employment in Japan, he places much emphasis on such institutional characteristics of the Japanese labor market as the long-term attachment between workers and firms, often referred to as the lifetime employment system; the half-yearly variable bonus, which encourages wage flexibility; the seniority system (*nenkō*), which (in its purest form) relates earnings solely to length of service; and the annual and roughly simultaneous wage negotiations during the "spring wage offensive." He concludes that: "Many of the labor-market arrangements selected by the economic theorist to achieve macroeconomic efficiency and high productivity appear to correspond rather closely to well-known features of the Japanese labor market" (p. 34). Kahn (1984) basically accepts these explanations of the greater flexibility of Japanese wages vis-à-vis other countries.

Although the degree of wage flexibility seems to depend on many factors, including the rate of economic growth, the resultant labor-market conditions, the movement of consumer prices, and the composition of wage payments, some authors (for example, Gordon 1982; Kahn 1984; Sachs 1979, 1983; and OECD 1984) emphasize variable bonus payments as an important source of Japan's greater wage flexibility. The argument derives from an empirical analysis by Hashimoto (1979), who finds that the ratio of special wage payments to total earnings is high, that it varies among different-sized firms, and that it has been rising for all firm sizes. He also notes that the ratio of bonuses to earnings is closely associated with human-capital variables, and that there is a positive correlation between the cyclic sensitivities in the production index and the ratio of bonus payments to earnings. He also argues that "the wide use of bonus payments in Japan reflects both the high profitability of investment and the low costs of reaching agreements, that is, low transaction costs, about fluctuating productivities" (p. 1103).

When proper attention is paid to the fact that the bonus, which accounted for 92% of special wage payments in 1980, is regularly paid in early summer and at the end of the year, it is clear that the importance of special wages should be assessed according to the ratio of annual special wages to monthly regular wage, namely (12 × monthly special wage/monthly regular wage, in months). According to figure 1, the sum of special wages in 1983 amounted to 4.6 months' regular wages in large firms with five hundred or more regular employees. In this respect, however, two important facts should be noted. First, the movement of the ratio over time is very similar across different-sized firms, which may suggest that the ratio of bonus payments to monthly regular wages is more closely connected with macroeconomic than firm-specific factors. Second, the ratio of bonus payments to monthly regular wage rose continuously with some exceptions from 1960 to 1974, and then stabilized around the level attained in 1972.

Perhaps the simplest way of measuring wage flexibility is to calculate the coefficient of variation (the standard deviation divided by mean, expressed in percentage terms) of the annual percentage change in wages for a specified period. But, if wage flexibility is expressed by the annual percentage change in total wages ($\dot{W}_1$), it cannot be concluded that special wage payments make a significant contribution to Japan's wage flexibility as a whole, because

$$\dot{W}_1 = r(\dot{W}_2) + s(\dot{W}_3). \tag{4}$$

FIGURE 1

RATIO OF ANNUAL SPECIAL WAGES TO MONTHLY REGULAR WAGES

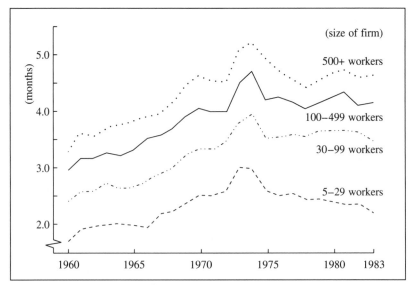

Source: Ministery of Labor, *Monthly Labour Report.*
Note: Ratio refers to [12 × monthly special wages/monthly regular wage].

It follows that when the proportion of $\dot{W}_3$ to $\dot{W}_1$ (namely s) is not high, $\dot{W}_1$ is chiefly regulated by $\dot{W}_2$ with a high value of $r = (1 - s)$). In fact, the correlation between $\dot{W}_1$ and $\dot{W}_3$ was stronger (0.983) than the correlation between $\dot{W}_1$ and $\dot{W}_3$ (0.836) for the period 1960–1983, and the ratio of special payments to total monthly wages (s) from 1960 to 1983 was only 24.1% on average, rising consistently over the 1960s and remaining relatively stable thereafter except in 1973 and 1974 (see figure 1). If we assume that, the coefficient of variation on the annual percentage change in respective wages for a period under consideration is V, then the numerical contribution of changes in special wages to overall wage flexibility can be measured as $(V_1 - V_2)/V_1$ or, alternatively, as the ratio of increase in special wages to increase in total wages (namely, $\Delta W_3/\Delta W_1$). In spite of the assertion by many authors that Japan's greater wage flexibility could be ascribed to the existence of variable bonus payments, up to now nobody with the exception of Suruga (1987) has attempted to estimate a quantitative contribution of bonuses to overall wage flexibility.

II. The Responsiveness of Wage and Employment to Changes in Nominal GNP

1. The Macroeconomic Experiences of the Japanese Labor Market

This section presents some empirical findings concerning the responsiveness of wage and employment changes to a declining growth rate of nominal GNP, relying on the results derived from equation (2).

If we take the Japanese case, a remarkable feature of figure 2 (which shows the annual percentage change for the variables related to equation [2]) is the distinct difference between the first and second halves of the period under consideration. For example, the economic growth rate ($\dot{Y}n$), measured in terms of net national income at factor cost, dropped from a high average level of 16.3% in the 1960s to 9.1% in the 1970s and continued to decline in the early 1980s. While compensation per man-hour ($\dot{W}$) showed an upward trend after 1966, it has continued to fall since the extraordinary peak of 1974. There was also a tendency for the growth rate in the number of employees ($\dot{E}$) to decline from the beginning of the period under consideration to the mid-1970s, reflecting the declining rate of economic growth and decreased labor-force participation rate as well as the slowdown in the rate of increase in the working age population. However, this trend has been reversed in recent years.

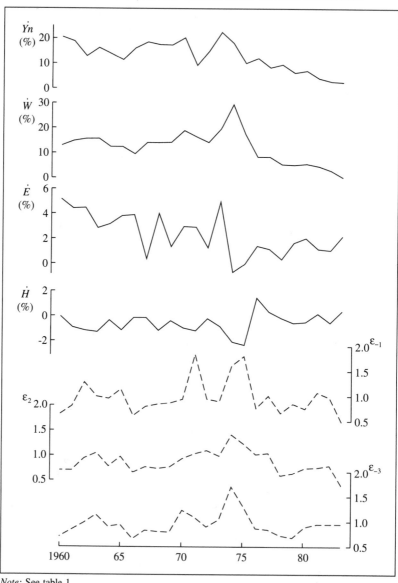

FIGURE 2
ANNUAL RATE OF CHANGE IN NATIONAL INCOME, COMPENSATION
PER MAN-HOUR, EMPLOYMENT AND HOURS WORKED, AND
COMPENSATION ELASTICITIES WITH RESPECT TO NATIONAL INCOME

Note: See table 1.

Especially striking is that, with declining economic growth, $\dot{W}$ became extremely flexible when expressed by the coefficient of variation, which was more than six times as high in the 1970s as it was in the 1960s (see table 1). In other words, wages are more volatile and more vulnerable to recession than are changes in employment. From a macroeconomic perspective this suggests that wage flexibility combined with the Japanese

TABLE 1

VARIABILITY OF GROWTH RATES OF NOMINAL GNP, EMPLOYMENT AND
WAGES, AND ELASTICITIES OF WAGES WITH RESPECT TO NOMINAL GNP

Variable	Item	1960–83	1960–69	1974–83	$\dfrac{1974\text{--}83}{1960\text{--}69}$
$\dot{Y}n$	M	13.455	16.302	9.141	0.561
	SD	5.347	2.723	4.221	1.550
	SD/M (%)	39.737	16.703	46.174	2.764
$\dot{W} + \dot{E} + \dot{H}$	M	14.892	16.482	11.209	0.680
	SD	5.630	1.563	6.594	4.220
	SD/M (%)	37.805	9.481	58.827	6.205
$\dot{W}$	M	12.619	13.465	9.873	0.733
	SD	5.845	1.642	7.747	4.717
	SD/M (%)	46.342	12.198	78.464	6.433
$\dot{E}$	M	2.655	3.591	1.434	0.399
	SD	1.576	1.354	0.910	0.672
	SD/M (%)	59.365	37.705	63.434	1.682
ϵ_1	M	0.955	0.851	0.995	1.168
	SD	0.321	0.186	0.367	1.972
	SD/M (%)	33.606	21.838	36.869	1.688
ϵ_2	M	0.896	0.844	0.878	1.040
	SD	0.203	0.130	0.266	2.053
	SD/M (%)	22.710	15.372	30.337	1.974
ϵ_3	M	0.941	0.839	1.005	1.197
	SD	0.229	0.133	0.307	2.311
	SD/M (%)	24.364	15.854	30.603	1.930
$\mu(\dot{W} + \dot{E} + \dot{H})/\dot{Y}n$	M	68.257	54.278	81.400	1.500
	SD	19.622	10.973	16.182	1.475
	SD/M (%)	28.748	20.216	19.880	0.983

Sources: Economic Planning Agency, *Annual Report on National Income*,
and *Annual Report on National Accounts*; Statistics Bureau, Prime
Minister's Office, *Annual Report on the Labour-Force Survey*.

Note: $\dot{Y}n$ = Growth rate of net national product at factor cost; $\dot{W}$ = growth
rate of compensation per man-hour; $\dot{E}$ = growth rate of employment
(employees); $\epsilon_i = \dot{W}/\dot{Y}n$ (see text); μ = Labor share; M = mean; SD
= standard deviation.

lifetime employment system seemed to contribute to the relative stability of employment.

Second, wages in percentage terms were not only flexible over time but were also very sensitive to percentage changes in nominal output. According to the figures shown in the lower part of table 1, the elasticity of nominal wages with respect to the change in nominal GNP ($\epsilon_1 = \dot{W}_t/\dot{Y}_{n_t}$) was 0.995 on average and was very close to unity in the ten years up to 1983. Although elasticity values vary according to the time-lag involved,

$$\epsilon_2 = \frac{\dot{W}_t}{\frac{(\dot{Y}n_t + \dot{Y}n_{t-1})}{2}}, \qquad \text{or } \epsilon_3 = \frac{\dot{W}_t}{\frac{(\dot{Y}n_{t-1} + \dot{Y}n_t + \dot{Y}_{t+1})}{3}},$$

wages in Japan are still very responsive to both rises and falls in the growth rate of nominal output, taking into account the recent rise in the coefficient of variation (SD/M, percent). In addition to this, as the mean values of this elasticity are generally high in the case without a time-lag, the change in wages in a given year seems to depend primarily on the contemporaneous change in nominal output. We present evidence below that this sort of intimate relation between $\dot{W}_t$ and $\dot{Y}n_t$ can be confirmed by international comparison.

Other things being equal, a close relationship between $\dot{W}$ and $\dot{Y}n$, especially during economic downturns, will bring about a smaller increase in employment than otherwise. Taking the higher ϵ values, $\dot{E}/(\dot{W}+\dot{E}+\dot{H})$ dropped from 21.8% in the 1960s to 12.8% in the ten years up to 1983 (when $\dot{W}$ was adjusted for gross domestic product [GDP] deflator and converted into the real terms, the corresponding figures are 33.0% and 26.8%, respectively). Thus a higher degree of nominal wage flexibility combined with higher ϵ will have an unfavorable impact on fluctuations in employment. When economic growth slows down it seems that any remaining benefits from the growth process are absorbed in wage increases.

Third, the effect of the share of labor income on the relationship between fluctuations in wages, employment, and output must be considered, because, as noted earlier, when labor's share of income is low the relationship between $\dot{Y}n$ and $\dot{W}$ or $\dot{E}$ will be neutralized or weakened through μ. Gordon (1982) neglects this important point. In Japan, the share of labor income rose consistently from 49.1% in 1960 to 71.0% in 1983, depending on the rise in consumer prices, the rising proportion of employees to total employed persons, and the decline of the ratio of income from private corporations to national income (Mizuno 1984). One question, therefore, is how the change in $\dot{Y}n$ is absorbed into the whole profile of labor market behavior; that is, $\mu(\dot{W}+\dot{E}+\dot{H})/\dot{Y}n$. Although these proportions are expected to be very high in the face of a sudden decline in the economic growth rate, around 55% of $\dot{Y}n$ was absorbed into the sum of labor's share of income, wage increases, employment change, and decreased working hours in the 1960s. But the proportion rose to about 80% in the ten years up to 1983, in spite of a relatively low value of $(\dot{W} + \dot{E} + \dot{H})$, reflecting the steady rise in labor's share of income.

Using the average of $\dot{Y}n$, $\dot{W}$, $\dot{E}$, and $\dot{H}$ shown in table 1 and the average labor's share of income over a decade, the following results can be computed using equation (2).

1960–69: $16.302=0.522\ (13.465+3.591-0.573)+(1-0.522)\ 16.105$

1974–83: $9.141=0.663\ (\ 9.873+1.434-0.098)+(1-0.633)\ \ 5.082$

This suggests the existence of a trade-off between wage increases and employment expansion. Generally, the lower the level of labor's income share, the greater will be the increase in employment generated by a given economic growth, even if the $\dot{W}/\dot{Y}n$ is high. But the connection between a higher labor share of income and a higher ϵ suggests that employment expansion is sacrificed during a recession. One of the distinguishing features of the ten years up to 1983, compared with the 1960s, is that with the decline in the growth rate of nominal output and the rising share of labor income, nominal wages respond very sensitively to the change in $\dot{Y}n$, which in turn brings about a higher ϵ and exerts an unfavorable effect on employment. Given that not only $(\dot{E}+\dot{H})/(\dot{W}+\dot{E}+\dot{H})$ but also $(1-\mu)\dot{K}$ were lower in 1974–83, Japanese workers and trade unions appear to have pursued wage increases at the expense of growth in employment and nonlabor incomes.

2. Fluctuations in the Growth Rate of Nominal GNP and Wage Flexibility

Are the macroeconomic experiences of the Japanese labor market unique or similar to that of other industrialized countries? Using table 2, which shows the macroeconomic behavior of the labor market for six selected countries, and adding further calculations, the following comments are warranted particularly for the period 1974–83. First, given the nominal growth rate of GDP, Japanese wages are most flexible in terms of the coefficient of variation based on annual wage changes ($\dot{W}$). The elasticity of wages with respect to nominal GDP ($\dot{W}/\dot{Y}n$) is just unity and differs somewhat from that in the United States and Canada, which have elasticity values below 1, or in the three European countries, which have values above 1. Second, reflecting the steady rise in the labor's share of income in Japan

TABLE 2
INTERNATIONAL COMPARISONS: VARIABILITY OF NOMINAL GROWTH RATE OF GDP, COMPENSATION PER MAN-HOUR, EMPLOYMENT AND WORKING HOURS, AND THE ELASTICITY OF WAGES WITH RESPECT TO NOMINAL GDP (1960–1983)

Period, country	$\dot{Y}n$			$\dot{W}$			$\dot{E}$			$\dot{H}$			$\dot{W}/\dot{Y}n$		
	M	SD	V	M	SD	V	M	SD	V	M	SD	V	M	SD	V
1960–83															
Canada	10.46	3.91	37.38	7.99	4.07	50.86	2.88	1.89	65.77	−0.24	0.84	350.56	0.79	0.41	52.32
France	11.91	2.22	18.61	12.24	3.83	31.30	1.30	1.14	87.50	−0.65	0.85	131.31	1.02	0.21	20.70
W. Germany	7.90	2.94	37.18	8.71	3.22	36.99	0.41	1.63	399.00	−0.48	1.47	304.19	1.33	1.02	76.91
Japan	13.46	5.35	39.74	12.62	5.85	46.34	2.66	1.58	59.37	−0.38	0.83	217.16	0.96	0.32	33.61
U.K.	11.15	5.07	45.42	11.62	6.49	55.85	−0.08	1.59	1,996.53	−0.45	1.02	224.50	1.04	0.25	23.56
U.S.A.	8.29	2.64	31.81	6.71	2.14	31.91	2.20	1.57	71.25	−0.45	0.59	131.19	0.86	0.32	37.34
1960–69															
Canada	8.04	2.46	30.61	5.21	2.38	45.64	3.50	1.25	35.84	−0.17	0.59	345.05	0.66	0.25	38.28
France	10.14	2.00	19.73	8.85	2.00	22.65	1.93	0.91	47.17	−0.02	0.59	294.97	0.89	0.19	21.75
W. Germany	8.25	2.98	36.08	8.50	1.99	23.35	0.88	1.62	184.93	−0.34	1.59	460.96	1.46	1.45	99.12
Japan	16.30	2.72	16.70	13.47	1.64	12.20	3.59	1.35	37.71	−0.57	0.50	87.72	0.85	0.19	21.84
U.K.	6.86	1.19	17.33	6.85	1.45	21.15	0.54	1.14	210.84	−0.58	0.97	168.38	1.01	0.21	20.24
U.S.A.	6.81	2.02	29.62	5.09	1.87	36.69	2.62	0.98	37.58	−0.34	0.57	168.21	0.76	0.20	25.57
1974–83															
Canada	12.43	3.88	31.21	10.76	4.21	39.16	2.03	2.18	107.51	−0.30	1.06	352.59	0.94	0.54	57.97
France	13.52	1.31	9.67	15.71	2.72	17.33	0.35	0.79	224.86	−1.21	0.81	66.95	1.16	0.17	14.59
W. Germany	6.18	1.85	30.01	7.09	2.93	41.31	−0.42	1.51	362.28	−0.54	1.54	286.49	1.26	0.60	48.00
Japan	9.14	4.22	46.17	9.87	7.75	78.46	1.43	0.91	63.44	−0.01	1.10	1,115.89	1.00	0.37	36.87
U.K.	15.12	4.90	32.38	15.78	7.5	48.09	−0.75	1.75	232.95	−0.31	1.03	331.04	1.03	0.27	26.31
U.S.A.	9.57	2.54	26.58	8.33	1.43	17.16	1.67	1.93	115.20	−0.53	0.55	104.78	0.95	0.38	40.21

Source: Mizuno (1986).
Note: See table 1.

the proportion of $\dot{Y}n$ going to labor is strikingly high, being about 80% in comparison with about 60% in other countries. Third, while the ratio $(\dot{E} + \dot{H})/(\dot{W} + \dot{E} + \dot{H})$ is comparatively similar to three countries, the United States (12.1%), Canada (13.8%), and Japan (11.9%), there is a large divergence between these countries and the three European economies. Thus these results, while being by no means definitive, lead us to believe that there are three different aspects to labor market performance when viewed in the light of the macroeconomic response of wages and employment to changing economic conditions.

In spite of the first comment mentioned above, we must note that the difference in the elasticity of wage changes, with respect to annual growth rate of nominal GDP, is not necessarily large among countries, being in the neighborhood of unity (for example, from 0.94 in Canada to 1.26 in West Germany on average in the subperiod 1974–83). In addition to this, during the 1960s when the Japanese economy experienced stable economic growth in the sense that it had the smallest coefficient of variation on $\dot{Y}n$, the dispersion of annual changes in wages was also at its lowest. These considerations lead us to expect a positive correlation between the variability of nominal growth rates of GDP, $V(\dot{Y}n)$, and the variability of rates of changes in nominal wages, $V(\dot{W})$. Using the average of the relevant variables over the two specified periods, we depict such an international relationship in figure 3. From the figure a close, positive correlation ($r = 0.812$) can be seen between $V(\dot{W})$ and $V(\dot{Y}n)$, and thus we may say that if the Japanese economy maintains a relatively stable economic growth without being disturbed by any exogenous shock like the sudden rise in oil prices, its wages would change smoothly. In other words, one of the major reasons for greater flexibility of wages in Japan should be ascribed to larger economic fluctuations in Japan in comparison to other industrialized countries.

III. The Determinants of Wage Flexibility and the Role of Bonuses

1. The Responsiveness of Wage Changes to Economic Factors

Even if it is concluded that compensation per man-hour measured by national income data was very flexible in Japan in the sense that $\dot{W}$ is highly sensitive to $\dot{Y}n$, this is simply a macroeconomic phenomenon, and thus some important problems remain to be resolved. In so far as the national labor market is stratified and composed of various subsidiary markets in

115

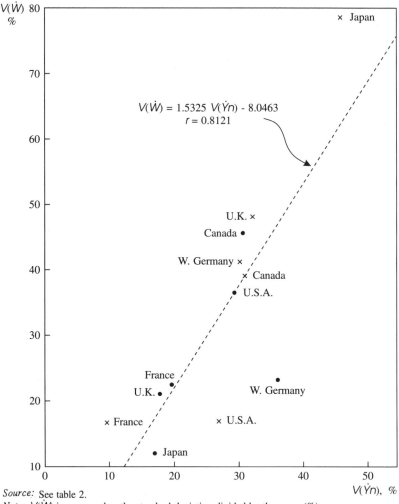

FIGURE 3
INTERNATIONAL RELATIONSHIP BETWEEN THE VARIABILITY OF
GROWTH RATE OF NOMINAL GDP AND THE VARIABILITY OF GROWTH RATE OF
COMPENSATION PER MAN-HOUR

$V(\dot{W}) = 1.5325 \ V(\dot{Y}n) - 8.0463$
$r = 0.8121$

Source: See table 2.
Note: $V(\dot{W})$ is expressed as the standard deviation divided by the mean (%),
in terms of the annual growth rate of nominal compensation per
man-hour.
$V(\dot{Y}n)$ is expressed as the standard deviation divided by the mean (%),
in terms of the annual growth rate of nominal GDP.
The mark ● and × refer to the average of $V(\dot{W})$ and $V(\dot{Y}n)$ for the
period 1960–69 and the period 1974–83, respectively.

which the supply of, and demand for, labor behave quite differently, it is important to determine which sector's wages tend to be rigid and which sector's wages tend to be flexible. Also, the contribution of special wage payments to wages in general must be assessed.

In order to give a substantive meaning to the problem of wage flexibility and to determine what factor contributes most toward the volatile wage changes in Japan, the Phillips-type wage-change functions have been estimated for six countries. The functions include two or three explanatory variables, including the reciprocal of the unemployment rate $(1/u)$; the growth rate of labor productivity $(\dot{\alpha})$, as measured by annual percentage change in real GDP per man-hour; and the annual percentage change in consumer expenditure deflator $(\dot{P}c)$. The results of regression estimations are presented in table 3.

Although the estimated results are satisfactory, as a whole, in the sense that the three variables adopted here are able to explain 85% or above of the average wage change over the period from 1960 to 1983, our major interest is in how far the relative contribution of each explanatory variable differs among countries. When the second type of regression result, which has three variables, is considered (given the independent effect of the intercept on wage changes), the annual percentage change in labor productivity $(\dot{\alpha})$ can account for from 63% to 75% of the average wage change in Canada, France, West Germany, and the United Kingdom. At the same time, the role of changing labor market conditions in regulating wage changes is considerably small. On the other hand, the most important factor contributing to wage changes in Japan is the variation in supply of and demand for labor, $1/u$, which accounts for about 45% of the wage change, followed by movements of consumer prices. The situation in the United States seems to differ not only from that in the three European countries but also from the Canadian case.

From Japanese wage statistics, annual percentage changes in three aspects of wages can be recognized: the total wage $\dot{W}_1$, the regular wage $\dot{W}_2$, and the special wage $\dot{W}_3$. If the same econometric method used above is applied to these different kinds of wage changes, we may be able to determine more clearly the important features of Japanese wage flexibility. The estimated results are for males and females working in firms with thirty and more regular workers. Following equation (3), the results are as follows:

$$\dot{W}_1 = -11.446 + 2.053 \text{ PRO} + 1.106 \ \dot{P}c_{-2} + 11.571 \ O/A$$
$$ (2.44) (7.85) (7.42)$$
$$ \bar{R}^2 = 0.9011 \ \text{D.W.}=2.10,$$

117

TABLE 3
REGRESSION RESULTS OF WAGE-CHANGE
FUNCTION FOR SELECTED COUNTRIES, 1960–1983

Country		Const.	$1/u$	$\dot{\alpha}$	$\dot{P}c$	$\bar{R}^2$	DW
Canada	(1)	−2.9902	27.3230		1.1259	0.7134	1.0811
			(2.791)		(7.537)		
	(2)	−2.1718	10.1269	0.7920	0.3615	0.8434	1.7763
			(1.224)	(4.293)	(1.725)		
			<17.486>	<62.968>	<19.546>		
France	(1)	5.2706	−0.0525		0.9650	0.7483	1.4285
			(−0.021)		(4.751)		
	(2)	−2.6617	1.6212	0.9075	0.4221	0.8666	1.8805
			(0.853)	(4.430)	(2.198)		
			<4.912>	<74.571>	<20.517>		
W. Germany	(1)	0.9568	3.7641		1.1141	0.5777	1.6748
			(5.070)		(4.138)		
	(2)	−3.5225	1.6997	1.0018	0.5527	0.8683	2.0763
			(3.321)	(6.879)	(3.230)		
			<12.468>	<69.791>	<17.741>		
Japan	(1)	−6.4197	18.2113		1.0563	0.8915	1.2956
			(7.482)		(10.025)		
	(2)	−5.1605	11.9457	0.2993	0.9202	0.9180	1.7652
			(3.873)	(2.792)	(8.871)		
			<44.730>	<21.387>	<33.883>		
U.K.	(1)	0.0538	5.1759		1.1245	0.7814	2.1620
			(1.670)		(8.377)		
	(2)	−4.3045	5.5759	0.9988	0.2183	0.8733	1.7346
			(2.361)	(4.029)	(0.884)		
			<15.133>	<73.493>	<11.374>		
U.S.A.	(1)	1.2095	9.8414		0.7612	0.8424	2.5212
			(2.711)		(11.062)		
	(2)	−0.0118	9.2635	0.3520	0.5402	0.8841	2.5397
			(2.971)	(2.928)	(5.639)		
			<25.403>	<35.667>	<38.930>		

Source: Mizuno (1986).
Note: $u =$ Unemployment rate.
  $\dot{\alpha} =$ Annual percentage change in labor productivity, as measured by the annual rate of change in real GDP per man-hour.
  $\dot{P}c =$ Annual percentage change in consumer expenditure deflator.
  $\dot{W} =$ Annual percentage change in compensation per man-hour. The figures shown in ( ) and < > indicate t-value, and the relative contribution of the respective variable to the change in wages, respectively.

$$\dot{W}_2 = \quad -7.144 + 1.050 \text{ PRO} + 1.026 \, \dot{P}c_{-2} + \quad 9.995 \, O/A$$
$$\qquad\qquad (1.45) \qquad\quad (8.49) \qquad\qquad (7.47)$$
$$\bar{R}^2 = 0.9107 \quad \text{D.W.} = 1.86,$$

$$\dot{W}_3 = -16.382 + 4.843 \text{ PRO} + 1.021 \, \dot{P}c_0 \quad + \quad 9.675 \, O/A$$
$$\qquad\qquad (5.05) \qquad\quad (6.37) \qquad\qquad (4.23)$$
$$\bar{R}^2 = 0.8693 \quad \text{D.W.} = 1.91,$$

$$\dot{W}_3 = -19.784 + 5.010 \text{ PRO} + 0.706 \, \dot{P}c_0 \quad + \quad 7.979 \, O/A$$
$$\qquad\qquad (6.32) \qquad\quad (4.28) \qquad\qquad (4.07)$$
$$+ \, 0.279 \text{ STR} \qquad\qquad\qquad \bar{R}^2 = 0.9109 \quad \text{D.W.} = 2.09.$$
$$(3.21)$$

Although the estimated result on $\dot{W}_3$ is better in the case of the equation including the variable STR, if we employ the equation excluding this variable (to ensure the comparability of explanatory variables contributing to the changes in regular and special wages), a macrobalance of supply of and demand for labor (namely $O/A = 1$) brings about a rise of 11.57% for $\dot{W}_1$, about 10% for $\dot{W}_2$, and 9.68% for $\dot{W}_3$. At the same time, PRO, $\dot{P}c_{-2}$, and O/A account for 25.7%, 31.8%, and 42.5%, respectively, of the changes in the total wage rate $(\dot{W}_1)$, given the independent effect of the intercept on wage changes. The corresponding figures are 16.6%, 37.2%, and 46.3% for $\dot{W}_2$, and 48.2%, 23.5%, and 28.3% for $\dot{W}_3$. Needless to say the explanatory power of these variables with respect to special wages would be reduced if we allowed for the effect of the STR variable on them.

From the above considerations, the following conclusions may be made. First, Japanese wages appear to be much more responsive to changes in labor market conditions than is the case in the other industrialized countries investigated. Second, while changes in regular wages are chiefly explained by movements in consumer prices, special wages, on the other hand, are more closely related to changes in the profit rate. However, the most influential factor regulating both types of wage changes is the change in labor market conditions.

2. Wage-Changes by Size of Firm

Our next step is to explore the problem of Japanese wage flexibility in relation to the size of firm, and to inquire whether wage changes have responded differently to changing economic conditions in large and small firms. No refined model or complex equation will be attempted because, as noted earlier, all the necessary disaggregated data by firm size are not available, so that aggregate data must be employed as the explanatory variables

119

of wage change by firm size. Thus it is assumed that wages in any sector will change in response to the movements of general economic conditions. Table 4 shows the regression results estimated according to firm size and type of wage payment.

Although there is room for improving the model in the case of the smallest firm size (five to twenty-nine regular workers), Table 4 nevertheless gives generally satisfactory results in the sense that this simple model can explain about 75% to 90% of wage changes in the long run. Original regressions were run for the model following equation (3), but no significant effect of the variable STR (the ratio of union members involved in industrial disputes to total union members) on the changes in regular or total wage could be observed. Table 4 therefore shows the estimated results for $\dot{W}_1$ and $\dot{W}_2$, excluding this variable.

We may then state that while in most cases the changes in regular and total wages are explained by three variables (PRO, $\dot{P}c_t$, and O/A), in the case of special wages it appears that union activity has a role to play. In the case of $\dot{W}_3$, the three basic variables are statistically significant for all sizes of firms, including large firms. This indicates that even large firms tend to pay bonuses according to movements in profitability. However, in the case of $\dot{W}_1$ and $\dot{W}_2$ the picture is different. Here the PRO does not play a significant role in wage determination for large firms. In fact, for $\dot{W}_2$ the PRO has a negative coefficient for large firms and, even in the case of $\dot{W}_1$, the t value of the coefficient for PRO is too low to be significant.

To conclude we may say that for large companies the profitability of the firm does not seem to have a significant influence on the determination of $\dot{W}_1$ and $\dot{W}_2$. There may be other forces at work deciding the level of wages, such as interindustry comparisons of the cost of labor unrest if adequate wages are *not* given. In other words, profitability is not the sole key to wage determination for $\dot{W}_1$ and $\dot{W}_2$. Also, from the table, it can be seen that consumer prices $\dot{P}c_t$ is a stable and significant factor in explaining wage changes in all cases ($\dot{W}_1$, $\dot{W}_2$, and $\dot{W}_3$) and for all sizes of firms, especially for categories of smaller firms. It can also be seen that the $\dot{P}c_t$ parameter is larger in the case of $\dot{W}_1$ and $\dot{W}_2$ than in the case of $\dot{W}_3$ for each size category. Finally, the job opening to applications ratio (O/A) is also a very important force in explaining wage changes in all sizes of firms and all wage categories. However, there seems to be some difficult theoretical problem here, as changes in O/A should be much *less* important for large firms than small firms because O/A measures the supply and demand for labor at the job centers, which are often not linked to the "internal labor" market of large firms. The contrary finding shown in these results needs further explanation.

TABLE 4

REGRESSION RESULTS OF WAGE-CHANGE
FUNCTION BY SIZE OF FIRM, 1960–1983

Wage	Size of firm	Const.	PRO	$\dot{P}c_t$	O/A	STR	$\bar{R}^2$	DW
$\dot{W}_1$	500 and more	−7.525	0.501	0.932	13.845		0.9079	2.18
			(0.60)	(6.73)	(9.03)			
	100–499	−11.747	2.255	1.154	11.173		0.9017	1.91
			(2.66)	(8.16)	(7.14)			
	30–99	−14.343	3.411	1.165	10.285		0.8664	1.86
			(3.49)	(7.13)	(5.68)			
	5–29	−18.239	5.615	1.356	6.601		0.7792	1.99
			(3.83)	(6.06)	(2.50)			
$\dot{W}_2$	500 and more	−2.624	−0.425	0.757	11.839		0.9054	1.70
			(−0.59)	(6.33)	(8.94)			
	100–499	−6.999	1.032	1.000	10.348		0.9210	1.37
			(1.52)	(8.84)	(8.26)			
	30–99	−10.215	2.246	1.064	9.448		0.8987	1.30
			(2.94)	(8.34)	(6.69)			
	5–29	—	—	—	—		—	—
$\dot{W}_3$	500 and more	−16.670	3.804	0.625	11.644	0.185	0.8968	2.42
			(4.50)	(3.56)	(5.58)	(2.01)		
	100–499	−20.071	5.326	0.801	7.344	0.264	0.8964	2.17
			(6.09)	(4.40)	(3.40)	(2.76)		
	30–99	−22.223	6.369	0.722	6.003	0.307	0.8305	2.02
			(5.47)	(2.98)	(2.09)	(2.41)		
	5–29	−25.207	8.319	0.881	10.321		0.7590	1.60
			(4.33)	(3.05)	(2.35)			

Sources: Ministry of Labour, *Monthly Labour Statistics, Annual Report on Labour Market,* and *Basic Survey on Trade Unions*; Statistics Bureau, Prime Minister's Office, *Annual Report on Consumer Price Index*; Economic Planning Agency, *Annual Report on Business Cycle Indicators.*

Note: PRO=Ratio of net profit to sales.
$\dot{P}c$ = Annual percentage change in consumer price index. In the cases of $\dot{W}_1$ and $\dot{W}_2$, they show the coefficient with respect to $\dot{P}c_{-2}$, but $\dot{W}_3$ shows the coefficient with respect to $\dot{P}c_0$.
O/A = Ratio of job openings to applicants.
STR= Ratio of union member involved in labor disputes to total union members.

3. The Effect of Bonuses on Japan's Wage Flexibility

In order to investigate which sector's wages are more flexible and how much special wage payments contribute to Japan's wage flexibility, measurements were taken of the means, standard deviations, and coefficients of variation of the annual percentage increases of three types of wages according to firm size. The figures in table 5 show that for the entire period (1960–83) the average rate of increase in the total wage was a little higher for small firms than for large firms, so that there should be a narrowing of wage differentials among firm sizes in relative terms. However, there is no significant difference among firms in the flexibility of total and regular wages, when expressed through the coefficient of variation. In contrast, special wages show somewhat greater volatility than regular wages and vary inversely with the size of the firm. It should also be noted that wage flexibility became more evident after the first oil crisis for all sizes of firms.

It appears from table 5 that wage flexibility in Japan is explained predominantly by movements in the regular wage. If the quantitative contribution of special wage payments to overall wage flexibility is defined as $(V_1 - V_2)/V_1$ in percentage term, the contribution of special wages to the variability of total wage changes is only 8.99% for large firms with five hundred or more regular workers (i.e., where the ratio of special wages to total wages is highest) during the period 1960–83. Even during the ten years up to 1983 it is only about 16%.

When the rates of increases in regular wages fluctuate to a greater extent than those of total wages (including special wages), such a measure yields the negative values for the 1960s as shown in table 5. This is in spite of the greater variability of special wage changes to those of regular wages. One possible method to overcome this sort of a defect (Suruga 1987) is to measure the ratio of the absolute changes in special wages to those in total wages $(\Delta W_3/\Delta W_1)$. From the following relations between ΔW_3 or ΔW_2 and ΔW_1, that is,

$$\Delta W_1 = 1{,}024.96 + 3.5135\ \Delta W_3, \qquad r = 0.9644,$$
$$\Delta W_1 = \phantom{1{,}0}16.27 + 1.3669\ \Delta W_2, \qquad r = 0.9952,$$

it is found that the annual average absolute increase in total wages was three and a half times that of special wages. When a measure such as $\Delta W_3/\Delta W_1$ is taken, the mean percentage contribution of special wages does not account for more than 25.9% of the absolute change in total wages for firms with thirty or more regular workers over the whole period considered. Moreover the corresponding figures are relatively lower for small firms, where bonus payments are not a major component of total wages (see figure 1).

TABLE 5

VARIABILITY OF THE ANNUAL PERCENTAGE INCREASES OF WAGES BY SIZE OF FIRM AND THE RELATIVE CONTRIBUTION OF BONUS PAYMENTS TO WAGE FLEXIBILITY

Period, firm size	Total wage ($\dot{W}_1$)			Regular wage ($\dot{W}_2$)			Special wage ($\dot{W}_3$)			$\frac{V_1 - V_2}{V_1}$	$\Delta W_3/\Delta W_1$ (%)		
	M_1	SD_1	V_1 (%)	M_2	SD_2	V_2 (%)	M_3	SD_3	V_3 (%)		M	SD	V (%)
1960–83													
500 and more	12.01	6.25	52.08	11.40	5.40	47.40	13.03	7.41	56.84	8.99	28.66	7.61	26.54
100–499	12.23	6.24	50.99	11.65	5.60	48.07	13.41	7.65	57.04	5.73	26.44	8.35	31.59
30– 99	12.24	6.22	50.80	11.73	5.46	46.49	13.65	7.96	58.34	8.48	22.41	9.77	43.60
5– 29	13.05*	6.49*	49.76*	—	—	—	13.78*	9.65*	70.05*	—	15.70*	8.46*	53.92*
1960–69													
500 and more	10.99	3.09	28.08	9.98	3.06	30.63	13.95	4.44	31.82	−9.08	30.84	7.59	24.60
100–499	11.81	2.70	22.85	10.86	2.78	25.60	14.83	3.66	24.66	−12.01	28.30	7.06	24.93
30– 99	12.44	2.59	20.79	11.38	2.35	20.67	15.84	4.67	29.50	0.01	23.97	5.83	24.31
5– 29	14.71**	3.59**	24.40**	—	—	—	17.81**	6.65**	37.36**	—	18.23**	5.55**	30.46**
1974–83													
500 and more	10.43	7.80	74.81	10.59	6.63	62.55	9.24	6.93	75.04	16.39	25.67	7.56	29.46
100–499	11.19	7.94	77.94	10.26	7.15	69.67	9.17	8.01	83.35	10.61	23.72	10.11	42.60
30– 99	9.57	7.67	80.18	9.88	6.85	69.35	8.49	8.00	94.24	13.51	19.32	13.60	70.39
5– 29	9.49	7.43	78.32	—	—	—	6.40	6.72	104.95	—	10.59	9.02	85.22

Source: Ministry of Labour, *Monthly Labour Statistics.*
Note: Size of firm is classified according to the number of regular workers.
Growth rates of total wage are adjusted for total hours worked.
Growth rates of regular wage are adjusted for contract hours worked.
* and ** mean the figure for the period 1961–83 and 1961–69, respectively.
$\Delta W_3/\Delta W_1$ is measured in terms of monthly wage.

Therefore, the argument that the greater flexibility of Japanese wages is attributable to the variability of special wages is not supported by empirical evidence. Although it cannot, of course, be denied that special wage payments are more flexible, in the sense that they have a larger coefficient of variation than regular wages, most of Japan's wage flexibility can be explained by the volatility of regular wages themselves, which formed around 75% of total wages on average, between 1960 and 1983. In assessing the degree of wage flexibility the relative weights of the different types of wages must be borne in mind and the role of regular wages should be studied carefully.

IV. Concluding Remarks

In order to investigate the realities of wage flexibility in Japan, the present paper has considered some characteristics of wage changes in Japan from an international perspective. The evidence shows that Japan's wage flexibility does not depend to a large extent on the existence of special wage payments, most of which come from the half-yearly bonus.

According to the empirical evidences presented in this paper, the elasticity of wages with respect to nominal GNP is high, being 0.96, on average, over the whole period under consideration. Wage changes became increasingly volatile in the ten years up to 1983, in combination with the relatively low and variable economic growth rates. On the other hand, the higher elasticity of wages experienced during the economic downturn brought about not only a smaller expansion of employment than was the case in the 1960s, but also strengthened the unfavorable impact on employment growth brought about by the rising share of labor income over time. Although the macroeconomic relations between changes in wages, employment, and nominal GNP differ remarkably from country to country, there is a close association between the variability of the annual percentage increase in wages and the movement of nominal economic growth rate across countries. This fact could explain most parts of Japan's wage flexibility without relying on the existence of the variable bonus payments peculiar to the Japanese economy.

In addition to this fact, wages are much more sensitive to changing labor market conditions in Japan than in the European or North American countries studied. When total wages are classified into two categories, the movement of the consumer price index and the changes in labor market conditions account jointly for 81% of the changes in the regular wage, while changes in special wages depend primarily on the behavior of the profit-related variables. Moreover, if disaggregated by firm size, special wages show somewhat more flexibility and vary inversely with firm size, though very little, if any, significant difference can be found between the flexibility of total wages and regular wages with respect to firm size.

Nevertheless, special wage payments cannot explain more than 25.9%, which closely corresponds to the value estimated by Suruga (1987), of the flexibility of the total wages during the period studied. Most of Japan's wage flexibility should therefore be ascribed to the large variability of the regular wage component, which constitutes around 75% of the total wages.

References

Blandy, R., and S. Richardson (1982). *How Labour Markets Work: Case Studies in Adjustment*, Melbourn: Longman Cheshire Pty Limited.

———— (1984). "How Labour Markets Adjust," in *Understanding Labour Market*, edited by R. Blandy and O. Covick, George Allen and Unwin.

Boehm, E. A. (1984). "Money Wages, Consumer Prices, and Causality in Australia," *The Economic Record*, vol. 60, no. 170 (September).

Freeman, R. B., and M. L. Weitzman (1986). "Bonuses and Employment in Japan," NBER Working Paper, no. 1878 (April).

Gordon, R. J. (1982). "Why U.S. Wage and Employment Behavior Differs from That in Britain and Japan," *The Economic Journal*, vol. 92 (March).

Hall, R. H. (1980). "Employment Fluctuation and Wage Rigidity," *Brooking Papers on Economic Activity*, vol. 1.

Hashimoto, M. (1979). "Bonus Payments, On-the-Job Training, and Lifetime Employment in Japan," *Journal of Political Economy*, vol. 87, no. 5, Part 1 (October).

Kahn, G. A. (1984). "International Differences in Wage Behavior: Real, Nominal, or Exaggerated?" *The American Economic Review*, vol. 74, no. 2 (May).

Koshiro, K. (1986). "Labour-Market Flexibility in Japan: With Special Reference to Wage Flexibility," Discussion Paper Series, 86-2, The Center for International Trade Studies, Faculty of Economics, Yokohama National University, April.

Mizuno, A. (1975). "External Wage Structure and Labour Market Conditions: The Experience of the Manufacturing Sector in Post-War Japan," *Keizaigaku Ronsan (The Journal of Economics)*, vol. 16, no. 1.2 (March).

———— (1984). "Rōdoshijyō Behavior no Bunseki (An Analysis of Labour Market Behavior)," in *Nippon Keizai to Fukushi no Keiryōteki Bunseki (Econometric Analysis of Japanese Economy and Welfare)*, edited by The Reseach Institute of Economics, Chuō University, Tokyo: Chuō University Press.

———— (1986). "Koyō Chōsei Pattern no Kokusai Hikaku (An International Comparison of Employment-Adjustment Pattern)," *Keizaigaku Ronsan*, vol. 27,

Asao Mizuno

no. 3 (May).

OECD (1965). *Wages and Labour Mobility: A Study of the Relation between Changes in Wage Differentials and the Pattern of Employment with A Foreword on the Implications for Incomes Policy*, Paris.

———— (1984). *Employment Outlook*, Paris, September.

———— (1985). *Employment Outlook*, Paris, September.

Okun, A. M. (1973). "Upward Mobility in A High-Pressure Economy," *Brookings Papers on Economic Activity*, vol 1.

Ono, A. (1981). *Nippon no Rōdōshijyō: Gaibu Shijyō no Kinō to Kōzō (Japanese Labour Market: The Functions and Structure of External Market)*, Tokyo: Toyokeizai Shinposha.

———— (1985). "Saikin no Tei Keizai Seichō to Rōdōshijyō (Recent Low Economic Growth and Labour Market," in *Senshin Kōgyōkoku no Koyō to Shitugyō (Employment and Unemployment in Advanced Industrialized Countries)*, edited by R. Minami and A. Mizuno, Tokyo: Ohkura Shobo.

Raisian, J. (1983). "Contracts, Job Experience, and Cyclical Labour Market Adjustment," *Journal of Labour Economics*, vol. 1, no. 2 (April).

Sachs, J. D. (1979). "Wages, Profits, and Macroeconomic Adjustment: A Comparative Study," *Brookings Papers on Economic Activity*, 2.

———— (1983). "Real Wages and Unemployment in the OECD Countries," *Brookings Papers on Economic Activity*, 1.

Suruga, T. (1987). "Japanese Bonus Payment System and Flexible Wage," *The Monthly Journal of the Japan Institute of Labour*, vol. 29, no. 5 (May).

Tachibanaki, T. (1986). "Labour Market Flexibility in Japan in Comparison with Europe and the U.S.," Discussion Paper, no. 215, Kyoto Institute of Economic Research, Kyoto University, October.

126

Richard N. Block

5

The Legal and Institutional Framework for Employment Security in the United States: An Overview

I. Introduction

Employment security has traditionally not been viewed as being associated with a public purpose in the United States. While employment for all citizens is always an important political issue, historically, government at all levels has always had a very circumspect role in providing employment security. As a result, there is no mandate in the United States that requires full employment, either guaranteed by the government or as a function of the private sector. The issue of employment security has been addressed piecemeal, through a variety of private and public vehicles.

The purpose of this paper is to present an overview of employment security in the United States. In order to focus the paper, it is limited to problems of employment security resulting from structural economic change in the United States. Employment security issues resulting from the business cycle (i.e., protection for layoffs of short duration) or for misconduct on the job (i.e., discharge) are not addressed. Some idea of the scope of the problem of unemployment due to structural economic change can be obtained from a U.S. government estimate that 11.5 million workers lost jobs between 1979

Richard N. Block

and 1984 due to plant closings, plant relocations, rising productivity due to technological change, and declining output. This accounts for roughly 10% of the labor force in the United States.[1]

Because the United States has generally been unwilling to view employment security for its citizens as a matter that has a substantial public purpose, part two of this paper discusses why this is so and establishes the cultural framework in the United State for viewing employment security. This framework is then used to analyze the different ways in which the United States addresses the matter of unemployment and employment security for its citizens. Part three applies this framework to examining employment security in the unionized sector in the United Sates, while part four examines employment security in the nonunion sector. Part five then looks at what the government has done to address the issue of employment security and unemployment. Part six presents a conclusion.

II. Cultural Norms and Employment Security in the United States

The United States has some well-established societal values regarding the functioning of the economic system. These values underlay any employment-security-related legislation that is considered and ultimately enacted in law. To a large extent, these norms also determine the range of options available to employers in determining employment-security-related practices. In general, since work and employment are viewed as primarily economic activities in the United States, these cultural norms are used to evaluate the issue of employment security. Therefore, it is appropriate to outline these cultural norms so that the legal and institutional framework for employment security can be placed in context.

In discussing these cultural norms, I do not contend that all people of the United States would subscribe to all of these propositions. Some might believe strongly in some but not in others. In addition, certain groups in society may attempt to ameliorate the adverse effects of these norms and values on themselves. But the United States is a democratic country; therefore, it is reasonable to believe that the government represents a rough consensus. Given this, I believe that an observer of the legislative process and the political debate, as it relates to the regulation of economic activity and employment security, would conclude that these cultural norms are present. An examination of the outcomes of the political process regarding employment and the nongovernmental institutions concerning employment security would further reinforce the proposition that these norms exist.

Individualism

In this context, I refer to individualism as the belief that the citizen should be free to pursue his or her own self-interest so long as that pursuit does not unlawfully prevent others from doing the same. Coupled with this value, is a belief in self-reliance (i.e., that an individual should rely on his or her own efforts to make a living and achieve status in society). Society, in turn, has only a minimal responsibility for the well-being of the individual.

The value placed on individuals and self-reliance spills over on to the corporation. The corporation, in the United States, is viewed as a legal individual, with most of the legal rights and obligations accruing to citizens. The corporation is viewed as an economic actor comparable to an individual citizen. But this legal status has been transferred to social status in the economic system. Thus, the corporation as the employer has the same right to pursue its self-interest as the citizen-employee. In establishing the employment relationship, the employer is viewed as legitimately acting with the same self-interest as the employee. The employment contract is fundamentally viewed as an exchange between two equal parties, each attempting to pursue their own self-interest. The fact that the employee may need the job more than the corporation needs the services of an individual employee is not viewed as of sufficient importance to modify the principle of equality of the actors and pursuit of self-interest by the employer and the employee.

As regards employment security, the value of individualism manifests itself in the principle of employment-at-will. Under this principle, the employee may resign at any time (either for personal reasons or to pursue a better employment opportunity), or the employer may terminate the employee at any time, so long as the termination is not for a reason that is unlawful.[2,3] Thus, the individual employee and the corporate individual are each pursuing their own self-interest, the employee in quitting to find a better job or leave the labor force, the employer in replacing the employee with another employee or by saving the wage costs.

Private Property

A second deeply held value in the United States is the importance of private property. This is closely related to principle of individualism. The person or corporation is entitled to use private property to pursue self-interest, so long as there is no unlawful interference with others who pursue their self-interest. Property, however, is generally viewed as being limited to physical property.[4] Therefore, the corporation has property rights in its

Richard N. Block

physical assets (i.e., machinery and buildings) but the employee does not have a property right in the job.

The employment relationship in the United States is a manifestation of the employer's property rights. In essence, the employer is permitting the employee onto the employer's property for certain purposes and/or for specified times. This permission can be rescinded at will.

The Virtues of the Market

There is a general consensus in the United States that the market is the most efficient, and therefore the preferred, mechanism for allocating economic resources. This does not mean that society believes in all cases that the market must be permitted to work in an unfettered manner. It does mean, however, that the market is the preferred method of allocating economic resources, including labor. The market, in turn, is considered to work best when individuals allocate their resources in the manner that they believe will maximize their personal profit.

Skepticism of Government Intervention

Consistent with the principles of individualism and self-reliance, there is no consensus in the United States that the government ought to be actively involved in regulating economic activity. Government involvement in the economy is viewed by some as an infringement on the rights of individuals to use their property as they see fit, since it means that the state is having a say, to some extent, in the disposition of private property.

While government has been permitted involvement in certain activities, the burden is always on the advocate of government intervention to show why the private decision makers in the market have failed. Moreover, as the round of economic deregulation that occurred in the late 1970s demonstrated, government regulation is constantly under scrutiny to determine if it is really necessary; that is, if the market failure that justified it still exists.[5]

For example, any governmental limitations on the right of employers to terminate employees may be viewed as governmental infringements on the rights of employers to control their property. Such government intervention is also viewed as interfering with the workings of the market, and therefore contributing to less efficient allocation of resources than would be ideal. The market works best when individuals are free to pursue their own self-interest. Government regulation impedes this pursuit.

130

Government regulation of the employment relationship does exist, of course. But no government regulation of the employment contract is preferred, and any government regulation must be seen as either remedying a clear social evil or enhancing, rather than impairing, the operation of the labor market.

Consumer Sovereignty

In the United States, the most efficient allocation of resources is considered to be that which minimizes the price consumers pay for the product. The value of low consumer prices is fundamental to the U.S. economic system. In making resource allocation decisions, the citizen's role as a consumer is given greater weight than the citizen's role as a producer or wage earner.

The value placed on low consumer prices is well-illustrated by the current debate in the United States over the decline of the manufacturing sector. It is widely accepted that one reason for the decline of the manufacturing sector in the United States is that wages and labor costs in manufacturing are too high, relative to the product market for manufactured goods. These labor costs contribute to prices for American manufactured goods being quite high relative to the prices of goods made outside of the United States. This has resulted in substantial unemployment among American workers. Yet, there is clearly a reluctance in the United States to decrease this price differential by raising the price of foreign goods via import restraints, even if such restraints would result in increased employment among U.S. workers. The differential must be decreased by lowering U.S. production costs through, among other things, a reduction in wages and labor content. Any unemployment resulting from this reduction is simply a byproduct of the operation of the market.

If the firm is unable to successfully compete and goes out of business, society does not view itself as having an obligation to help the firm in order to maintain employment.[6] If the firm decides to shift resources away from some markets as a result of competition, the firm must be moving toward a more efficient allocation of resources, and society is better off. The workers will simply shift, over a period of time, into those sectors where there are jobs.

Assumption of Abundance and Growth

Traditionally, the United States economy has been characterized by abundance and growth. Indeed, excluding occasional cyclical downturns,

131

the economy of the United States has generally exhibited continued growth over the last century. The major exception to this was the long depression of the 1930s, the government embarked on a series of programs to increase aggregate demand, employment, and wages, all under the rubric the "New Deal." Although some important social legislation that was enacted under the New Deal (social security old age insurance, minimum wage legislation, unemployment insurance) remains, the job creation programs were either declared to be in violation of the country's constitution or were abandoned by the late 1930s. World War II and continuing economic growth from the end of the war until the early 1980s continued to obviate the need for job security programs. The unemployment that existed (unemployment rates of roughly 5%) was considered to be primarily frictional (i.e., normal search between jobs) and to a small extent, structural (a mismatch between employee skills and employer needs). But, in general, job insecurity due to a fundamentally inadequate demand was not considered to be a national problem that required government intervention.

III. The Institutional Framework for Employment Security in the United States: Collective Bargaining

The values discussed above seem to place great value on market flexibility and employee freedom of choice. They work best when employees have numerous labor market options. Many employees, especially the less skilled and the less educated, do not have such options. These labor market groups bear the burden of the economic effects of these cultural norms; that is, long- and short-term unemployment, loss of income, and reduction of standard of living. In addition, many employees have economic and family interests (i.e., home ownership, health of elderly parents, and careers of spouses) that tie them to a geographic area, thus making it difficult for them to pursue labor market options to the extent that those options are in a different geographic area. Workers who have these obligations are also likely to be older, and therefore less attractive to a new employer than younger employees who might be willing to work for lower wages. In short, there are many institutional barriers to labor mobility for people, and these barriers are greater the less skilled the employee.

The lack of opportunity perceived by blue-collar employees was observed sixty years ago by Selig Perlman, a well-known theorist of the labor movement in the United States. Taking at his fundamental assumption that unions in the United States were essentially democratic and reflected the will of their membership, he observed that unions often attempted to control the relevant collection of job opportunities for their membership through such devices as requiring a minimum number of workers on particular jobs or limiting entry into the union. By such devices, unions attempted to increase job opportunities for their membership. Perlman viewed this as indicative of a "scarcity consciousness" among workers, a consciousness of scarcity in the relevant collection of job opportunities. Perlman contrasted this with the "opportunity consciousness" of the capitalist class.[7]

To this day, job security remains a high priority of unions in negotiations with employers. But unions have traditionally been cautious in placing too much weight on job security in collective bargaining. Normally employers place at least as much importance in remaining flexible to reduce the size of their labor forces as corporate needs change as do unions on job security. Thus, job protection for employees, if obtainable, will normally come at a steep cost in wages. Given the long-term economic growth in the United States between World War II and the late 1970s, the period during which the present-day collective bargaining system in the United States developed, unions during this period were less concerned about long-term employment declines. Thus, the emphasis was placed on obtaining high wages.

Data from the file of collective bargaining agreements covering 1,000 workers or more maintained by the Bureau of Labor Statistics (BLS) in the U.S. Department of Labor support this. Although the data are from the 1960s and 1970s, they represent the only detailed data available on the extent of the provisions. Moreover, as will be discussed below, although the severe economic dislocations in the early 1980s encouraged unions to place a greater concern on job security than in the previous three decades, with one exception, there is no indication that this dislocation led to formal employment guarantees.

The matter of job security has been addressed in a variety of different ways under collective bargaining in the United States. This part of the paper first discusses the legal framework for collective bargaining over job security in the United States. It is important to understand this so that the parameters of collective bargaining can be understood. Following this, the paper discusses collective bargaining agreements that are designed to provide direct employment guarantees to workers. Finally, there is a discussion of collective bargaining methods for alleviating income loss resulting from short-term unemployment caused by cyclical downturns in the economy.

The Legal Framework

The collective bargaining system in the United States is highly regulated, with an enormous amount of legal doctrine on the issues that are

Richard N. Block

"mandatory subjects" of bargaining. If a subject is considered mandatory, a party must bargain over it if requested by the other party. A failure to reach agreement on such a matter may result in a strike or an employer lockout in support of the proposal. On the other hand, if a subject is considered "nonmandatory" or "voluntary," either party may raise it, but there is no obligation for the other party to bargain about it. Neither party may insist on a nonmandatory subject of bargaining to the point of a strike or a lockout.

Under Section 8(d) of the National Labor Relations Act, as amended, "wages, hours, and terms and conditions of employment" are mandatory subjects of bargaining. What is considered to be a mandatory subject of bargaining has been the subject of much litigation over the past fifty years. As a rule, unions prefer an interpretation of the phrase that brings as many matters as possible under the aegis of bargaining. Employers, on the other hand, prefer a narrow interpretation so that they can act without the necessity of negotiating with the union. As the law has evolved regarding employment security during the past twenty years, this phrase has been given an interpretation that can fairly be said to favor employer interests over union interests.

The earliest case that addressed this matter, the 1964 Fibreboard case,[8] was actually decided in favor of the union position. In that case, the Supreme Court ruled that an employer could not subcontract to an outside firm work done by bargaining unit employees without first negotiating with the union. In that case, the employer had arranged with an outside firm to take over its maintenance work, with the work being done on the employer's premises and under the supervision of the employer. There was no change in the nature of the business, nor any change in the capital structure of the business.

Where there are such changes, there is no obligation to bargain over the decision, although there is an obligation to bargain over the effects of the decision. In other words, the fact that an employer's decision may result in loss of employment does not make the decision a term or condition of employment over which the employer must bargain. Such decisions are viewed as being central to the control of the business and strictly the function of management. For example, in the case of Otis Elevator Company, the employer was not obligated to bargain with the union over a decision to consolidate its research and development operation and close a New Jersey facility.[9]

The foregoing would suggest then, that formal employment guarantees and restrictions on employers that result in enhanced employment opportunities should be rare in collective bargaining agreements. That this is indeed the case is indicated below.

134

Employment Guarantees

A 1963 BLS study of 1,773 agreements covering over 7.4 million workers indicated that only 139 agreements, covering 602,000 workers contained any sort of guarantee of wages or employment. Of these 139 agreements, 117 contained only weekly guarantees. With the exception of the agreement between West Coast longshoremen and the stevedoring companies on the West Coast,[10] the rest contained guarantees for longer periods of time, but never more than two years. Moreover, these were found disproportionately in the food processing, transportation (exclusive of railroads and airlines), and retail trade industries.[11]

Collective bargaining provisions concerning subcontracting were given impetus by the 1964 Fibreboard case[12] that made subcontracting a mandatory subject of bargaining. A 1969 BLS study of subcontracting provisions in major collective bargaining agreements (Major Collective Bargaining Agreements: Subcontracting, BLS Bulletin 1425-9) showed that the percentage of agreements in its file with provisions addressing the employer's right to subcontract increased from 22.6% in 1959 to 43.9% in 1965–66. Seldom, however, was subcontracting prohibited. Rather, the provisions limited subcontracting when the regular work force was not completely utilized, such as when there were employees on layoff or employees who would be laid off as a result of the subcontracting.

Provisions regarding interplant and intracompany transfers were examined in 1966–67. Of 1,823 agreements covering 7.3 million workers, 586, covering 3.4 million workers, contained such provisions. Even when such provisions exist, however, they simply redistribute rather than increase employment opportunities. Layoffs occur among employees in the receiving facility.

The severe economic problems of the 1980s in the United States resulted in a change in union priorities in collective bargaining. Many companies in the heavily unionized manufacturing industries faced severe financial pressures due to the recession of 1981–83 and the increasing penetration of the U.S. market by imports. The prevailing view among employers, the public, and, possibly, some union leaders was that the cost of manufacturing in the United States was too high relative to foreign producers, and that the high labor costs associated with collective bargaining were the prime contributor of this U.S. disadvantage.

Faced with the prospect of major employment losses associated with a loss of market share, firms extracted wage and benefit reductions and work rule changes from unions, all designed to reduce the cost of production and make the companies more competitive. The incentive for unions to

Richard N. Block

provide these concessions was job security. But it was not job security in the formal sense. Rather, unions were put in the position of facing almost certain job loss if the concessions were not forthcoming. But there were few job security guarantees associated with these concessions. Unions were, in essence, providing these concessions based on nothing more than an increased probability that the company would be able to compete; therefore, there would be fewer job losses than without the concessions.

Similar pressures on unions were present in the domestic airline industry, which was deregulated in 1978. As a result, airlines were free to drop and start routes as they saw fit, without the need of government approval. As a result, small nonunion airlines, using low labor costs and low fares as a marketing tool, were established and began to compete with the major, high-cost, unionized carriers on heavily traveled routes between major cities.

As noted, almost none of the concession agreements contained formal job guarantees. Outside of an increased probability that layoffs would be avoided in return for the wage concessions, unions generally received some voice in the governance in the firm, usually through representation on the Board of Directors, or a profit-sharing plan, under which some portion of the worker's compensation would be determined by the financial performance of the firm.[13] Some attempt to increase the number of jobs was made in the steel industry collective bargaining in 1983, when the parties agreed that all savings resulting from wage concessions would be invested in the domestic steel business, but this notion has not been further developed in the 1986 steel industry agreements.[14]

The only collective bargaining negotiations in the United States that specifically provided job security were the auto assembly negotiations in 1984–85. In that year, the United Auto Workers (UAW) and General Motors Corporation (GM) included in their agreement a Job Opportunity Bank Security Program (JOBS Program). Under the program, any worker with at least one year of service who loses his or her job because of technological change, contracting out of work, negotiated productivity improvements, transfer of work, or consolidation of work, or because of internal displacement by another employee who lost a job for one of the above reasons, is entitled to be placed in the JOB Bank, which is financed by GM. While in the Bank, the employee draws the wage in the last position. The employee may be placed in a training program, replace another worker to facilitate training of the displaced worker, transfer to another GM plant consistent with the collective agreement, be placed in an assignment not covered by the union contract, or take an assignment otherwise consistent with the program. The bank was funded by a six-year $1 billion commitment from GM.

The program does not apply to layoffs for cyclical reasons or layoffs due to a decline in product demand. Ford Motor Company and the UAW negotiated a similar agreement later in 1984, while Chrysler Corporation and the UAW followed suit in 1985.[15]

This provision, which is unique to the auto industry, is a classic example of the way that the U.S. collective bargaining system can address job security issues. The interests of both the auto companies and the workers are protected. The companies may now implement whatever productivity-enhancing changes they believe are necessary. The workers are protected in their jobs, and thus have little incentive to resist these changes through shop-floor actions or other obstructionist tactics.

Employment security was also a prime concern of the Communications Workers of America (CWA) in their Spring 1986 negotiations with AT&T. In their June 1986 agreement, CWA and AT&T agreed to a four-part employment security program.[16] The program reflects many of the attributes that have been learned through human resource management in the nonunion sector. First, the program provides for an annual employment opportunities outlook report, which provides a forecast on growth or reductions in each AT&T line of business, and associated estimates of employment levels by job category and by geographic area. Second, the program has a training component, with a company-financed independent, nonprofit corporation established to provide career development training to help CWA members plan future employment. The corporation will be jointly administered by CWA and AT&T.

Third, the employment security plan permits CWA members to transfer jobs across AT&T corporations and subsidiaries. Fourth, and in furtherance of the transfer plan, the parties have created an Employment Opportunities Review System (EORS) by which employees who are laid off or who are candidates for layoff may nominate themselves to be placed in a transfer pool. Under EORS, qualified employees in the system must be hired by an AT&T unit before any new employee is hired "off the street."

The AT&T-CWA plan, although not providing the employment guarantees of the auto industry plan, moves in the direction of protecting current employees by offering those employees the jobs associated with any corporate restructuring. The program seems to rely strongly on information and will require growth in AT&T in order to avoid involuntary layoffs. Given AT&T's current downsizing,[17] the extent of employment security offered through this plan remains an open question.

Restrictions on Plant Movement

There are no major collective agreements that use a prohibition on plant closure or movement as a means of providing employment security. An analysis of 522 agreements covering at least 1,000 workers (2.4 million employees overall), indicated that 189 major agreements, covering almost 1.2 million workers, addressed plant movement in some manner. The majority of these agreements left such decisions to management. Only 10 agreements, covering 94,000 workers, required union approval of a closing or relocation, while two agreements, covering 2,400 workers, required consultation but no union agreement before a shutdown.[18]

The rest of the agreements that addressed plant closing dealt with the impact of the closing on the employees. For example forty agreements required notice and consultation with the union on the impact of a plant closing. In addition, it is generally presumed that when a plant closes, severance pay and interplant transfer provisions, which, in turn, operate through seniority provisions, will apply.[19] These latter provisions, however, do not increase the number of job opportunities. They do, however, determine how the resulting unemployment will be distributed.[20]

Seniority Systems

Seniority systems are well-established in the collective bargaining system in the United States. In essence, these systems provide certain benefits to employees that are associated with length of service in the firm. One of the major uses of seniority is determining who shall be laid off in the event layoffs are necessary and who shall be recalled. Thus, although these systems do not normally result in an increase in the total number of jobs available, they do determine how the jobs are distributed. Thus, as a result of the existence of such systems, it is reasonable to believe that long-service employees have a type of effective lifetime employment security so long as the company remains in business or the plant operates; that is, their seniority is so great that it is extremely unlikely that they will ever be laid off so long as the company remains in business. Even if they are laid off, they will be the first recalled.

BLS data from 1970–71 provide some idea of the extent and scope of these provisions.[21] Of 1,845 agreements (concerning at least 1,000 workers) covering 7.2 million workers, 1,476, covering 6.2 million workers, made some provision for procedures concerning layoff and recall. If one excludes the construction industry, where the short terms of employer attachment

138

make layoff and recall provisions unnecessary, 90% of all agreements had layoff and recall provisions.

The BLS examined 364 layoff provisions in detail, and all but one assigned seniority a role in determining who shall be laid off. Ninety-nine (27%) of the provisions made seniority the sole factor in layoffs, and 83 (23%) made it the sole factor in recalls. Another 44% of the agreements made seniority the major factor (as compared to skill, ability, and qualifications) to be considered in layoffs, and 48% made it the major factor in recalls.

These layoff provisions also include substantial "bumping rights" for laid off employees. By bumping rights, we mean the number of subdivisions in the plant or company to which a laid-off employee can move and displace a less senior employee. Nineteen agreements permitted bumping across plants. One hundred fifty-one of the 364 agreements, covering 623,000 workers, allowed the exercise of bumping rights throughout a plant, 95 permitted bumping in a department only, 70 permitted bumping only in a job or occupation, and 19 left the matter to local negotiations. As regards recall rights, one-third of the agreements studied specified the plant as the unit of recall, one-fifth specified the department, and one-fourth the job or occupational classification.

It is important to realize that these systems do not have the force of law; they are solely the creatures of collective bargaining, and they can be modified by the parties. Indeed, at the termination of a collective agreement, these systems also terminate. In other words, an employee has no legal seniority independent of the collective bargaining agreement, and where there is no collective agreement, the concept of seniority has no legal or contractual meaning.[22]

IV. The Institutional Framework for Employment Security in the United States: The Employer-Dominated System

Given the small size of the unionized sector in the United States, a complete discussion of the institutional framework for employment security in the United States requires an examination of the employment security practices that are not directly associated with collective bargaining. As noted above, labor is generally viewed as a variable cost, and there is no societal consensus that employers should provide security to their employees. Therefore, where such systems exist, it is usually because corporate tradition or concern over unionization dictates these employment practices.

Richard N. Block

Therefore, where they exist, it is because the corporate executives wish it to be that way, presumably because the corporation believes that such practices enhance the long-run performance of the firm. In a study of twenty-six large, nonunion companies, ranging in employment from 2,200 to 300,000, Foulkes found that nine had never had a layoff, and six had never even reduced the hours of employees.[23]

What are the advantages of such practices from the point of view of the firm? They are seen as minimizing the potential for a conflict between the firm's interest in productivity and efficiency, and the employee's interest in job security. By practicing employment security, the expectation is that employees will cooperate with the firm and be flexible, since no decision of the firm will adversely affect the employee's job.

There are several established personnel practices that contribute to employment security in these firms. Most of the firms maintained a lean permanent workforce, using overtime, temporary employees, and subcontractors to meet excess labor requirements. Thus, any unemployment was shifted to the nonpermanent workforce, a group of employees to whom the company felt no obligation. Attrition, through retirements and normal turnover, accompanied by substantial internal transfer rights to provide an adequate distribution of labor within the firm, was another method that firms used.[24]

An approach that may be viewed as a compromise between permanent employment security and layoffs is the establishment of an early retirement program. Where such programs exist, the firm may encourage or require employees to retire prior to the regular company retirement age. The incentive for voluntary retirement may be an increase in retirement benefits.

When firms that value employment security must lay off employees, it is normally done on the basis of seniority and with a severance bonus based on length of service. In addition, some companies retain job placement specialists to aid laid off employees in finding new employment.[25]

Two of the best-known firms that have adopted a practice of employment security are IBM and Hewlett-Packard. Indeed, IBM, in its internal documents, states that maintenance of steady employment for regular IBM employees is a commitment on the part of the company. Consistent with this commitment, IBM has not laid off an employee since 1940. This IBM commitment requires the full cooperation of all IBM business units, so that a unit with staff redundancy can count on other units to absorb the extra personnel.

The foundation of IBM employment security practice, however, was continuing long-term growth in sales and earnings. The company, however, has never *guaranteed* total job security for its employees. The lower projected growth rates for the company, due, to a large extent, to saturation

140

and competition in the personal computer market, suggest that the company may be reaching the limits of its commitment. In September of 1986, IBM announced that it was seeking volunteers for early retirement. The company hopes that the early retirement program will eliminate 4,000 of an expected reduction of 8,000 jobs to be made by 1988. The reduction will mean that IBM's U.S. employment would be reduced to 230,000.[26]

If IBM must initiate layoffs in order to meet its employment reduction targets, the company will join some other well-known U.S. companies that have downsized. The list includes such corporate giants as General Electric, Exxon, and AT&T. Significantly, none of these companies are in financial distress, although all have experienced declines in financial performance associated with the broad structural changes that have occurred in the world economy in recent years. For example, General Electric's downsizing was due to the company's belief that it was necessary to concentrate on fewer lines of business. GE reduced employment by approximately 100,000, or about 20% of its workforce worldwide.[27] Exxon, apparently believing that the price of oil will remain at current levels for the foreseeable future, will restructure itself into three parts, a U.S. unit, a Canadian unit, and an international unit. The U.S. unit will reduce its staff by 15%, or six thousand jobs. Exxon prefers to use resignation or early retirement, but has said that it will use layoffs to meet its targets.[28]

AT&T, in response to deregulation, has announced that it must make large-scale reductions in its workforce of approximately 330,000, with many of these outside its traditional long-distance service business. For example, in 1985, employment was cut by 24,000 in the unit of the company that sells computers and private communications systems. The composition of the reduction was 14,000 layoffs, 7,000 early retirements, and 3,000 transfers.[29]

The foregoing suggests conflicting pressures on organizations. On the one hand, they need employees to cooperate in implementing strategic changes that they must make in order to remain competitive. On the other hand, the firms also may be attempting to reduce their labor input, suggesting some layoffs among employees. Some large firms have attempted to manage this pressure by developing a "core-periphery" approach to employment. Employees within the "core" are provided employment security, while employees in the "periphery" are treated in more traditional ways; that is, as a variable cost. The "periphery" may also contain part-time workers, temporary workers, and subcontractors. Presumably, employees in the "core" are seen as more important to the organization than employees in the "periphery."[30]

Richard N. Block

V. Employment Security in the United States: The Role of Government

With the exception of the large public service employment programs that the government established during the 1930s, providing direct employment security for its citizens, has never been viewed as the task of government. Although the Employment Act of 1946 stated a public policy that government in the United States has a role in helping to insure full employment, this has generally been interpreted to mean full employment through overall macroeconomic growth rather than through intervention in labor markets at the micro level. Moreover, the full employment policy has traditionally been balanced with the government's interest in minimizing inflation. On the other hand, at least since the 1930s, government in the United States has been viewed as having a role in helping workers who are displaced, because of the technological change, adjust to their new labor market status. Each of these two issues is briefly discussed in this section of the paper.

Government and Employment Security

As noted, provision of direct employment security has not been viewed as a role of government in the United States. In other words, the rights of management to make decisions on corporate resource allocation in the best interests of the stockholders are paramount. Any impacts on labor are to be addressed by private parties, presumably through collective bargaining. This is consistent with the strong preference in the United States against governmental involvement in the functioning of the market.

An important illustration of this principle can be found in considering the labor relations implications of the Airline Deregulation Act (ADA) of 1978. Prior to 1978, airlines in the United States were heavily regulated as regards fares and routes. The ADA deregulated the industry, permitting unlimited entry into the industry, entry to and exit from routes, and almost total deregulation of fares. With strong political pressure from the airline unions, the ADA included a provision that would have provided income protection for employees who were laid off primarily because of deregulation and where the carrier had at least 7.5% of its employees laid off within a twelve-month period. The ADA also established preferential hiring rights at the major carriers for employees who lost their jobs after deregulation.[31]

When enacted, the labor provisions of the ADA represented an unprecedented role for government in apparently guaranteeing to workers adversely affected by an employer's strategy some measure of protection

142

against job loss. But no worker has ever been found to be laid off primarily because of deregulation, and rules governing the preferential hiring program were not issued until 1986, despite the fact that the program ended in 1988.[32]

In the Department of Transportation's most important decision to date, employees of Northwest Airlines and Republic Airlines were denied labor protection for the employment impact of the merger of the two airlines.[33] The Department of Transportation determined that the private collective bargaining mechanisms were sufficient to protect the workers and no disruptive labor strife would result. Thus, even in situations in which government involvement in job security is mandated as public policy, the government views its role narrowly and will avoid intervention if a reasonable argument can be made against it.

Government in the United States has been equally reluctant to enact policies that would protect worker job security less directly by placing some constraints on the rights of companies to close facilities and eliminate jobs. At the present time, there are no such restraints on employers. Employers need not even bargain over the decision to close a facility with the union that represents employees at that facility.[34]

Although there are no prohibitions in the United States against closing a facility, legislation to provide advance notice to employees was enacted in 1988, after being introduced in every Congress since 1973. Advance notice provides the opportunity for employees and other interested parties to reverse a company's decision. If reversal is impossible, advance notice at least provides the workers and localities the opportunity to make the necessary adjustments. The major employer arguments against advance notice were that the company might lose credibility with customers, may lose access to credit, and may lose key employees who are necessary to facilitate the closing. There was also a concern that morale and productivity would drop during the period between an announcement and a closing.[35]

The advance notice legislation, The Worker Adjustment and Retraining Notification Act, requires that business establishments with one hundred or more employees provide at least sixty days notice of (1) a closure affecting at least fifty full-time employees, (2) a layoff of six months or longer affecting fifty employees comprising one-third of its full-time employees, or (3) a layoff of six months or longer affecting at least 500 full-time employees. Because the legislation covers only establishments with 100 or more employees, the U.S. General Accounting Office estimates that only 44% of U.S. workers, and only 2% of U.S. business establishments, are covered by the advance notice requirement. The exclusion of establishments with less than 100 employees indicates that the

Congress accepted the traditional company arguments as they applied to smaller firms.[36]

Although five states have legislation dealing with advance notice, the legislation is quite weak. Maine and Wisconsin are the only states to require advance notice, but the penalties for noncompliance are minimal, $50 per employee in Wisconsin and $500 per firm in Maine. Laws in Michigan, Massachusetts, and Maryland are voluntary.[37] It should be noted, however, that in the absence of national standards that apply to all states, individual states may believe that there are costs to enacting such legislation. If corporate executives believe that such legislation makes it more expensive to produce in those states than in states without such legislation, then states with such legislation may believe they are at a disadvantage in competing with other states for business investment and, ultimately, jobs.[38]

Government and Displaced Workers

Although government in the United States has never had a substantial interest in providing workers with employment security, it has long had an interest in aiding workers who are considered disadvantaged in the labor market, or who are displaced due to economic change, and who bear the burden of adjustment to economic change.

The history of federal involvement in aiding and training workers viewed as difficult to employ dates back to 1962 with the Manpower Development and Training Act (MDTA), under which programs were administered at the national level. The MDTA was replaced in 1973 by the Comprehensive Employment and Training Act (CETA), under which state, regional, county, and local governments administered federal training funds. The CETA was replaced by the Job Training and Partnership Act (JTPA) of 1982, which brings private industry into the administration of these programs through a local private industry council associated service delivery area.[39]

In general, what one can observe is a continuing decentralization of the training function, consistent with the dominant value systems in the United States of opting for less government intervention rather than more, whenever possible, and of opting for lower-level government involvement rather than higher-level government involvement, whenever possible. Thus, the 1962 MDTA left most the authority to the federal government. The CETA shifted programmatic authority to the states and localities, and the JTPA brought the private sector into the process.

It is probably too soon to assess the impact of the JTPA. A government study estimated that the JTPA served 96,100 workers in 1983 and 132,200 workers in the period from July 1984 to June 1985. According to the study, this was less than 5% of the eligible population. The study suggests that the major emphasis of the states and localities in administering the JTPA has been on placement rather than training. Placement is the more cost-effective activity, but will tend to benefit those workers who are easiest to re-employ. The study suggested that this also reflects in the interests of the private sector.[40]

The JTPA is one of several federal programs that help displaced workers. Trade Adjustment Assistance (TAA) aids workers who are displaced by foreign competition by providing income supports. However, the level of funding for TAA has been declining for several years. It has dropped from $1.6 billion in 1980 to approximately $27 million today. The unemployment insurance system provides income supplements for twenty-six weeks to workers who are laid off.[41]

VI. Conclusions

The purpose of this paper has been to provide an overview of employment security in the United States as it relates to adjustment to structural economic change. As indicated by the paper, there is a strong cultural value system in favor of the operation of private markets, and against governmental intervention in the functioning of those markets. There is also a strong presumption in favor of individual actions unconstrained by the role of government. Since employment is viewed as a market function, essentially an economic transaction between the individual employee and the corporate individual, any government intervention can be justified only if there is strong evidence of a failure of the market to operate properly.

These values underlay the legal and institutional framework for employment security in the United States. The legal framework for collective bargaining requires union involvement in a decision affecting employment only if that decision does not involve a change in the capital structure of the employer's business. In addition, because it is important to employers to maintain flexibility in the allocation of labor resources, in only a small percentage of union contracts have unions been able to obtain anything approaching employment guarantees. While employees with substantial seniority do have employment security, in the practical sense, provided the facility or firm in which they are employed remains in business, the operation of seniority systems does not normally increase the total number of job opportunities.

Richard N. Block

While some nonunion employers and employer policies for nonunion employees have traditionally placed a high value on job security, recent changes in the market have resulted in the relaxation of these practices as firms have found it necessary to reduce employment costs and adjust to changing markets. There is a possibility that in the future such firms may apply job security practices to a smaller number of key employees.

As would be expected, the government has taken almost no role in providing employment security. The government, however, has traditionally had an obligation to provide aid to workers displaced by corporate adjustments to changing markets.

In conclusion, the United States places a high value on flexibility of all resources, including labor. A byproduct of this has been a reluctance to provide employees with employment security to the extent that this might inhibit the movement of resources toward what is viewed as the most efficient allocation. American workers clearly bear a substantial share of the costs of this system. Whether or not the benefits to the United States are worth it is a question for another paper.

Notes

1. "Summary of Office of Technology and Assessment Report on Reemployment of Displaced Blue Collar and Nonprofessional White Collar Workers," reprinted in BNA *Daily Labor Report*, no. 26, 1986 (February 7, 1986), pp. D-1 to D-30.
2. The doctrine of employment-at-will has begun to be modified in some states through court decisions. Courts have found that a promise to discharge only for just cause is enforceable. Also, a discharge of an employee for refusing to carry out an unlawful directive is itself, unlawful. See, for example, Jack Stieber, "Employment-at-Will: An Issue for the 1980's," *Proceedings of the 36th Annual Meeting of the Industrial Relations Research Association, San Francisco. California. December 28–30, 1983*, pp. 1–13 (Madison, Wis.: Industrial Relations Research Association, 1984) and Andrew D. Hill, *"Wrongful Discharge" and the Derogation of the At-Will-Employment Doctrine*, Labor Relations and Public Policy Series, No. 31 (Philadelphia, Pa: Industrial Research Unit, the Wharton School of Business, University of Pennsylvania, 1987). Key cases in selected states include: California—Pugh v. See's Candies Inc. 116 Cal. App. 3d 311, 171 Cal. Rptr 917 (1981); Illinois—Palmeteer v. International Harvester Co. 85 Ill. 2d 124, 421 N.E. 2d 876 (1981); and Michigan—Toussaint v. Blue Cross & Blue Shield, 408 Mich. 579, 292 N.W. 2nd 880 (1980).
3. For example, it is unlawful in the United States to discharge an employee because of his or her race, sex, religion, national origin, or union sympathies. There are other prohibitions, but these are the major ones.

146

4. See, for example, Ivar Berg and James Kuhn, *Values in a Business Society* (New York: Harcourt, Brace, 1965).

5. The airline and trucking industries in the United States were deregulated in the late 1970s. For a discussion of this, see, for example, Richard N. Block and Kenneth McLennan, "Structural and Economic Change in the United States' Manufacturing and Transportation Sectors Since 1973," in *Industrial Relations in a Decade of Economic Change*, edited by H. Juris, M. Thompson, and W. Daniels (Madison, Wis.: Industrial Relations Research Association, 1985), pp. 354–62.

6. Witness the enormous controversy about government loan guarantees to Chrysler in 1980–81.

7. See Selig Perlman, *A Theory of the Labor Movement* (originally published 1928) (New York: Augustus M. Kelley, 1966), pp. 154–233. The inconsistency between the union interest in controlling the relevant collection of job opportunities through group action and the prevailing cultural norm in the United States favoring individual and free markets may provide some insight into why the unionized sector in the United States has never been as large, as a percentage of the labor force, as in other countries. In 1985, only about 19% of the labor force in the United States was unionized. This percentage has shown a consistent decline since 1956, when the percent unionized in the United States reached an historical high of approximately 29%.

8. Fibreboard Paper Products v. NLRB, 379 U.S. 203. See also, for example, Block and McLennan, op. cit.; First National Maintenance Corporation v. NLRB, 452 U.S. 666 (1981); and Donna Sockell, "Two Decades of the Mandatory-Permissive Distinction in Bargaining: Reflections on the Wisdom of Borg-Warner," unpublished paper, Graduate School of Business, Columbia University, 1984.

9. United Technologies, Inc., 269 N.L.R.B. 162 (1984). A complete discussion of the legal framework for employment security should also point out that in the event a strike occurs, the employer has the legal right to hire permanent replacements for the strikers. Thus, if the employer and the union cannot agree on the appropriate labor relations adjustments, the strikers risk being replaced and possibly losing their jobs unless the union agrees to accept the employer's terms. Recent examples of large-scale striker replacements resulting from the employer adjustments to structural economic change include the Continental Airlines and Phelps Dodge (a major producer of copper).

10. In return for the right to mechanize the unloading of ships on the West Coast, the stevedoring companies guaranteed to fully registered longshoremen average weekly earnings up to thirty-five hours per week. See Paul T. Hartman, *Collective Bargaining and Productivity* (Berkeley and Los Angeles, Cal.: University of California Press, 1969).

11. See U.S. Bureau of Labor Statistics, *Major Collective Bargaining Agreements: Supplemental Unemployment Benefit Plans and Wage Employment Guarantees*, Bulletin 1425-3 (Washington, D.C.: Government Printing Office, 1965).

Richard N. Block

12. Fibreboard Paper Products v. NLRB, 379 U.S. 203. U.S. Bureau of Labor
    Statistics, *Major Collective Bargaining Agreements: Subcontracting*, Bulletin
    1425-8 (Washington, D.C.: Government Printing Office, 1969).
13. See, for example, Block and McLennan, op. cit., pp. 337–82.
14. Ibid. See also, for example, "Steelworkers Settle with Bethlehem on Cuts Total-
    ing $1.96 per hour, Repayment Guaranteed," BNA *Daily Labor Report*, no. 102,
    1986 (May 28, 1986), pp. A6–A7. It appears, however, that one of the reasons
    for the strike at USX Corporation's steel facilities (formerly US Steel) was
    doubt on the part of the union that the company truly has a commitment to the
    steel industry and the jobs of steelworkers. See, for example, J. Ernest Beazley
    and Mark Russell, "Steel Union is Balking at Further Givebacks, Terming Them
    Futile," *Wall Street Journal*, July 29, 1986, p. 1.
15. See Block and McLennan, op. cit.
16. "Statement of CWA President Bahr and CWA Summary of AT&T Agreement,"
    BNA *Daily Labor Report*, no. 117, 1986 (June 18, 1986), pp. E-1–E-3.
17. See, for example, "Variety of Methods Used by AT&T in Cutting Workforce
    by 25,000," BNA *Daily Labor Report*, no. 127, 1986 (July 2, 1986),
    pp. A-1–A-3.
18. See U.S. Bureau of Labor Statistics, *Major Collective Bargaining Agreements:
    Plant Movement, Transfer, and Relocation Allowances*, Bulletin 1425-20
    (Washington, D.C.: Government Printing Office, 1981).
19. Ibid.
20. For a somewhat more detailed discussion of issues involving plant closing, see
    pp. 143–44..
21. See U.S. Bureau of Labor Statistics, *Major Collective Bargaining Agreements:
    Seniority in Promotion and Transfer Provisions*, Bulletin 1425-11 (Washington,
    D.C.: Government Printing Office, 1971).
22. See Richard N. Block, *The Impact of Union-Negotiated Job Security Provisions
    on Labor Turnover and Labor Mobility*, unpublished Ph.D. dissertation, Cornell
    University, 1977, p. 47.
23. Fred Foulkes, "Large Nonunionized Employers," in *U.S. Industrial Relations,
    1950–1980: A Critical Assessment*, edited by J. Stieber, R. B. McKersie, and
    D. Quinn Mills (Madison, Wis.: Industrial Relations Research Association,
    1981), pp. 129–58.
24. Ibid., pp. 141–44.
25. Ibid.
26. See, for example, "A Lifetime at IBM Gets a Little Shorter for Some," *Business
    Week*, September 29, 1986, p. 40.

27. See, for example, "Can Jack Welch Reinvent GE?" *Business Week*, June 30, 1986, p. 62.

28. See, for example, Allanna Sullivan, "Exxon's Sleeker Look Starting to Emerge," *The Wall Street Journal*, June 2, 1986, p. 6.

29. See, for example, "A Leaner AT&T Could Cost Thousands of Jobs," *Business Week*, September 15, 1986, p. 50.

30. See, for example, Paul Osterman, "Turnover, Employment Security, and the Performance of the Firm," in *Human Resources and the Performance of the Firm*, edited by Morris Kleiner, Richard N. Block, Myron Roomkin, and Sidney Salsburg (Madison, Wis.: Industrial Relations Research Association, 1987), pp. 275–318.

31. Peter Capelli, "Airline Industrial Relations After Deregulation," in *Collective Bargaining in American Industry*, edited by D. Lipsky and C. Donn (Lexington, Mass.: D.C. Heath, 1987).

32. Ibid.

33. See "Excerpts from Department of Transportation Opinion and Order in NWA-Republic Acquisition Case," BNA *Daily Labor Report*, no. 149, 1986 (August 4, 1986), pp. F-1–F-5.

34. See United Technologies, op. cit.

35. See *Special Report of Office of Technology Assessment on Advance Notice and Rapid Response in Connection with Plant Closing*, reprinted in BNA *Daily Labor Report*, no. 180, 1986 (September 17, 1986), pp. D-1–D-60. See also Edgar Weinberg, *Employment Security in a Changing Workplace*, Work in America Institute Studies on Productivity, no. 34 (New York: Pergamon Press, Work in America Institute, 1984).

36. United States General Accounting Office, *Dislocated Workers*: Report to the Committee on Education and Labor, House of Representatives, November, 1989, pp. 35–36.

37. Ibid.

38. Of course, some firms voluntarily provide advance notice of shutdowns. A United States General Accounting Office study of advance notice in five hundred firms with a 70% response rate found that 25% gave from one to fourteen days notice, 19% gave from fifteen to thirty days notice, 18% gave from thirty to ninety days notice.

39. *Ibid.*

40. *Ibid.*

41. *Ibid.*

Werner Sengenberger

6

Revisiting the Legal and Institutional Framework for Employment Security: An International Comparative Perspective

Introduction

Few people would object to the argument·that employment security is one of the most profound and critical institutional aspects of labor markets and, more widely, of economies as a whole. However, security provisions written into legal or collective agreements have become a major subject of controversy in recent years, particularly in Europe. There are those who feel that the pertinent regulation is excessive and rigid and is stifling the labor market and the competitiveness of enterprises. Others, notably the unions, have come to defend the existing rules and standards and have regarded attempts to relax them as socially retrogressive. In their view, employment security is of vital importance for the satisfactory functioning of the labor market, and therefore there is no basic conflict, in this view, between efficiency and security. On the contrary, efficient arrangements in the labor market presuppose a minimum level of security and social acceptability.

There are, however, serious questions to answer in this area. For example, what should constitute security provisions and who should benefit

150

from them? Also, in what way and how should they be adjusted in order to bring them in line with the changing economic and social environment of the labor market? From this perspective, employment security is a kind of institutional arrangement that attempts to meet conflicting interests and has thus to be continually reset or redeveloped.

In this study employment security is discussed from two perspectives. First, in terms of its relationship with adjustment occurring in the labor market and, second, in terms of its relationship to the distribution of labor market opportunities. These two aspects are related to each other but are clearly not the same.

I. Systems of Employment Security

In considering employment security, discussion often centers on certain aspects of workers' protection from dismissal or lay-off, such as advance notices, rules and procedures for fair dismissal, requirements of reporting to public authorities, financial compensation for job loss, and the like. This focus is hardly surprising since rules and regulations of this kind have been introduced or considerably extended, notably in European countries, during the 1960s. During the late 1970s these very same rules came under severe attack on the grounds that they seriously impaired labor market flexibility and stood in the way of employment expansion and the fight against unemployment.

However, in revisiting the issue of employment security and, in particular, in setting the stage for the design of adequate security provisions and systems for the future, it is necessary to take a broader perspective. Such a perspective would look at national provisions for security as being the outcome, or even the historical heritage, of a country's social institutions and the interaction between them. Also such provisions would have to be placed into the context of economic conditions and regulatory regimes. Thus, for example, the expansion of legal and contractual provisions of employment protection in many countries over the past two decades may be interpreted against the background of enterprise-internal labor markets that were developed and extended during periods of high rates of economic growth, unusually low unemployment, and stable, mass produced product markets. In this period, the provision of job or employment security written into contracts or into law often did not amount to much more than the codification of already existing managerial practices, based on company strategies of employment stabilization and the creation of company career lines. When the security provisions were introduced they did not severely impair the flexibility of firms with regard to labor adjustment. Employers, however, began to complain about labor rigidities stemming from these rules after larger cyclical swings, greater market turbulences, and a more rapid rate of change of products and processes began to become more common by the mid-1970s. In addition, as unemployment rose and more qualified labor resources were available on the external labor market, employers became more choosy and selective in their hiring and termination policies. New opportunities arose to improve the quality of their incumbent workforces with respect to age, skill, and performance levels through an extended exchange of labor between internal and external labor markets. But again, security provisions that impaired such labor substitutability were considered a barrier to this exchange.

In conceptual terms, how can employment security be provided? What basic strategic options exist? What solution in terms of a mix of options can be observed in various countries that have attempted to provide coherent systems of employment protection?

When approaching the question of employment security from an analytical standpoint it may be useful to keep in mind that, just like wage structures and wage payment systems, employment security provisions are multi-faceted. They affect the adjustment of labor and other productive resources as well as the distribution of employment and income opportunities. They also greatly influence worker motivation, productivity, and acceptance of rationalization and modernization measures. Moreover, they are instruments that influence worker loyalty and discipline.

A second important aspect of employment security provisions relates to the organizational level and scope according to which such security is defined. Thus, for example, one worker may feel secure through having privileged access to particular jobs, job categories, or job territories and receiving reallocation preference within an establishment or a company. Conversely, another worker may feel secure by being independent from employment in a particular establishment or firm and being able to move freely between different employers without incurring costs or losses. In other words, worker security is closely connected with prevailing mobility channels and chains as well as institutional mobility barriers in the employment system. This is why a meaningful way of looking at employment security systems should start from an analysis of labor market structures.

Strategy I: Restricting the Substitutability of Labor

A first, and probably the most widespread, option for establishing worker security in the labor market is to curb in some way the employer's freedom to substitute or exchange workers for each other. Under this type of normative regime the employer is bound to employ in the short run, and sometimes even in the long run, particular persons or particular categories of labor.

Within this strategic option, three major devices of historical importance may be observed in Western countries.

(a) *Rule of job demarcation and jurisdiction.*
Under the concept of "job control," a group of workers or a trade union claims as its employment "territory" (demarcation) particular tasks such as the handling of a particular equipment or materials and, furthermore, claims for its members the exclusive right to perform the requisite work (jurisdiction). Employers are bound to recognize the resulting division and allocation of labor. This system typically occurs where professions or craft unions and craft principles of work persist, as has been the case in Britain and other Anglo-Saxon countries even after the decline of traditional crafts. Craft principles are both a prerequisite and a consequence of this device. For if one group of workers or one craft effectively establishes control over a particular job territory the employment opportunities of the remaining workers will be reduced unless they also succeed in establishing exclusive rights over some type of work. Therefore, quite often, craft principles carry with them an inner dynamic for expansion.

While the degree of worker control under this device may be very intense and unshakable in the short run, the strategy tends to be vulnerable in the long run to the extent that employers will be tempted to free themselves from such worker monopolies. They will try to replace the base for the job territory through alternative skills, alternative technologies and production methods, alternative materials and equipment, or subcontract the work to "unconquered" territories, so that they make a particular category of worker superfluous. This practice, in turn, may provoke workers to resist innovation and modernization.

(b) *Seniority rule.*
A second principle of gaining job control for the worker consists of making worker allocation decisions in the company dependent on the date of entrance and the length of service of the worker in a particular plant or enterprise. In this case, management is obliged to observe the order or sequence in which layoffs and recalls of workers, transfers and promotions, upgradings and downgradings, and the assignment of particular tasks occur.

153

This form of job control tends to be used most often by industrial unions or worker groups who, unlike craftspersons, have no specific occupational or technical skills that they can use to claim particular domains of work or employment. The technical substitutability of unskilled workers is high to begin with and, consequently, one of the few means of curbing employer discretion is to establish a rule as to who is considered first and last for particular jobs or assignments. The resulting allocational system gives senior workers security at the expense of junior workers. It generally does not improve the level of security, as such, but rather operates on the principle of pure redistribution of security among workers. It protects the older, less mobile and possibly more fatigued or low-performance worker. It restricts the arbitrary or disciplinary playing of workers against each other, and also prevents discrimination against particular types of workers, such as union members, and the like.

Seniority rules have been more widespread in some sectors and countries than in others. They have gained great significance in countries such as the United States, France, and Italy where seniority provisions are often included under collective agreements or even under law. In Germany, on the other hand, seniority rules, where they exist at all, are mostly of an informal nature and are often overruled by other allocative principles, such as worker skill or performance.

The effective employment protection provided by seniority provisions tends to be limited just like the demarcation device; it depends on the continued existence of particular companies, establishments, departments, or job ladders. It may also depend on a sufficient number of job categories or a sufficient differentiation of workers according to their position within the firm. A lack of job or worker differentiation leaves management much room for arbitrary worker allocation and task assignment. But, precisely because of this requirement for an extensive division of labor, seniority systems tend to preserve a low skill content or low range of competency for each job, and in this way increase the technical substitutability of workers. Job control positions resting on the seniority rule can also be undermined, evaded, or neutralized through rationalization of work, plant relocations, and the like. Thus, they often provide only localized and vulnerable systems of worker security especially when high unemployment and a low rate of vacancies discourage workers from changing jobs.

154

(c) *Protection from dismissal and loss of employment status.*
A third device for curbing employee substitutability is to limit the possibility that a worker's contract with a particular employer can be terminated, to protect the particular employment or income status already achieved by the worker, or to cushion the impact of worker layoff or dismissal. Where such provisions as these exist there is often a distinction made between individual dismissal and mass (or collective) dismissal. Worker protection provided in the case of mass dismissal usually goes far beyond that of individual dismissal.

Particular measures of worker protection from dismissal include:

- early notice given to workers or prenotification given to works councils;
- protection from "unfair," "socially unwarranted," or "unjustified" dismissal;
- requirements for informing of, or consulting with, works councils or other worker representation;
- requirements for reporting to state and public authorities and rights of approval by these authorities;
- requirements for internal or external retraining of redundant workers;
- financial worker compensation (indemnity, severance payments);
- rights of appeal of managerial decisions to labor courts or tribunals.

The effective protection provided by these instruments is often limited and usually depends on the employment practices in particular establishments or firms.

Employment protection legislation exists in nearly all European countries and also in Japan. It is almost absent in the United States where the "hire-and-fire-at-will" doctrine prevails and advance notice provisions are written into only a minority of collective contracts. In one attempts to portray the mix of legal and institutional provisions of job security in major industrialized countries, one might picture the distribution of security devices as in figure 1.

The figure presents Japan and the United States as opposite cases in terms of approach towards employment security. In the United States, there is little if any limitation on the termination of employment. Rather, worker security depends on limited internal allocation and reallocation governed by rules of seniority, especially in the unionized sector. In Japan, on the other hand, management enjoys a large degree

Werner Sengenberger

FIGURE 1
NATURE AND DEGREE OF REGULATION OF EMPLOYMENT SECURITY
IN SELECTED INDUSTRIAL COUNTRIES IN THE 1970S

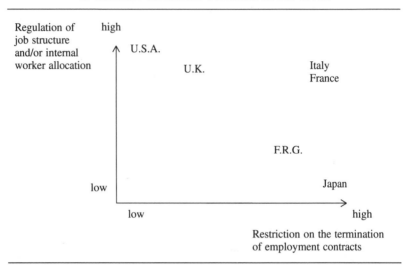

of freedom to change internal worker assignment and allocation within the enterprise, but is severely limited in its opportunities to dismiss or lay off workers. This is especially true for large- and middle-sized companies. The prevailing regulation and practice in Great Britain is more akin to that of the United States (i.e., job control through demarcation and jurisdiction is fairly pronounced). Redundancy legislation exists but it is not as highly developed as in many other European countries. Germany has had substantial protection regarding dismissal of workers, but by and large, management is fairly free to organize work and allocate workers internally on the basis of skill and performance.

France and Italy are alike in that, especially during the early 1960s and early 1970s, extensive regulation, partly through law and partly through collective agreement, was introduced with regard to both worker mobility and redundancy. Collective dismissal in Italy is considered almost impossible, and in France it has to be approved by the labor inspectors. In both countries, internal work organization and allocation are subject to collective work rules. The resulting fairly rigid regulation schemes in these two countries have recently triggered

156

many reactions and measures of deregulation and flexibilization have been introduced.

Strategy II: Improving the Mobility Potential of Workers

As we have seen, the effective security provided by the "nonsubstitution strategies" aspect of employment protection hinges very much on the continued existence of particular jobs or job categories, particular types of work, or particular companies and/or establishments.

There is an alternative principle of organizing worker security that, instead of curbing the substitutability of workers across particular employment areas, attempts to improve worker mobility, especially beyond the boundaries of particular jobs, establishments, and enterprises. Instead of preventing one employee being replaced by another, the thrust of this strategy is to provide the worker with easier access or lower costs when taking up alternative employment. The objective is to prevent the worker from becoming dependent on, or trapped into, particular areas of employment. His security is based on the possibility of leaving particular employers and moving on to new or better job opportunities elsewhere.

Practically all Western countries have attempted to increase or improve worker mobility mainly by way of manpower and other active labor market policies, and by making information on job opportunities and job openings available through placement services. This policy has also been promoted through improved worker training and by attempting to improve the regional mobility of workers. Nevertheless, a great deal of variation may be observed across countries in relation to the effective functioning of local or regional occupational labor markets.

Going beyond these minimum essential requirements, for increasing mobility in occupational labor markets, two other sets of instruments or measures are of importance in enhancing such mobility:

(a) *The standardization of the terms of employment between firms or establishments, with regards to wages, fringe benefits, and working conditions.* Contrary to neoclassic economics, which expects the growth of interfirm or interregional mobility of labor as a result of differentials in wages and other terms of employment, one might argue that more balanced terms of employment, especially those concerning the removal of enterprise-specific pay elements, could also foster sectoral worker mobility.

(b) *Standardized and broad basic vocational education and training.* The broader the base of skill and competency a worker commands, the larger is his potential mobility in the labor market. Thus, policies for promoting more comprehensive worker skills or greater polyvalence may improve the worker's mobility both between firms and within firms by allowing him or her to adapt more easily to new products and processes. Increasing worker competence also tends to lower resistance to economic or technological change because being made redundant by one firm does not leave the worker without hope of finding employment elsewhere. In other words, employment risks are more diffused the wider the potential mobility of the worker. Therefore, instead of defending a strong point in the employment system, worker security can also stem from the opportunity to use the "exit" option in the labor market.

Taking a look around the industrialized world since the 1950s one might say that the strategy of standardizing and equalizing wages, fringe benefits, and other conditions of employment was most advanced in Sweden. Under the concept of a "solidaristic" wage policy, wages were balanced according to region, skill, industry, and gender. It was expected that as a consequence of compressing labor cost differentials between firms the least efficient, least profitable, or least competitive firms would be squeezed out of the market, thus improving the overall efficiency level of the economy. The resulting increased reallocation of manpower across firms was supported financially by active public labor market policies, and potential labor demand deficiencies were eliminated by active macroeconomic policies.

The second strategy for the promotion of mobility was to provide a broad and standardized skill base for the average worker that would enable him or her to master a wide range of different tasks and to allow him or her to adjust easily to new skill requirements. This policy is being pursued mainly in West Germany. Within the so-called "dual system of vocational training" (in vocational schools and enterprises) about 60% of West German youth in each age cohort receive vocational training in one of the more than four hundred recognized occupations for which training schemes and curricula are provided. Another 20% of each age cohort go to vocational schools, 10% to universities and other academic institutions, and only 10% receive no vocational training at all. The extensive provision of vocational training for a large share of workers has led to the preservation or re-establishment of occupational type labor markets in Germany. Recently the skill content of a number of occupations, especially in the metal industry, has been increased so as to extend horizontal flexibility and mobility of workers.

In contrast to seniority-based systems of employment security, which depend on an extensive division of labor and a large number of job categories, a low division of labor and few job categories are considered conducive to, rather than a threat to, worker security under a system geared to a strategy of mobility. However, the weakness of the mobility strategy surfaces when high unemployment and low vacancy rates discourage workers from changing employers, thus binding them to particular firms. The mobility strategy is also less suited to older workers, to those who are geographically less mobile, and to those who do not have the requisite vocational skills necessary for interfirm mobility. Therefore, in those countries where the mobility approach is important, such as Sweden or West Germany, this strategy has been combined with a strategy to protect workers from dismissal and to take account of those workers who do not benefit from the mobility approach.

Strategies III and IV: Strategies of Exchange: Participation and Cooperation of Workers

The strategic choices for employment security discussed so far have been characterized by two main features: first, they are based on regulations involving normative standards, obligations, or minimum requirements for the employers. Since they are based on either legal or contractual norms they tend to be of a long-run nature and, as such, resist rapid change or adjustment. Second, they relate exclusively to the employment system.

An alternative to such normative employment-related systems of worker security are institutions and forms that *involve workers in the decision-making process*, either at the enterprise level or at the industry or even national level. These strategies may be called strategies of exchange between employers and employees or their respective agents. Sometimes they even involve third parties such as governments or state authorities. They presuppose the existence of collective organizations in the labor market and a degree of autonomy and power of the various agents that would allow them to participate in the decision-making process.

The thrust of these strategies is not only through the imposition of substantive regulations but also, and more importantly, through the provision of *procedural frameworks* that allow the parties to bargain over joint matters with a view to discovering the best solution for all concerned.

159

Werner Sengenberger

Within this range of strategies of exchange, employment may be positively affected by

(a) *Trading one type of worker reward against another (for example wage levels against security).* An example of this variant is the number of concessionary bargains struck in the United States in the early 1980s, under which unions temporarily yielded wage improvements or fringe benefits in order to stabilize or re-establish the profitability of particular enterprises or industries.

(b) *Entering into trade-offs between worker rewards, on the one hand, and the improvement of productivity, efficiency, modernization, and other measures that bear on the competitive position of firms, on the other.* This usually means that worker representatives or the state get involved in production or even investment policies.

Exchange strategies at the establishment or enterprise level appear to be of critical importance for employment security in Japan, notably in the large firms. Given the decentralized, enterprise-centered system of industrial relations and the commitment of firms to the life-long employment of at least part of the workforce, the vitality and survival of the particular company is of crucial importance to worker security. Plant closures, and particularly bankruptcies, would in this case mean a major loss not only to the worker's income position and social security but also to the worker's future employment opportunities. Therefore, the employees may tend to be especially cooperative when it comes to organizational and technical changes that are deemed necessary for maintaining or improving the competitive position of the firm in the product market.

In West Germany, the so-called "cooperative" conflict resolution at plant or enterprise level has also been a predominant feature of industrial relations. The Factory Constitution Act gives works councils information, consultation, and codetermination rights not only in matters of worker utilization but also in economic matters. In return, the law require works councils to cooperate with management over organizational changes and commits the works councils to "mutual trust and confidence." Within this legal procedural framework, it is fairly common for higher wages, employment security, and other improvements to be traded against worker acceptance and active worker involvement in product innovation measures, production rationalization, and change in work organization. Any organizational change that adversely affects either job numbers or work quality is subject to bargaining. The law specifies that managerial and worker interests have to be equally balanced, and, if necessary, a social plan is to be developed in which the specifics of the resulting compromise are laid down in a written plant agreement.

Similar exchange relations may be established among the parties at the industrial or national level. Cooperative arrangements, involving employer federations, union associations, and public authorities are found in many areas in Germany. They range from tri-partite relations within the German Productivity Center (RKW) to structural adjustment policies, social policies, regional policies, humanization of work and training, and labor market policies. Over the past ten years, however, cooperative relations have given way to more conflict-oriented situations. For example, the practice of so-called "concerted action," a kind of summit talk involving employers, national trade union federations, and the federal government on economic and labor market issues, has become rare and has lost political significance. The deterioration in the industrial relations climate may be seen against the background of increased unemployment, power structures changing in favor of employers, and the spread of political philosophies that would give more emphasis to decentralized and individual resolutions than to collective conflict resolutions.

Supra-enterprise policies that influence worker security may also be geared toward the structural reconversion of the economy. Through corporatist relationships or unilateral government activities, the reallocation of capital and labor resources from economically declining to economically expanding sectors may be facilitated or promoted. The risk of structural change is thus not borne exclusively by individual workers or firms, but tends to become more socialized and often more easily accepted. Perhaps the best known case of active public structural reconversion policies is that of the one pursued in Japan by the Ministry of Labor, in cooperation with MITI.

Exchange strategies generally function only where the parties involved in the exchange process possess a certain amount of autonomy and influence, and as long as the exchange produces results that are considered gainful to each party. Exchange strategies tend to deteriorate in periods of high unemployment,when the position of the workers' side is usually weakened and employers may be tempted to seek dominance rather than participation and cooperation. In one way or another, all of the strategic options regarding employment security discussed

FIGURE 2
STRATEGIES FOR WORKER SECURITY:
A SYNOPSIS OF AVAILABLE OPTIONS

Orientation of Strategy / Type of Strategy	Enterprise-centered	Labor-market centered
Control strategies	Restricting worker substitution through • craft principles • seniority rule • protection from dismissal	Promoting worker mobility across firms, occupations and regions
Exchange strategies	Internal exchange: bargaining at plant or enterprise level	External exchange: bargaining at industry or national level (corporatism); stabilization policies, structural policies, demand policies

in this section have limitations and are in some way dependent on particular institutional or economic presuppositions. In figure 2 an overview of the various strategic choices is given. Strategies for providing worker security may be based on the principles of control or exchange, and they may be organized on an individual establishment or company level or may even be based on arrangements that go beyond the scope of the individual firm.

II. Employment Security and Work Force Adjustment

Having highlighted the principal strategies for employment security, we now turn to the question of how the various strategies, or more precisely the mix of strategies, influences actual behavior in the labor market. In the following, we show, in particular, how enterprises respond to cyclical variations of demand in adjusting their labor resources and how these reactions vary systematically with the system of employment security.

162

1. Employment Adjustments in Relation to Cyclical Variations of Demand (Numerical Flexibility)

Work Force Adjustment in the United States and West German Automobile Industry

In table 1, details are given of the key results of a major study of U.S. and German auto industries, covering the entire period from 1945. For the period of 1971 to 1980 employment elasticities relating the level of employment and the number of weekly hours worked to output (number of vehicles produced) changes are shown. The main findings are the following:

• *Employment* is much more sensitive to output changes in the United States than in Germany. Thus, the employment elasticity in the United States is about twice as high with regard to variation of production when

TABLE 1

ESTIMATES OF EMPLOYMENT ELASTICITIES IN TERMS OF THE
NUMBER OF EMPLOYED WORKERS, THE NUMBER OF PAID
WEEKLY HOURS, AND THE TOTAL LABOR INPUT IN THE UNITED
STATES AND GERMAN AUTOMOBILE INDUSTRY, 1971–1980
(ANNUAL RATES OF CHANGE)

| Dependent variables | Country | Independent variable: output change during | | R^2 | F | DW |
		the previous year $(t-1)$	the same year (t)			
Employed production workers	USA	0.21 (2.41)	0.57 (7.23)	0.89	28.86	2.04
	FRG	0.38 (5.01)	0.28 (3.55)	0.83	19.49	1.82
Paid weekly hours	USA	0.02 (0.30)	0.17 (3.83)	0.68	7.37	2.18
	FRG	−0.06 (−1.83)	0.34 (9.51)	0.92	46.37	1.84
Total labor input: workers × weekly hours	USA	0.22 (3.43)	0.74 (12.70)	0.96	86.18	1.89
	FRG	0.32 (4.10)	0.62 (7.66)	0.91	38.86	1.74

Source: Köhler and Sengenberger, 1983.
Note: Output is measured in terms of the number of vehicles produced.
    ( ) shows t-values.

Werner Sengenberger

unlagged data are used. However, if the data is lagged by one year, the elasticity level is higher in Germany than the United States, which suggests a delayed adjustment process in the former country.

- *Weekly working hours* are more elastic in Germany than in the United States on an unlagged basic. The elasticity coefficient turned out roughly twice as high in Germany as in the United States for the 1970s.
- *For the total amount of labor input* (i.e., number of workers times weekly hours per worker), the elasticity figures for the United States are slightly above the ones for Germany. Another test shows that the difference is not statistically significant.

The findings mean that while the composite measure of cyclical sensitivity of employment to output changes does not show great differences between the two countries, the method of adjustment differs strikingly. In brief, U.S. firms accomplished employment adjustment primarily through changes in the numbers of workers employed, which is not surprising in light of the hire-and-fire-at-will doctrine that has predominated in the United States. German firms, in view of company stabilization policies and dismissal protection, are much less able to adjust work force levels within short periods of time. They compensate for this lack of adjustability by greater variation in weekly working hours and, thereby, on balance, reach an almost equivalent adjustment potential to that of U.S. auto companies. Average weekly hours vary between forty-three in boom periods to thirty-two in slack periods and hence permit substantial numerical scope for adjustment.

Roughly comparable results, especially with regard to the rank order of countries under consideration, may be gained from computing short-run employment functions for manufacturing in selected OECD countries (see tables 2 and 3). Again, with regard to the size of the labor force as well as the *total* number of hours worked, Japan and France show low elasticities, Germany and Great Britain medium elasticities, and Canada and the United States high elasticities for the unlagged model. Results for the lagged model indicate that in Japan and France, the adjustment process takes a long time, whereas in North America most employment adjustment is done in the same year of output change.

The distribution of countries with respect to the adjustment pattern is well in accord with the predominant type of employment security system portrayed in figure 1. Enterprises in countries like Japan, France, or Italy, in which firms follow strong employment stabilization policies on their own or under pressure from work force protection provisions, vary their employment levels slowly in relation to changing economic conditions;

164

TABLE 2

EMPLOYMENT ELASTICITY (EMPLOYEE BASED) IN THE MANUFACTURING
SECTOR OF SELECTED OECD COUNTRIES, 1974–1983

Country	Constant	Output (t)	Lag ($t-1$)	Time	R^2	DW
Japan	−0.13 (0.14)	0.06 (0.01)	0.96 (0.026)	−0.00037 (0.00015)	0.9862	1.31
France	0.68 (0.24)	0.07 (0.01)	0.79 (0.05)	−0.00130 (0.00026)	0.9966	1.17
Germany	−0.08 (0.08)	0.17 (0.01)	0.84 (0.016)	−0.00104 (0.00008)	0.9972	1.91
United Kingdom	−0.14 (0.09)	0.26 (0.02)	0.82 (0.023)	−0.00072 (0.00015)	0.9986	2.06
Canada	0.29 (0.17)	0.33 (0.00)	0.60 (0.05)	−0.00197 (0.00018)	0.9756	1.54
U.S.A.	0.34 (0.02)	0.38 (0.015)	0.54 (0.023)	−0.00182 (0.00009)	0.9931	1.42

Source: Hotz-Hart, 1987, S. 36.
Note: Standard errors in parentheses.

TABLE 3

EMPLOYMENT ELASTICITY IN RELATION TO THE NUMBER OF HOURS WORKED IN
THE MANUFACTURING SECTOR OF SELECTED OECD COUNTRIES, 1974–1983

Country	Constant	Output (t)	Lag ($t-1$)	Time	R^2	DW
Japan	0.86 (0.25)	0.09 (0.03)	0.71 (0.06)	−0.00075 (0.00041)	0.8790	1.689
France	0.89 (0.34)	0.13 (0.02)	0.68 (0.08)	−0.00263 (0.00058)	0.9949	2.664
Germany	−0.23 (0.17)	0.33 (0.03)	0.70 (0.04)	−0.00230 (0.00026)	0.9844	2.346
United Kingdom	−0.80 (0.26)	0.65 (0.08)	0.48 (0.07)	−0.00219 (0.00049)	0.9889	1.821
Canada	0.32 (0.18)	0.46 (0.04)	0.45 (0.06)	−0.00285 (0.00027)	0.9721	1.611
U.S.A.	0.31 (0.09)	0.58 (0.03)	0.34 (0.03)	−0.00299 (0.00016)	0.9877	1.743

Source: Hotz-Hart, 1987, S. 36.
Note: Standard errors in parentheses.

whereas the North American countries, which have almost no regulation restricting dismissals or lay-offs, adjust quickly and more fully.

There may, however, be some underestimation of effective adjustment potentials through working hours in some countries. As indicated by Koshiro (1985) and others, there is a very large scope for the use of overtime hours as an instrument of adaptation in Japan. Part of this overtime may not be registered in the official statistical figures so that the de facto range of flexibility may exceed the recorded one.

2. Employment Adjustment in Relation to Qualitative Changes in Demand (Functional Flexibility)

In addition to affecting the quantitative (or numerical) adjustment process, employment security systems also impinge on qualitative adjustment (i.e., the capacity of enterprises and establishments to introduce and implement new products and processes and to use the productive capacity of labor resources as effectively and efficiently as possible). More recently, the flexibility associated with this capacity has been termed "functional."

Quantitative-type and qualitative-type flexibility of firms may not work in the same direction. On the contrary, they may be inversely related. If the numerical adjustment is based on an easy and rapid exchange of labor between the internal and external labor market, this variation of personnel may inhibit the firm's ability to reallocate its capital and manpower resources internally. Conversely, enterprises with low external mobility may find it easier to adjust their workforces to new types of work organization or job requirements if the stability of employment provides a high rate of job security. This would imply that long-term employment relationships are not necessarily an impediment for structural adjustment. Fixed labor resources may become an obstacle to organizational or technical changes only to the extent that there are obstacles to the internal reallocation of workers.

In Germany, labor adjustment by altering working time arrangements is publicly supported by a subsidy for short-time work. In this context, short time is defined as anything less than the regular hours per week, so that firms have to bear only a minor part of the adjustment cost. It is believed that this subsidy is beneficial to both workers and employers because the former keep their jobs during slack or reorganization periods and, therefore, do not add to the number of unemployed, while the latter retain their experienced incumbent work forces through the critical period. Some firms in Germany use periods of slack or excess labor for purposes of work force training and the scheduling of repair and maintenance work.

166

A Multi-Country Comparison

The extent, speed, and method of employment adjustment in the largest OECD countries, including those represented at this Conference, can be gathered from tables 2, 3, and 4.

Table 4 is derived from OECD data, and illustrates cyclical swings of output and employment over the period 1969 to 1983 for both the aggregate economies and for their manufacturing sectors. In addition the average time-lag of employment adjustment is documented.

The results show Japan, France, and Italy having a comparatively low rate of adjustment in terms of the number of employees and, with the exception of Japan, a large lag in the adjustment of employment. For example, the ratio of production to employment variations in manufacturing was 0.15 in Japan, 0.18 in France, and 0.26 in Italy and the average lag of employment vis-à-vis production output changes in manufacturing amounted to six months for Japan, nine months for France, and eleven months for Italy. Canada and the United States, on the other hand, adjusted their employment levels very rapidly and to a relatively large degree. It took only zero and one month, respectively, to adjust, and the adjustment rate in manufacturing amounted to 0.62 and 0.68, respectively. West Germany and Britain held intermediate positions.

The internal capacity of firms to adjust their labor stock to new or changing qualitative demands (such as new products or a new product mix, new processes, or new markets) depends mainly on two organizational variables:

(a) The capacity to change the internal division of labor and to allocate or reallocate resources in response to changing internal or external pressures; and

(b) the "polyvalence" of the workforce (i.e., the extent to which workers can replace other workers temporarily or take over their tasks).

Needs for rapid qualitative adjustment may originate both from the demand and the supply side of the labor market. Needs may arise due to shortage of materials, insufficient quality of supplies, machine breakdowns, energy supply problems, quick revisions in the production program, and the like. Supply-side related needs for adjustments may be due to absenteeism or shortages of labor.

Employment security strategies that rest on highly specified job structures or rigid rules of worker allocation, such as job control and seniority systems, have more recently come into conflict with increased flexibility

167

TABLE 4

CYCLICAL VARIATIONS AND SPEED OF ADJUSTMENT IN THE SEVEN LARGEST OECD COUNTRIES, 1969–1983

| Country | Cyclical variation (average cyclical amplitudes[a]) | | | Manufacturing sector | | | Lag of adjustment of employment (in months) |
| | National economies | | | | | | In relation to output in manufacturing |
	Gross domestic product (GDP) (1)	Employment (2)	Ratio (2)/(1)	Output (3)	Employment (4)	Ratio (4)/(3)	(5)
Japan	5.6	1.9	0.34	17.0	2.5	0.15	6
France	3.9	1.9	0.49	13.5	2.5	0.18	9
Italy	8.5	3.0	0.35	19.6	5.1	0.26	11
F.R.G.	7.0	3.2	0.46	13.5	6.5	0.48	7
U.K.	7.1	3.2	0.45	13.0	7.2	0.55	7
Canada	6.9	4.4	0.64	16.5	10.3	0.62	0
U.S.A.	8.0	5.0	0.63	18.9	12.9	0.68	1
Total	5.6	2.8	0.50	13.0	5.9	0.45	6

Source: OECD, Employment Outlook, September 1984, and the author's computations.
[a] Measured by the percentage deviation of the maximum and minimum values from the trend line.

requirements. Stabilized workforces, on the other hand, may be more able to respond quickly to changing qualitative conditions of demand and supply.

The stability of the workforce may also affect the level or growth rate of productivity. From various studies we know that productivity is not fully determined by technology, but may vary significantly given the same type of capital equipment. This is especially true where productivity does not primarily depend on individual worker effort or performance, but is a joint or *collective product* emanating from cooperation and problem-solving by work teams. The most critical variable may be the level of cooperation between individual workers, or workers and managers, when it comes to resolving bottleneck situations, machine downtime, or other operational disturbances. The higher the capital stock per worker and the greater the systemic, interrelated character of production or services, the more often will the smooth and continuous operations of capital and equipment influence efficiency levels. Similar operational requirements are given where the value of the product or service is strongly time-dependent or perishable.

In all of these instances, pure numerical flexibility tends to be of secondary importance compared to the "problem-solving" or innovative capacity of work groups, or sometimes the entire workforces in the plant. Under modern production systems, productivity potentials are very much "incorporated" into work teams. They are of a profoundly "social" nature. These capacities, in turn, usually require not only experience but also long-term, stable personnel relations; high turnover of the staff may be a source of inefficiency.

In this context, it may not be altogether accidental that those countries that have come up with employment systems with high average labor turnover have tended to face problems of insufficient productivity growth in the past decade. In table 5, a positive correlation can be observed between the average stability of employment and productivity growth rates in the period between 1969 and 1983. Japan, which had the most long-term and stable employment relations in this period, also reached the highest rates of productivity improvement. Of course, the causation may run in the opposite direction as well (i.e., high productivity growth may promote employment stability), but the results are at least compatible with the view that security arrangements affect productivity.

Although the manufacturing sector in the United States started with rather high productivity levels, over the past two decades it has been at the lower end of productivity growth rates among the large OECD countries. Many efforts have been made by economists to resolve this "productivity puzzle." The usual production and economic development models, which include variables like the size and vintage of capital stock, R & D

169

TABLE 5

EMPLOYMENT STABILITY, THE STRUCTURE AND DISTRIBUTION OF UNEMPLOYMENT, AND PRODUCTIVITY GROWTH

Country	Indicators of employment stability			Structure and distribution of unemployment						Average annual rate of productivity growth[e] 1959–82
	Cyclical stability[a] 1969–83	Average number of years of service in year (. .)[b]	Rate of turnover in year (. .) (in %)[c]	Rate of Unemployment[d]		Youth unemployment as a percent of total unemployed 1970–82	Average duration of unemployment (months) 1973/1982			
				Total (1982)	Youth (up to 25 years) 1982		1973	1982		
Japan	1.9	66.8 (1982)	25(1971) 18(1983)	2.4	4.4	46.2	—	—		4.69
France	1.9	62.5 (1978)	20(1971) 14(1982)	8.0	20.2	39.2	9.1	13.4		3.20
Italy	3.0	50.3 (1972)	28(1971) 11(1982)	8.9	29.7	—	—	—		2.81
F.R.G.	3.2	51.0 (1972)	33(1971) 25(1982)	6.1	9.6	26.0	4.8	8.2		2.91
U.K.	3.2	52.4 (1979)	30(1971) 20(1984)	12.4	23.1	27.1	8.7	11.2		1.99
Canada	4.4	45.3 (1983)	—	10.9	18.7	37.2	2.3	3.6		2.24
U.S.A	5.0	45.8 (1983)	48(1971) 40(1981)	9.5	17.0	47.5	—	4.0		0.58

Source: OECD, *Employment Outlook*, September 1983; September 1984; September 1985; OECD Historical Statistics.

[a] Measured by amplitudes of variations of employment (see table 4).
[b] Proportion of employed with more than five years of service.
[c] Average annual percentage of accessions and separations.
[d] Standardized according to ILO procedure.
[e] Real GDP per employed.

expenditures, compositional variables, and the like, could not adequately explain the lack of productivity growth. "Numbers alone won't solve it," as one analyst concluded (Adler 1982).

During the 1980s there were increasing signs that, under pressure stemming from product markets, foreign and domestic competition, and new technologies, changes have been occurring in the U.S. system of industrial relations (see Kochan, Katz, and McKersie 1986).

(1) In a number of collective agreements a new quid-pro-quo arrangement has been reached with regard to efficiency and worker security. Seniority rules as a basis for employment security were replaced by guarantees of employment. In return, the union accepted the relaxation of formal seniority-based rules governing internal worker assignment and allocation.

(2) In some cases, the division of labor in the plant was also changed through job redesign. GM, for example, has reduced the number of craft classifications from twenty to three at the refurbished NUMMI plant in Fremont. GM's Delco-Remy plant recently cut its assembly job classifications from seventy-five to one (Capelli and McKersie 1986, p. 7). The redesign of work organization may be at its most complete at GM's new Saturn plant.

The restructuring of labor is especially significant in U.S. manufacturing industries since, under Taylorism and "scientific management," the division of labor was more pronounced there than elsewhere. With the decline of "mass production" and the spread of "flexible specialization" the need for reorganization appears to be extensive (see Piore and Sabel 1984).

Provisions of employment security, especially because of its effect on personnel stabilization, may appear too costly and cumbersome to some people. There is, however, no security system that in some way or other does not entail costs; seniority systems may be similar to or even more expensive than restrictions or compensation for dismissal. The "loss of market efficiency," greatly emphasized by the neoclassic stream of economics, has to be balanced against the "loss of production efficiencies" that normally result from the absence of security provisions, and that show up through low productivity or problems of resistance to or even obstruction of innovation and modernization.

There is, however, still another, far reaching dimension of employment security that has been termed *dynamic efficiency*. If, as a result of security clauses, management is prevented from adjusting the workforce level without any restriction or friction to external market conditions in terms of quantities and prices, it may be challenged or forced to compensate for this lack of maneuverability by increased efforts to seek competitive advantages through more efficient production or better and novel products. For example, many German firms that, in the face of employment protection clauses, experienced limited discretion and scope for workforce reduction in the recession of 1974–75, decided to diversify their product mix and extend their production capacity to be able to put the existing workforce to new uses. As a consequence of this diversification, firms became less specialized to particular buyers. These firms moved some way from static efficiency, which rests on the external elasticities of the labor market, to more dynamic efficiency, which is based on greater autonomy of the enterprise from market forces and opens up new choices and avenues for strategic behavior.

III. Employment Security and the Distribution of Opportunities and Risks in the Labor Market

There is, finally, a link between employment security systems and the distribution of opportunities and risks in the labor market.[1] With the growth and spread of labor market segmentation we have become more familiar with the *redistribution* of income and employment opportunities. Workers in some quarters of the employment system may enjoy enhanced security at the expense of others. There may be winners and losers in the labor market, which result from institutional arrangements not attributable to individual education and training, effort, motivation, and the like. There is, in other words, a rather stable, institutionalized inequality in the labor market from which the individual worker cannot easily escape. Thus, workers who are totally equal in their individual performance capacity may be treated rather differently in terms of income or employment opportunities, depending on whether they are employed in big or small firms, in region A or region B, in one or the other industry, or whether they are young or old, male or female, and the like.

Although there are all kinds of rules and regulations affecting the distribution of opportunities, those regulating employment security have a major impact.

1. The Impact of Security Provisions on the Structure and Distribution of Unemployment

To give one illustration of the effects of institutional security arrangements, one may consider the structure and distribution of unemployment in various countries.

Table 5 lists various indicators of unemployment, including the relative significance of youth unemployment and the average duration of unemployment. The figures in the table indicate that there ar wide variations of these two measures within the large OECD countries and, furthermore, that the aggregate level of unemployment cannot explain this variation. There must be other determinants in addition to the unemployment rate that affect the structure and distribution of unemployment.

The data suggest that the stability of employment patterns prevailing in a country, together with the predominant skill formation (training) system, are fairly good predictors of the characteristics of unemployment. The stability of employment is itself closely associated with security systems as was shown above.

On average, spells of unemployment tend to be short where there is no regulatory limitation or restriction of dismissal and where, as a consequence, the average stability of employment tends to be low, and the rate of personnel turnover high. Thus, the United States and Canada, which rank lowest on the stability indicators, also show by far the lowest average duration of unemployment. On the other hand, the average spell of unemployment in France lasted more than three times as long as in the United States in 1982, although the aggregate unemployment rate in France was lower at that time. The French employment security provisions, as we have seen above, are some of the most extensive of the major countries. Great Britain and Germany once again hold the middle ground in terms of both employment security and the length of unemployment spells.

Moreover, employment security systems tend to exert an influence on the distribution of unemployment among various categories of labor. For example, they influence the extent to which young workers, relative to older workers, are affected by unemployment. Two institutional variables are of vital significance in this context. First, unemployment tends to be more concentrated among young workers if employment patterns are governed by the principle of seniority. Second, the distribution of unemployment (as well as employment opportunities) hinges on the system of skill formation. In other words, if training is specific to a particular firm, and is provided "on the job" in the course of an employment career, the workers's relative value rises in the eyes of his employer with his length of service in the firm. Thus, workers tend to move with growing tenure into more secure employment positions or posts in the firm.

If, conversely, as is the case in West Germany, worker skill formation rests primarily on standardized vocational training acquired at the beginning of the employment career, then young workers tend to be less disadvantaged in relation to older ones. Young workers reach high-productivity levels fairly rapidly if they undergo an apprenticeship period. In contrast, skill formation is slower and more gradual under enterprise-specific training, which has predominated in France, Japan, and the United States. Thus, in a country like West Germany, the rate of youth unemployment as well as the proportion of young workers among the unemployed tended to remain comparatively low despite sizeable increases in total unemployment figures during the 1980s.

2. Patterns of Labor Market Segmentation

The distribution of unemployment among various groups of workers can be seen as merely one symptom of labor market segmentation. However, it does not tell us how segmentation comes about. Basically, there are two essential mechanisms through which a lasting and stable differentiation of opportunities and risks may emerge in the labor market:

(a) *Indirect.*

Labor market segmentation may arise from divisions in the product market. Some enterprises may be in a position to externalize costs or risks onto other enterprises, resulting in a clear hierarchy of enterprises emerging. This genesis of segmentation patterns is, of course, well known from the dual product and labor market literature.

(b) *Direct.*

Labor market divisions may stem from strategies that treat various worker segments *within* an enterprise or establishment differently. Thus, the differentiation of employment or income opportunities may emerge even in cases where all enterprises in a national economy are in the same or equal economic positions. Firms may deal with risks and uncertainties, such as cyclical swings or fluctuating demand, by dividing their workforces into a stable core segment with permanent employment and a peripheral or fringe segment of workers fluctuating in accordance with labor needs.

In reality, we almost always find a combination of the two strategies of risk and cost redistribution or "buffering." Yet, the particular mix of the two strategies may differ substantially; in some countries the internal company-based division of workforce constitutes the predominant mode of separating the labor market, while in others labor market segmentation is primarily the outcome of "dominating" and "dominated" enterprises and the concomitant redistribution of employment opportunities.

174

For example, from various kinds of empirical studies it has been concluded that the classical dual labor market model presents a fairly good description of the labor market structure in the United States (e.g., Reich 1984; Buchele 1983; Rosenberg 1980; Doeringer and Piore 1971). The dispersion of income and employment opportunities is strongly linked to the prevalence of monopolized and competitive (or central and peripheral) sectors in the economy. Inequality patterns in the West Germany labor market, on the other hand, have much less resemblance to the dual model; they are, instead, primarily based on intracompany divisions of labor. Thus, there are big discrepancies in both earnings and employment risks between white-collar and blue-collar workers and between workers with and without vocational training. It is safe to say that the level of vocational training is the foremost distributor of opportunities in the German labor market. Sexual differences in opportunities can also, to a large extent, be explained by the lower access of women to particular vocational training schemes.

Japan, in my view, is significant in this respect because it has a combination of strategies both *within* and *across* enterprises, as shown by Koshiro (1985) as well as in numerous other studies of the Japanese labor market. There exist both a clear-cut hierarchy of enterprises and establishments in the Japanese economy, as well as a hierarchy of employees within each establishment. Competitive risks and burdens are shifted to particular firms (such as small enterprises or suppliers) as well as to particular categories of labor, such as temporary or subcontracted workers, or to both. Thus, the secondary labor market comprises both particular employers and particular groups of employees.

This is not the place to enter into a detailed discussion of the origins and genesis of the various patterns of segmentation. It is sufficient to point out what I would view as *the most significant institutional prerequisite for labor market segmentation, that is, the degree of centrality and uniformity in the regulation of the terms of employment.* In the United States and Japan, wages, employment security, and other areas of employment regulation are more or less determined within a system of decentralized, enterprise-centered industrial relations and collective bargaining. The influence of trade unions is limited to particular areas of the economy (i.e., to particular industries, enterprises, and even regions). As a result, large sectorial differentials between unionized and nonunionized enterprises have emerged, in terms of both wages and fringe benefits as well as job security. Conversely, in West Germany (and a number of other European countries, notably the Scandinavian ones) the terms of employment are regulated much more widely by law or by a large-scale, comprehensive collective agreement within a more centralized system of industrial relations. It follows

175

Werner Sengenberger

that wages and other elements of labor costs, as well as employment security provisions, are spread much more evenly across sectors, industries, occupations, regions, and enterprises of different sizes. Skill formation is also subject to uniform, nation-wide regulation. The extensive standardization of wages and employment conditions sets an effective minimum-term base for practically all employers. Until very recently it was almost impossible for an individual employer to undercut this standard. Thus, in a way, the system did not permit downward adjustment or downward depressive forces in the labor market. Competition among workers was not eliminated but severely curbed, at least as far as labor costs were concerned. Also, as long as all firms were exposed to the same competitive conditions, wide differentials of productivity, efficiency, technological standard, and the capacity for modernization could not arise. In fact, compared to Japan, differentials in productivity or capital/labor ratios for varying size classes of establishment in manufacturing remained small in European countries (Sengenberger 1987, p. 238).

Being prevented from resorting to a low-labor cost strategy, enterprises in Germany and in other European countries opted mainly for very selective personnel policies to gain competitive advantages. That is to say, employers tended to be extremely choosy when it came to hiring, dismissal, promotion, transfer, and internal training decisions. Price competition, which, due to the standardization policies, could only occur in an upward direction, was effectively replaced by "quality" competition in the labor market. The key criterion of selections, therefore, has been the level of vocational training. Workers with pertinent certified skills tended to form the core work forces whereas nonapprenticed workers were bound to form the fringe segments or remained unemployed. Selection according to vocational skill was widely accepted and was usually something that management and works councils within the codetermination framework could agree upon.

3. Recent Changes in Labor Market Structure in Germany

The "traditional" German employment system, including the security provisions, has increasingly come under pressure during the 1980s. It has been claimed that the uniformity of wages and working conditions is grossly inconsistent with the requirements of labor market flexibility. The regulatory framework was blamed for the large job losses and the rising unemployment. Wage structures were regarded as too rigid and worker protection too excessive to permit a sufficiently rapid restructuring of the economy.

Following this logic, a series of changes and revisions in the labor law were introduced and social benefit levels cut back, especially after the Conservative-Liberal Coalition Government took over in the autumn of 1982. As far as employment security goes, the most significant revision of standards has been implemented through the "Employment Promotion Act," which became effective on 1 May 1985. The key stipulations of this law are the following:

(a) *Creating opportunities for more flexible utilization of workers*:
- by arranging during a transitional period from the 1 May 1985 to the 1 January 1990, for the extended use of fixed-term contracts for unemployed workers and apprentices who had been given employment upon completion of vocational training, and by permitting such contracts to be concluded for up to eighteen months (from the previous level of six months) without any need for justification; and
- by extending until 1 January 1990, the maximum permissible period for the use of "personnel leasing' (i.e., temporary utilization of agency employees from three months to six months).

(b) *Flexibilization of working time arrangements and work scheduling*:
- by making part-time work more attractive; and
- by increasing the possibilities for job sharing and the short-run scheduling of working hours in line with labor demand (so-called "capacity-oriented variable working hours").

(c) *Special relief from restrictive deployment rules for small firms and newly established firms*:
The law grants special relief for small firms, which are seen as suffering most from the current restrictions in terms of unbearable labor costs (though it should be emphasized that very small firms have hitherto been exempted from most of the protection rules and from works council representation). Moreover, the small and the newly established firm is said to be given special treatment because it is expected to spearhead the move toward employment expansion. In essence, the various changes proposed under this heading are geared toward further exemption of the small firm from worker protection; for example, by excluding part-time workers when determining the number of employees and, thereby, allowing more firms to remain below the size threshold for which protection rules apply; by giving newly established small firms special permission to use workers on fixed-term contract for a period of up to two years; or by relieving small firms

Werner Sengenberger

from the obligation to provide wage or salary payment during worker illness.

(d) *Relaxing the requirement for social plans*:
In addition, section 112 of the Employee Relations Act has been altered so as to relax the requirement for employers to negotiate a social plan with works councils in the event of workforce reductions or other organizational changes that would have negative consequences for the workforce. Thus, for example, the proportion of workers to be dismissed in an economic downturn, which requires negotiation between management and the works council, has been increased from 5% to 10% or 20% of the workforce (depending on the size of the establishment) (section 112a). Newly established enterprises are totally exempted from the obligation to make social plans during the first four years of their existence.

All of these legal revisions were justified on the grounds of the need to remove barriers from the profitable deployment of labor. Unless such restrictive rules were relaxed, so it was argued, there would be no new areas opening up for economic growth and the expansion of employment.

So far, the positive employment effect expected from changes in the law have not been very encouraging. There are no clear signs that many new jobs have been created as a result of the alterations. The main effect of the legal revisions has been one of substitution as full-time jobs have been replaced by part-time jobs, and regular, indefinite employment contracts have been replaced by fixed-term contracts.

No matter whether the act has a positive impact on the level of employment or not, it will definitely affect the structure of the labor market. It has, among other things, led to an increase in the more casual, precarious types of employment that started in the mid-1970s. Thus according to figures from the Federal Employment Institute, for example, incidence of personnel leasing (agency labor) increased from 140,000 cases in 1975 to 380,000 cases in 1981 (when this statistical series was discontinued). The total number of man-hours worked by agency labor in 1985 was four times greater than in 1975. Furthermore, the proportion of employees holding fixed-term contracts steadily increased from the mid-1970s to reach a level of 4.1% in June 1984 (WZB-Mitteilungen 1986).

By the end of this century the German labor market may in some respects more closely resemble the Japanese one. As a result of the recent legislative changes, formalized distinctions between the regular, permanent workforce and the temporary, much more insecure fringe workforce have already grown. Also, various types of enterprises are treated differently by labor law. However, more important moves are yet to come. There is growing pressure from neoclassic economists and neoliberal political forces, calling for changes in, or even abandonment of, those instruments that created the basis for standardized regulations in the past. Industry-wide bargaining is to give way to local enterprice-based negotiations; the legal enforceability of collective contracts is to be abandoned; small- and medium-sized firms are to be freed from further social obligations; unemployed workers are to get lower wage rates; and the like. Deregulation and decentralization is the common rationale behind these proposals (for an overview of changes already enacted and changes being discussed, see Sengenberger 1984a).

What are the likely effects of extended interfirm differentials of wages and other terms of employment? Those who advocate a more decentralized regulatory approach claim that employment would expand if wages and other conditions were brought more into line with individual productivity and profitability of enterprises; and the use of labor relative to capital would become more expedient if there was unrestricted downward adjustment of wages and other terms of employment. On the other hand, it may be argued that Germany has had a viable and competitive small firm sector *because* small firms had to be as efficient and innovative as large ones in order to stay in the market. They could not escape the standard labor cost regime and there was no "easy way out" through low wages.

While the neoclassic arguments stress "static-type" flexibility in the sense of an easy and unrestricted responsiveness of enterprises to external market conditions, the latter argument emphasizes "dynamic" flexibility in the sense that firms that are unable to take the "easy way out" by reducing wages are forced to become competitive, primarily by creating new or better products and seeking new markets. These methods, in the end, assure more dynamism in the economy than the pure market model, particularly in national economies that are as much exposed to international competitive pressure as the EEC countries are.

Conclusion

There are various ways of organizing employment security, and these often relate to basic differences in the structures of the labor market in various countries. In terms of basic approaches, strategies limiting worker substitution and mobility may be distinguished from those that attempt to promote interfirm mobility of workers. In addition, strategies of exchange must be considered that are essentially geared toward reaching a better utilization of resources through better trade-offs between labor and capital, either on the enterprise level or on the industry or national level.

Different strategies for employment security have different economic and social impacts. In the absence of restrictions or other obligations relating to the dismissal of employees, adjustment with regard to quantitative changes in demand may be easier and faster. However, low stability of employment may run into conflict with more qualitative objectives such as productivity improvement and internal restructuring and innovation within the enterprises.

The decline of external labor mobility in many industrialized countries over the last ten years, as indicated, for example, by the declining rate of accessions and separations, has been interpreted as increased inflexibility of the labor market. Rigid protectionist legislation and collective agreements have been considered responsible for this tendency. However, it may well be that the causation runs quite differently. The decline of worker mobility may be the result of increased unemployment and the concomitant reduction of opportunities for the worker to change jobs.

Flexibility is often equated with the ability of firms to externalize the costs or risks of adjustment (i.e., to pass them on to other enterprises or establishments or to particular categories of workers, such as casual labor. The growth of such negative externalization may indeed augment the flexibility of a number of businesses, yet it is doubtful whether it can enhance the functioning of the labor market as a whole. It mainly redistributes the burden of costs and risks among various firms or workers, and, in addition, a segment in the labor market that is characterized by low-productivity and low-performance standards emerges. From a macroeconomic perspective, an alternative mode of organization would be to emphasize "dynamic efficiency." This would imply taking some competition out of the labor market and, thereby, challenging firms to channel competitive efforts toward efficient production, competitive products, and the search for new markets.

Note

1. In this study I will not discuss the issue of the impact of employment security provisions on the *level* of employment and unemployment. I find the state of research on this question, both in theoretical and empirical terms, too shaky and inconclusive at the present time.

References

Adler, Paul S. (1982). "Numbers Alone Won't Solve It," *Monthly Labor Review*, October.

Buchele, Robert (1983). "Economic Dualism and Employment Stability," *Industrial Relations*, vol. 22, no. 3.

Doeringer, Peter B., and Michael J. Piore, (1971). *Internal Labor Markets and Manpower Analysis*, Lexington.

Hicks, John R. (1956). "The Instability of Wages," *Three Banks Review*, no. 31, London.

Hotz-Hart, Beat (1987). *Modernisierung von Unternehmen und Industrien bei unterschiedlichen industriellen Beziehungen*, Bern and Stuttgart.

Kochan, Thomas A., Harry C. Katz, and Robert B. McKersie (1986). *The Transformation of American Industrial Relations*, New York.

Köehler, Christoph, and Werner Sengenberger (1983). *Personalanpassung-Betriebliche Beschaftigungspolitik in der deutschen und amerikanischen Automobilindustrie*, Frankfurt/Main-New York.

Koshiro, Kazutoshi (1984). "Reality of Dualistic Labour Market in Japan: Scarcity of Good Employment Opportunities and Industrial Relations," *East Asia-International Review of Economic, Political and Social Development*, vol. 2, Frankfurt.

———— (1985). "Job Security: Redundancy Arrangements and Practice in Japan," *Discussion Paper Series*, 85.3, The Center for International Trade Studies, Faculty of Economics, Yokohama National University.

OECD (1986). *Labour Market Flexibility*, report by a High-Level Group of Experts to the Secretary-General, Paris.

Piore, Michael J., and Charles F. Sabel (1984). *The Second Industrial Divide, Possibilities for Prosperity*, New York.

Piore, Michael J. (1986). "Perspectives of Labor Market Flexibility," *Industrial Relations*, vol. 3.

Reich, Michael (1984). "Segmented Labour: Time Series Hypotheses and Evidence," *Cambridge Journal of Economics*, vol. 8, March, pp. 63–81.

Rosenberg, Sam (1980). "Male Occupational Standing and the Dual Labor Market," *Industrial Relations*, vol. 19, no. 1.

Sengenberger, Werner (1984a). "West German Employment Policy: Restoring Worker Competition," *Industrial Relations*, vol. 23, no. 3.

———— (1984b). "Vocational Worker Training, Labor Market Structure, and Industrial Relations in West Germany," *The Keizai Gaku*, Tokyo, July.

———— (1987). *Struktur und Funktionsweise von Arbeitsmärkten-Die Bundesrepublik Deutschland im internationalen Vergleich*, Frankfurt/Main.

Thurow, Lester (1985). *The Zero-Sum Solution: Building a World-Class American Economy*, New York.

Werner Sengenberger

Tokunaga, Shiegeyoshi (1984). "The Structure of the Japanese Labour Market," in *Industrial Relations in Transition*, edited by J. Bergmann and S. Tokunaga, Tokyo.

WZB-Mitteilungen (1986). (Wissenschafts-zentrum Berlin für Sozialforschung): Befristete Beschäftigung, Heft 32, June, o.v.

Yasuhiko Matsuda

7

Job Security in Japan

I. Overview of Legal Restrictions on an Employer's Power to Discharge Employees

Despite the long standing civil law principle, demonstrated by Article 627 of the Japanese Civil Code, that an employer has the right to terminate an employment contract, the term of which is indefinite, virtually all Japanese employers cannot discharge their employees at will or without a just cause.

First of all, Japanese companies employing ten or more employees are required to provide rules of employment under Article 89 of the Labor Standards Law, and such rules, almost without exception, include discharge clauses in which the reasons for discharging an employee are enumerated. Since Article 93 of the Labor Standards Law proclaims that standards for working conditions provided in the rules of employment have a normative effect on an employment contract, in so far as the standards provided are more favorable than the terms and conditions provided in an individual employment contract, a discharge in violation of such a discharge clause shall be regarded as invalid and, thus, null and void. Moreover, in companies that are unionized, such a discharge clause is most likely to include a consultation clause under which an employer is required to meet and confer with a union before discharging a union member in pursuance of a discharge clause present either in a company's rules of employment or in a collective agreement. Also, discharging a member in violation of such a consultation clause is generally treated as void by many courts.

In addition to the above-mentioned contractual limitations, there are a series of statutory restrictions on an employer's power to discharge employees. First, an employer is prohibited by Article 7 of the Trade Union Law from discharging an employee for his/her union activity or for his/her participation in remedial or adjustment procedures that are provided in the Trade Union Law. It has long been established that an unfair labor practice such as discharging an employee is not only subject to an administrative remedy, as provided by Article 27 of the Trade Union Law, but can also be an issue for a judicial decision in which such an illegal act by an employer can be declared null and void (Shinko-Kai Case, Supreme Court, April 9, 1968; Minshu vol. 22, no. 4, p. 845).

Second, Article 3 of the Labor Standards Law provides that an employee should not be discriminated against by reason of nationality, creed, or social status. A discharge during a period of absence due to work-related injury or sickness as well as a maternity leave, or thirty days thereafter, is also prohibited under the Labor Standards Law. By the same token a retaliatory discharge of an employee for filing a charge against an employer's violation of the Labor Standards Law is also regarded as void under Article 104, Paragraph 2 of said law.

Third, Article 11 of the Men's and Women's Equal Employment Opportunity Law of 1985 flatly prohibits discrimination against women with regards to discharge and retirement.

Finally, even when contractual limitations or statutory restrictions may not be applicable, an employer's power to discharge employees is also limited under the doctrine of "the abusive exercise" of an employer's right to terminate an employment contract, provided under Article 1 of the Civil Code. In the Nihon Shokuen (Salt) Company Case of 1975, the Supreme Court invalidated the discharge of an employee made in compliance with a union shop agreement, saying that since the expulsion of the plaintiff from the union on the grounds stated was found illegal and, thus, null and void, the said discharge had therefore lost an "objectively and socially reasonable cause" and was, therefore, an abusive exercise of employer's right to discharge an employee (on April 25, 1975; Minshu vol. 29, no. 4, p. 56). Again, in the Kochi Hoso (Broadcasting) Company Case of 1977 the Supreme Court confirmed its position, declaring that a discharge of a radio announcer for his repeated failure to arrive at a studio in time to read the news should be invalidated because the said discharge was an abusive exercise of an employer's right to discharge employees. The Court maintained, "even when an employee's conduct constitutes a cause for discharge (which is stipulated as such in a company's rules of employment), an employer may not always discharge the employee. It should be noted that when the said discharge is found to be significantly unreasonable in the specific situation, so that it could not be approved as being appropriate in the light of the socially accepted view, such a discharge should be considered an abusive exercise of an employer's right to discharge an employee and, thus, to be invalid" (on January 31, 1977; Rodo Hanrei no. 268, p. 17).

Under this ruling, the Supreme Court had finally decided to apply the doctrine of an abusive exercise of a right in order to limit, in a general sense, an employer's right to terminate an employment contract at will. The criterion used was that an exercise of an employer's power to discharge an employee should be objectively and socially reasonable because the abuse of such power would be disproportionately detrimental to an employee's life. It should be pointed out, however, that the rationale adopted by the Supreme Court to limit an employer's right to discharge employees is not the Constitutional guarantee of the people's right to work (provided by Article 27, Paragraph 1) but the traditional doctrine of abusive exercise of a right, so that an employer's right to discharge employees was not denied, as such. Note also that, being very much aware of the existence of the lifetime employment system in Japan, the Supreme Court was determined to set forth a criterion to control the abusive exercise of an employer's power to discharge an employee by using the criteria of "objectivity and social unreasonableness."

Finally, judging from the way in which lower courts have been applying such criteria to discharge cases, we can conclude that a Japanese employer may have virtually no power to discharge employees without just cause despite the legal principle of an employer's freedom to terminate an employment contract. Also, it seems that the only difference between a legal requirement of just cause and a judicial application of the doctrine of an abusive exercise of an employer's right is that in the latter case the burden of proof lies with the employee. However, this difference has also tended to decrease because many courts have been inclined to shift the burden of proof toward the employer on the ground that an employer is in a better position to obtain evidence.

Yasuhiko Matsuda

II. Development of Legal Restrictions on an Employer's Power to Discharge Employees

Almost all legal restrictions on an employer's power to discharge an employee emerged in the early postwar period under the substantial influence of Japan's new Constitution, which was promulgated in 1946 and which proclaimed the people's fundamental right to wholesome and cultured living (Article 25).

1. Contractual Restrictions on an Employer's Power to Discharge Employees as Interpreted by the Court

Even in the prewar period, many of Japan's companies had rules of employment that provided a discharge clause. This was so partly following the government's administrative direction under the Factory Law of 1911, but it was mainly for the purpose of maintaining order and high morale in the workplace. Governmental policy to promote the inclusion of a discharge clause in the rules of employment bore fruit soon after World War II when the Labor Standards Law was enacted with a provision that required an employer to include a discharge clause in the rules of employment (Article 89).

Such discharge clauses were soon interpreted by the court in a way that limited an employer's power to discharge employees. According to many courts, an employer can no longer discharge employees for any reason other than the ones enumerated in the discharge clause, and this is particularly so regarding disciplinary discharges.

One of the most controversial issues arising from collective bargaining agreements concerns the legal effect of a union consultation clause concerning the discharge of union members on an individual's employment contract. Right after the war, the Japanese labor union movement, dominated by the left, advocated a policy of joint management/worker control of factories and demanded that all sorts of consultation clauses be included in collective agreements. As the occupation policy brought pressure to bear on the Communists and their sympathizers, employers started trying to discharge such worker factions from their companies, sometimes with complete disregard for consultation clauses and against union opposition. Also, during the postwar reconstruction period, many instances of redundancy dismissals were conducted in violation of union consultation clauses. The majority of earlier court decisions declared such discharges, in violation of union consultation clauses, invalid on the grounds that such consultation clauses should be a normative part of labor agreements as provided by Article 16 of the Trade Union Law, which reads, in part, "Any provision of an individual employment contract contravening the standards concerning conditions of work and other treatment of workers provided in the collective agreement shall be void." As time progressed, an increasing number of court decisions found that a union consultation clause had a contractual effect on an employer and, therefore, an employer who had discharged a union member in violation of the clause should be liable for a breach of contract, while the said discharge itself was valid.

It should be noted that, over time, the courts have developed a general theory of legal restriction on an employer's power to discharge employees through their actual experience with contract violation cases. For instance, when a court found that an alleged reason for a discharge had been supported by evidence produced by an employer and also that it could be regarded an appropriate cause for discharge, it tended to decide in favor of an employer even though such a cause was not exactly the one that was enumerated either in the rules of employment or under a collective agreement. On the other hand, even when the alleged conduct of the employee was found to fit the cause for discharge that was provided in the rules of employment, a court has often decided against the employer for the reason that the discharge was too harsh a sanction for such conduct.

Also, some courts, in determining the legal effect of a union consultation clause, maintained that such a clause, even though it was not exactly the same as a "just cause" clause, should be construed as having a normative effect on an individual employment contract since one of the most important tasks for a union is to limit an employer's power to discharge employees in one way or another. However, as an employer's freedom to discharge employees has become more restricted under the doctrine of an abusive exercise of an employer's right to discharge employees, such a view has become less persuasive and more courts have tended to decide that such union consultation clauses have a merely contractual effect on an employer and, accordingly, to find that a discharge in violation of such a clause should not necessarily be void.

2. Statutory Restriction on an Employer's Power to Discharge Employees

One of the most significant feature of Japan's legal restrictions on an employer's power to discharge employees is that nearly all such illegal acts of discharging employees have been declared null and void by the court, whereas a common practice in the Western nations is that, illegal or not, an employer's act of terminating an employment contract could not be made null and void unless otherwise provided by a statutory law. This unique interpretation of "Willensdogma" by the Japanese court, which no doubt has something to do with the emergence of our lifetime employment system, has prevailed since the early postwar period.

From 1945 through 1949, when the old Trade Union Law of 1945 was amended, an employer's unfair labor practice was not made the subject of administrative remedy at the Labor Relations Commission as is the case today, but was only a subject for criminal prosecution. Discontented with the slow and often reluctant criminal procedure under the old unfair labor practice system, employees who had been discharged under the criterion of "unfair labor practice" brought civil suit against their employers. As will be explained in more detail later in the paper, it seemed to the court that reinstatement of the discharged employee was the only desirable legal remedy in the midst of sky-rocketing inflation and the tremendous job insecurity that was experienced in the early postwar period. Accordingly, the court did not hesitate to declare such an employer's "unfair labor practice" discharge of an employee illegal and, thus, null and void. As mentioned at the beginning of the paper, the Supreme Court confirmed such a position even under the new remedial system of unfair labor practice in Shinko-Kai Case of 1968 (April 9, 1968; Minshu vol. 22, no. 4, p. 845). It should be also pointed out that, since a prima facie case was established relatively easily in such civil procedures involving a charge against an employer's unfair labor practice, an accused employer was more likely to be put in a position where he/she had to show other strong reasons for such a discharge. The same would be true in other civil cases where an employer was alleged to have committed an illegal discharge in violation of Article 3 of the Labor Standards Law, which prohibits an employer from discriminating against an employee for his/her nationality, creed, or social status.

It can be seen, therefore, that the framework for the legal protection of employees from an employer's arbitrary discharge grew out of the economic and political background in Japan during the early postwar period. Employees were able to use the statutory protection guaranteed to unions as a means to furthering their case, while, at the same time, the courts were reluctant to agree to discharges during periods of severe economic dislocation.

3. Other Legal Restrictions on an Employer's Power to Discharge Employees as Implemented by the Court

Of all the institutional factors perhaps the one that has had the most significant impact on the development of legal restrictions of an employer's power to discharge employees is Japan's unique procedure for labor litigation, namely, a provisionary disposition, which is a Japanese version of the injunction procedure. Almost all the civil litigation referred to above was carried out under the legal procedure by which one party seeks a provisionary disposition order, or an injunction, from the court. As a matter of rule in civil procedures, one cannot appeal a case involving a provisionary disposition order to the Supreme Court. This is part of the reason why the Supreme Court was so late in rendering a decision on the theory of an abusive exercise of an employer's right to discharge employees, which had so long been adopted by lower courts. As is explained elsewhere, the provisionary disposition procedure, which is primarily a device for temporarily securing a legal claim that is presently at issue *in a case on merit* pending in the court, was originally made use of immediately after the war by employers who sought court orders to evict sit-in strikers or workers engaging in production-control tactics on company property.

As time progressed, employees, impressed by the effects of the provisionary disposition procedure, made increasing use of it particularly to secure wages and/or employment status for employees who had allegedly been illegally discharged. The court often responded favorably and issued provisionary disposition orders to the effect that the employer should keep paying wages, or otherwise treat the discharged person as an employee, whenever the petitioner successfully produced prima facie evidence for his/her claim or showed urgent necessity of obtaining such an order.

The economic chaos of postwar Japan seems to have been particularly conducive to the development of legal restrictions on an employer's power to discharge employees, and in particular on the development of the doctrine of abusive exercise of an employer's right to terminate an employment contract. In this respect, two points are worth making.

First, the court, well aware of the economic hardship a discharged employee was likely to suffer as a result of accelerating inflation during the early postwar period, was inclined to approve an allegation that the said discharge was an abusive exercise of an employer's freedom, unless the employer could justify such a discharge by showing either an appropriate or just cause for the discharge.

Second, under the provisionary disposition procedure a petitioner who was able to show successfully that his/her family has been suffering hardship since being discharged because of the severe economic situation in Japan, often promptly convinced the court of the necessity to issue an order for an employer to either keep paying wages or else treat the discharged employee as if no discharge had ever been made.

189

Once the court decided in favor of issuing a provisionary disposition order for an employer to keep paying wages to the petitioner or to maintain his/her status as an employee, it was only a matter of logic that the said discharge would be declared null and void by the court. By the same token, the court's presupposition that the said discharge was null and void made it possible for the court to issue an order that the employer should treat the petitioner as an employee. Despite strong criticism that such an order could never be legally enforced unless an employer voluntarily complied with it, it became one of the most popular judicial remedies for illegal discharges. This was because it was believed that such an order was the most appropriate for maintaining peace and harmony in employer-employee relations, since such an order could not be enforced unless an employer voluntarily complied with it.

III. Doctrine of Abusive Exercise of an Employer's Right to Discharge Employees in Practice

The last part of the paper deals with a few significant aspects of the legal framework concerning the discharge of employees. In particular, it looks at the complex difference between an ordinary and a disciplinary discharge and at the problem of the exclusion of temporary and part-time employees from the application of the doctrine of an abusive exercise of an employer's right to discharge. Finally, it touches on the far reaching impact of the legal restrictions on an employer's power to discharge employees on Japan's labor case law as demonstrated by court decisions concerning the legal nature of the rules of employment.

1. Ordinary Discharge vis-à-vis Disciplinary Discharge

The *theoretical* distinction between an ordinary discharge (which is an exercise of an employer's right to terminate an employment contract for an indefinite period at will) and a disciplinary discharge (an exercise of an employer's power to discharge an employee under a disciplinary clause in order to maintain order in the workplace) is firmly established. However, in *practice* the difference between them has been gradually obscured by the development of legal restrictions on an employer's power to discharge employees. On the other hand, the court tends to see more clear distinction between a discharge for a reason for which an employee is responsible and a discharge due to a business necessity, such as a redundancy dismissal.

Now that an employer may not discharge employees without an appropriate or a just cause, the discharging of an employee is more or less disciplinary in origin unless it is made for reasons such as redundancy due to business reasons. In fact, there has been a certain lack of distinction between provisions concerning ordinary and disciplinary discharge under the rules of employment. In many cases, the most severe punishment stipulated in a disciplinary clause is known as a "disciplinary discharge" and the next one is an "ordinary discharge," which involves less severe punishment (it is interesting to note that the court, in deciding on the validity of a discharge, has often compared a disciplinary discharge with capital punishment under criminal procedure). The main difference between the two types of discharges in practice is that under the former type the discharged employee is generally not entitled to severance pay.

In recent years, however, employers have tended to modify disciplinary discharges into ones providing varying percentages of severance pay, while, at the same time, depriving employees who have quit for another job of severance pay. What makes the situation more confusing is the statutory distinction between an instant dismissal (or a discharge on the spot) and a normal dismissal where thirty days' advance notice, or the equivalent pay, is required under Article 20 of the Labor Standards Law. The Labor Standards Law extends the period of advance notice required for an employer to terminate an employment contract, the term of which is for an indefinite period, from the two weeks provided under the Civil Law to thirty days. However, this does not apply to a discharge that is unavoidable for business reasons such as the discontinuation of a business or the discharging of an employee because of reasons for which an employee is responsible (e.g., misconduct, etc.). This instant dismissal is understood as the Labor Standards Law's attempt to modify (or to restrict) an employer's right to cancel (rather than terminate) an employment contract for an employee's breach, which is provided in Article 628 (a cancellation of an employment contract for "unavoidable necessity") as interpreted in the light of Article 541 of the Civil Law (a cancellation of contract for its breach). Therefore, instant dismissal may be allowed only when an employee has committed a serious offence, or a breach of contract.

In statutory terms, the doctrine of an abusive exercise of employer's right to terminate an employment contract is concerned with only a normal dismissal, but the court usually makes no distinction between the two types of statutory dismissals when it applies the doctrine to actual discharge cases. Moreover, employers have not always used an instant dismissal even in a case of disciplinary discharge, partly for fear that the courts would adopt a narrow interpretation of the discharge provisions in the rules of employment and mainly because employers have often found it troublesome to obtain approval for such dismissals from the local labor standards office, as required by Paragraph 3 of Article 20 of the Labor Standards Law. Such being the case, it seems appropriate to distinguish between the two types of discharges in terms of whether severance pay is given or not, regardless of whether it is an ordinary discharge or a disciplinary discharge.

2. Scope of the Doctrine of Abusive Exercise of an Employer's Right to Discharge Employees

As Japan's economic growth became sluggish after the oil crisis, employers tended to use more and more part-time employees, seasonal workers, and temporary workers who were sent from various kinds of manpower supplying agencies (about one sixth of all employees are so-called irregular workers according to the 1986 White Paper on Labor). The most common device that employers use to secure their substantive freedom to hire and fire employees against the legal restrictions is to set up a definite time period for employment and to renew it regularly.

The court's attitude has oscillated between the earlier Supreme Court decision that an employer's refusal to renew a contract for a definite term after repeated renewal was tantamount to a discharge and, therefore, should be treated as such under our legal principle concerning a discharge (Toshiba Yanagicho Factory Case, July 22, 1974; Minshu vol. 28, no. 5, p. 27) and the more recent Supreme Court decision, after the oil crisis, that, even after repeated renewals, such employees may be discharged more freely than those who are employed for indefinite time periods (Hitachi Medico Co. Case, December 4, 1986: Rokeisoku no. 1280, p. 3). By and large, it can be said that during a period of economic growth the court is inclined to treat the discharge of temporary employees in the same manner as that of regular employees probably because an employer can afford to treat both temporary and regular employees equally in a period of growth, whereas in an economic slump the court tends to decide differently in each case, stressing the fact that temporary workers were employed primarily to provide a flexible work force to cope with such as economic recession.

Likewise, the manner and degree to which the court applies the "abusive" doctrine to part-time workers is far from settled, particularly when a dismissal for business reasons is involved. Some courts insist that part-time workers should be the first to be dismissed and made redundant, whereas other courts maintain that the reasonableness of a dismissal should be determined from an objective and social viewpoint by studying the hardship caused to the individual by the discharge regardless of whether he/she is a full-time or a part-time employee.

3. The Doctrine of Abusive Exercise of an Employer's Right to Discharge Employees as Reflected in the Court's Interpretation of the Company's Rules of Employment

Perhaps one of the most serious problems arising out of employer-employee relations is the one concerning an employer's unilateral change of the rules of employment against an employee's interest, because in Japan every change in working conditions is generally preceded by a revision of the company's rules of employment and every company order is issued pursuant to the provision in the rules of employment. Putting it in legal terms, an employment contract is usually executed in the manner that is prescribed in detail under the rules of employment and it can be altered mainly by means of revising the rules of employment. After long and heated controversies over the question of whether employees should still be bound by such a unilateral change of the rules of employment if it was unfavorable for them, the Supreme Court finally rendered its decision in 1968, maintaining that, in so far as such a change of the rules of employment is reasonable as a whole, it should have a binding effect on all concerned employees, regardless of whether they had disapproved of such a change or not. In the very controversial decision given in the Shuhoku Bus Company Case, the Supreme Court found that a compulsory retirement system, which was newly adopted by revising the company's rules of employment, should be applicable to the employee who refused to comply with such a unilateral changes of his/her working condition (on December 25, 1968; Minshu vol. 22, no. 13, p. 3459).

In a further case, the Supreme Court, basing its judgement on the same reasoning, refused to enforce a revised part of a taxi company's rules of employment, which provided for a reduction of the amount of severance pay for those who had already been employed before such a change was made and were opposed to it, on the ground that such a change was not deemed reasonable (Mikuni Taxi Company Case, on July 15, 1983; *Hanrei Times* no. 515, p. 117). Also, in another decision involving a company's unilateral change of women workers' menstruation leave from being fully paid to begin partially paid, the Supreme Court maintained that a unilateral change of the rules of employment against the interest of employees was reasonable both in terms of its content and reason for such a change. It found that the said revision of the company's menstruation leave system successfully met such requirements and, thus, had a binding effect on the employees (Takeda System Case, November 25, 1983; *Hanrei Jiho*, no. 1101, p. 114).

It can be concluded that the Supreme Court, while maintaining that, as a rule, an employer's unilateral change of the rules of employment against the interest of employees should not be enforceable on the employees concerned, admitted that an exception to such a rule may be applied through the criterion of the "reasonableness" of the change. It seems that the Supreme Court's attitude has something to do with the development of legal restrictions on an employer's power to discharge employees. In other words, if no legal restriction on an employer's freedom to discontinue the employment relationship with employees had ever been developed, the court would never have admitted an exception to the rule that an employer's unilateral change of the rules of employment against the interest of employees should be unenforceable on the employees concerned, because, but for the legal restrictions on an employer's right to terminate an employment contract, an employer might as well always discharge an employee who has refused the employer's offer to change the terms and conditions in an employment contract. Putting it in other way, while Japanese employees are enjoying a considerable degree of job security under our legal system, at the same time, they have had to comply with unilateral changes of the terms and conditions of employment against their own interests made by employers unless the changes were unreasonably disadvantageous to them.

Conclusion

Summing up, the development of the doctrine of abusive exercise of an employer's right to discharge employees is attributed to our long-existing employment practice that workers have been employed not in terms of engaging them in a particular job or work but under expectation of life-long commitment between workers and employers, and, accordingly, that it has had a far-reaching effect not only on the theory and practice of our discharge system but also on every aspect of our employer-employee relations.

Finally, it is noteworthy that a theory applied by the court to limit an employer's power to discharge employees is constructed in such a manner that the socioeconomic situation underlying a discharge in question should be taken into consideration in determining its legality. In this respect, it is yet to be seen how the Japanese court will deal with legal disputes arising out of dismissals for business reasons made by employers who have been seriously struck by the "appreciation of yen" in recent years.

References

Azuma, Mitsutoshi (1950). "Futo Kaiko no Koryoku (Legal Effect of Unfair Dismissal)," *Hogaku Kyokai Zasshi*, 67, (3): 493.

Hanami, Tadashi A. (1979). *Labour Law and Industrial Relations in Japan*, Deventer, The Netherlands.

Konishi, Kunitomo (1969). "Kaiko no Jiyu (Freedom to Discharge)," *Hogaku Kyokai Zasshi*, 86 (9): 1628.

Matsuda, Yasuhiko (1973). "Judicial Procedure in Labor Disputes in Japan (1), (2)," *Japan Labour Bulletin*, Japan Institute of Labour, May 1973, p. 7, and June, 1973, p. 4.

Matsuda, Yasuhiko (1983). "Conflict Resolution in Japanese Industrial Relations," in *Contemporary Industrial Relations in Japan*, edited by Taishiro Shirai, Madison, Wisconsin, p. 187.

Sugeno, Kazuo (1985). *Rodoho (Labor Law)*, Tokyo.

Tanabe, Koji (1969). "Rodo Karishobun no Horitsuteki Mondai (Legal Problems on Provisionary Disposition Order in Labor Cases)", *Rodo Funso to Saiban (Labor Conflicts and Litigation)*, Tokyo, 305.

Yamaguchi, Koichiro (1968). "Hanrei Hyoshaku (Comment on Labor Law Case)," *Hanrei Times* no. 228. p. 76.

Abbreviations

Minshu: Saiko Saibansho Minji Hanreishu: Supreme Court Reports, Civil Cases. (Secretariat of Supreme Court)

Rominshu: Rodokankei Minji Saibanreishu: Lower Court Reports, Civil Cases on Labor. (Secretariat of Supreme Court)

Rokeisoku: Rodokeizai Hanrei Sokuho: Labor Economy Case Report. (Japan Management Association)

Rodo Hanrei: Labor Cases Report, Tokyo: Sangyo Rodo Chosasho. (Industry Labor Research Institute)

Hanrei Jiho: Labor Cases Journal, Tokyo: Hanrei Jihosha. (Labor Cases Journal Publishing Co.)

Jocelyn F. Gutchess

8

International Comparison of Employment Adjustment

The issue of employment security and its concomitant, employment adjustment, has become a top priority issue in most of the industrialized nations today—for employers, for workers and their unions, and for governments. Employment security, as used here, concerns those positive policies and practices that can be undertaken in both the private and public sectors to assure that workers have the opportunity to continue working with minimal disruption at productive jobs, if that is what they want to do, for as long as they want to do so. Employment adjustment measures are a necessary, indeed basic element of an effective employment security policy.

This paper will explore the reasons why employment security and employment adjustment have become so important; review some of the policies and programs, both public and private, that have been developed to deal with these issues; and make a tentative assessment of the role of employment security and adjustment issues in the conduct of industrial relations in the future. Though the discussion will focus primarily on the employment security adjustment practices and policies in the United States, adjustment programs of other industrialized nations will also be discussed.

Employment Security/Adjustment—A Priority Issue

Several trends, some global, some more parochial, have increased interest and concern with employment security adjustment. On the global scale three significant trends can be identified:

1. The rapid pace of technological change over the past two decades which has changed both the nature of work and the way in which it is organized. The computer-led technological revolution has brought about fundamental changes not only in the way business is conducted but, particularly significant, in the way products are made and marketed. Competition is fierce, and it is clear that the only way an employer can stay in the race is to be able to develop and utilize new technology better and faster than the next employer. Under these circumstances, jobs can very quickly become obsolete. Whereas formerly workers could expect to continue at the same job with the same employer throughout their work lives and certainly to be able to use the skills and experience developed from youth on, today no such expectations are possible, nor is the situation expected to get any better. According to some forecasters we are already nearing the end of the electronic age and will soon move into the photonics age, with the result that once again both workers and managers will have to learn new skills and techniques.

2. The increasing industrialization among the nations of the world, including the Third World nations—helped by the revolution in communications and transportation—has led to sharper competition and greater global economic interdependence. This in turn has required changes in employment patterns not only in the emerging nations but in the older industrialized nations as well, along with a greater need for effective adjustment measures.

3. The rapid transference across national borders of the impact of economic decisions and events over the past two decades has also increased the need for and interest in employment security and adjustment. Economic fluctuations have become both more violent and more frequent. Sound predictions are increasingly more difficult. Old economic theories do not seem to be working, making for uncertainty and inhibiting planning for the future.

The convergence of these global trends has helped to create the adjustment problems currently facing the industrialized world. Added to these are several more parochial, and perhaps more controversial developments

197

that have affected the course of adjustment. In each of the following three cases, the impact on adjustment can be either positive or negative. Very likely it is a bit of both.

1. There has been a shift in the general opinion away from a belief and trust in direct government action as a means of solving social and economic problems toward a reliance on market forces to correct economic imbalances, and on individual and other private sector efforts to deal with social problems. Although the reasons for the shift differ among countries, there is a commonality of experience among the industrialized nations. In the United States this shift has meant that the burden of responsibility for promoting a smooth process of adjustment is now being borne—to the extent it is borne at all—by the private sector, rather than the government. Government is not entirely out of the picture, but certainly as far as the Federal government is concerned, its role has diminished. This is not as true in European nations where governments have traditionally intervened in economic affairs to a greater extent than in the United States. But even in those countries, the private sector is being forced to deal more directly with the issues of employment security and adjustment than in earlier years.

2. A loss of union power appears to be taking place in all of the western industrialized countries. Organized unions currently represent a diminishing percentage of the work force throughout the industrialized world. For example, in England, where unionization has traditionally been very strong, only half of the work force still belongs to a union. In West Germany about one third belongs to unions, while in the United States and France the figure is closer to one fifth. Even in the Scandinavian countries, where unionized workers once comprised from 80 to 90% of the work force, the unions have lost members in recent years. As a result of this decline, unions, which formerly were able to protect their members through collective bargaining and union-instigated government support programs, can no longer do so. Granted that union weakness can facilitate adjustment—at least in theory—if it means that impediments to labor market flexibility are removed (e.g., union insistence on outdated work rules or manning levels). On the other hand, the decline in power can force union leaders into even more extreme protectionist positions. A strong union operating in a high growth economy can afford to take a long view toward adjustment, secure in the knowledge that its members facing a need to "adjust" can find new employment without sacrifice of earnings or skills. A weak union, losing members and power, is more likely to take the short view, resisting adjustment and moving toward a more protectionist stance.

3. Media attention to adjustment problems can also impact on policy. In the United States, plant closings and layoffs are big news. The

same is true for other western countries. In the United States, the general public is treated—sometimes weekly—to a series of heart-rending stories of worker dislocation, on television, in the newspapers, and on radio. As a result of this media attention and interest, adjustment problems, when they occur, are no longer reserved for the workers and employers directly involved, but become a high drama played out in the public eye. Politicians, especially those running for office, cannot ignore these problems; nor can employers. As a result, employment security and adjustment policies and programs are being developed and are being carried out not only in response to an immediate adjustment crisis, but are increasingly being planned in advance.

All of the factors mentioned above can and have had an effect on the employment security/adjustment issue. However, perhaps the single most important factor affecting the course of adjustment involves costs—not the costs of implementing employment security and adjustment measures, but the costs of *not* doing so. These costs can affect workers, employers and society as a whole.

For the worker who is unemployed because of a layoff or plant closing and unable to make a reasonably quick adjustment to other employment, the costs can include loss of income, loss of fringe benefits (such as health care and pension coverage), loss of savings, potential loss of skills, loss of self-esteem, and increasing likelihood of deterioration of individual and family health, both physical and mental. An employer who does not provide some degree of employment security for his employees, preferring instead to leave any necessary adjustment to the worker himself, risks the increased costs of higher taxes to pay for increased unemployment benefits and other government support programs. He also risks forfeiture of employee loyalty, which in a constantly changing high tech society can be very damaging. The high costs of recruitment and training make reduction of turnover an important cost consideration for most employers. Moreover, not only loyalty but productivity can be at risk. The link between employment security and productivity has been demonstrated repeatedly by employers in competitive industries. Lacking employment security, including measures to provide assistance when adjustment is necessary, workers are apt to resist changes to improve productivity such as the introduction of new technology. With such assurances, however, the workers themselves may very well take the lead in suggesting changes.

For society as a whole, an absence of employment security/adjustment policies can impose all of the recognized costs of high unemployment such as increased government expenditures for unemployment compensation and other government support programs; higher taxes, particularly on employers;

a decline in the general standard of living; and a potential increase in such social problems as crime, alcoholism, and drug abuse.

Where Does Responsibility for Employment Security and Adjustment Lie?

Since it is in the interest of workers, employers, and society to assure that the adjustment process, such as moving workers from where they are no longer needed to where they can be employed with their skills and talents productively utilized, is as smooth as possible, responsibility for providing effective employment security and adjustment policies must be shared by the public and private sectors. The emphasis as between a public or private sector approach may change from time to time, and, of course, there are different patterns of responsibility among the different industrialized nations. However, there is no doubt that all parties—unions, employers and government—have a role in meeting the employment security responsibility. In the United States, where this principle is fully recognized and accepted, the government role is complicated by the reduction of the Federal involvement over the past few years and the increased importance of state and local governments. This U.S. pattern differs from the European situation in many other important respects.

In the United States, the government, at whatever level, does not assume responsibility for nor intervene in labor market management to the extent that occurs in most European countries. For example, the employment service in the United States, although funded by the Federal government and operated by the states, is not the primary labor exchange instrument as is the case in European countries. Indeed the U.S. employment service tends to operate on the periphery of the labor market, serving disadvantaged workers, those who are least able to compete effectively in the labor market.

Another important difference between the United States and other western nations concerns government restrictions on hiring and dismissal practices based on race, religion, sex or age. American employers, unlike their European counterparts, can dismiss employees for economic reasons at will. Although this has tended to reduce rigidities in the U.S. labor market, it may also have produced more severe adjustment problems.

In the United States, training and retraining are almost entirely a function of the employer, whereas in European countries, the government is deeply involved in both of these aspects of labor market management. Perhaps the best-known example is the West German system of vocational and technical training, which is directly linked to the skill needs of local employers. In the United States, vocational training has by and large been carried out by local educational authorities without any reference to the job needs of employers. To some extent this is changing, as vocational schools and community colleges strive to find new support for their programs. One example is a program initiated and operated by General Motors, in which approximately fifty community colleges throughout the country have been enlisted to train automobile and truck maintenance workers needed by GM dealers, incorporating new and different technology.

Finally, there appears to be a greater degree of joint activity between government and employers in regard to employment security and adjustment in the western European nations than in the United States. In many European countries, for example, government and employers have worked together to establish job replacement programs in which former employers such as British Steel and Pilkington Glass in the United Kingdom, Thomson and Rhone-Poulenc in France, and the Oresund Shipbuilding Company in Sweden, have established, with government support and often direct participation, programs to encourage the development of new businesses in locations where they have closed plants and laid off workers. No such activity has taken place in the United States.

Current Employment Security/Adjustment Strategies

The kind of policies and programs adopted by either governments or the "social partners"—employers and unions—to provide employment security and facilitate adjustment can be grouped into three classifications. The first group are the defensive measures, measures designed to avoid or prevent layoffs. These are usually based on private sector initiatives and involve a commitment by the employer to employment security for his employees, and a willingness by both management and workers to work together to maintain the company's ability to .compete. The second group of security adjustment strategies can be called containment measures. These policies come into play when it is clear that a major adjustment must be made. The assumption is that workers are going to have to move; their old jobs are gone and they will have to find new ones. Containment measures are designed to limit or alleviate the adverse impact of restructuring changes. The third group of strategies includes the more aggressive, positive adjustment measures, undertaken to enable displaced workers to move into new careers, and new businesses. Rather than focussing on the adjustment that must be made on an individual basis, these strategies are aimed at speeding up the entire economic adjustment process.

Jocelyn F. Gutchess

Defensive Strategies

In using the term "defensive" to describe these strategies, no negative connotation is implied. The intended context is defense against layoffs and unnecessary unemployment, not defense against change. Adjustments may have to be made by individual workers, but a defensive strategy permits the adjustment to be made in-house; the worker remains employed by his employer. Indeed, it can be shown that companies that have implemented these policies have usually done so as a means of facilitating change. A list of such strategies includes, in no particular order:

- Buffering strategies

- Work sharing and voluntary reduction of work time

- Redeployment

- Retraining programs

- Advance warning schemes

Buffering strategies are certain employment policies or "buffers" used by an employer to protect a core work force and thus avoid layoffs and dismissals for economic reasons. Effective use of buffers is really nothing more than careful, prudent management, plus a dedication by the employer to the principle of employment security for his employees. The general concept is to staff lean; that is, employment starts at a level less than necessary to meet normal anticipated market demand, and then, by using buffers, the work force is expanded or contracted as needed. Buffering techniques include the use of regularly scheduled overtime; hiring (and dismissal) of temporary staff; internal job assignment shifts,; subcontracting (to outside vendors when things are going well, with the option to call the work back in-house when they are not); above or below inventory building; and re-scheduling of deliveries.

IBM provides one of the best examples of effective buffering to keep its staff employed, although many other companies also use these techniques. The IBM policy is rooted in the company's history and was established in the belief that only by providing employment security could the company achieve the productivity improvements that would allow it to grow and prosper. The experience of managers at the IBM typewriter plant in Lexington, Kentucky in the 1960s is typical. At that plant, at a time when IBM was having a hard time meeting its competition, the introduction of an employment security program relying, among other things, on the use of employment buffers, resulted in a 45% reduction in costs and

202

65% reduction in the time it took to manufacture the product. The Lexington managers started with a staff that was about 85% of the level deemed necessary to meet normal demand. Scheduled overtime brought the total number of available man-hours up to 95%, and the remaining 5% was met by the use of subcontracting.

Another computer company has adopted a similar buffering system, but starts with a 70% staff level. Some defense contractors concerned about over-reliance on government procurement staff as low as 50%, using buffering techniques to make up the difference.

Another defensive measure widely used in both the United States and in Europe is *work sharing*, accomplished through a program to reduce work time. In the United States, work sharing is accomplished most often by the private sector, operating without government involvement. In European countries, the government generally plays a more important role, usually through the implementation of short time compensation programs. Voluntary work sharing in the United States typically occurs in non-union companies, since the unions historically have preferred to rely on negotiated seniority systems as a way of reducing a work force when and as economic conditions demand. A seniority system can work well when the layoff is temporary. However, it can be an impediment to adjustment if the layoff is permanent. This is particularly true in those cases where the union has negotiated supplemental unemployment benefit schemes which add to and extend regular unemployment insurance benefits for unemployed workers, thereby dampening the interest and enthusiasm of laid-off workers in seeking new jobs. On the other hand, in a seniority system it is the younger workers who are the first dismissed and of course this is the group most apt and most able to make changes. In this respect, therefore, it can be said to facilitate adjustment.

A good example of a successful work sharing policy is provided by the Nucor company, the tenth-largest steel company in the United States. Manufacturing specialty steel using high technology mini-mills, the company has been profitable every year of its fifteen-year history, and prides itself in never having laid off any worker for economic reasons. The company works hard to foster an atmosphere of shared responsibility and shared rewards: bonuses are paid when things are going well, and everybody takes a cut—managers as well as workers—when they are not. Also, as needed, work time and compensation are reduced across the board, sometimes to as little as three days per week. But morale and productivity remain high.

In Europe, work sharing is usually accompanied by government-supported short time compensation schemes. Under these plans, the state unemployment insurance system is used to pick up the decline in employees' income when a company goes on short time because of a temporary decline in demand. Widely used in such countries as France and West Germany, the program has spread in recent years to Canada and the United States. In the United States, however, implementation of short time compensation requires legislation on a state-by-state basis. So far, only ten states have enacted such legislation despite the passage several years ago of a Federal statute encouraging the program.

Redeployment and retraining provide additional avenues for enhancing employment security and facilitating adjustment. These strategies can be considered defensive if they occur in-house and are successful in preventing layoffs or dismissals. When they are carried out externally, they fall into the third group of strategies, the aggressive adjustment measures.

Redeployment simply involves moving employees from where they are no longer needed to where they are. Such moves almost always require some retraining. In the early 1980s, British Airways successfully carried out an extensive redeployment–retraining effort, slimming the company from some 60,000 employees to about 36,000, and in the process, improving productivity and operational efficiency. The task was not easy, and indeed met with considerable resistance, both from affected workers, and even more from managers and line supervisors who did not like to see "their" employees moved to other parts of the company. Training was provided, for the most part by the company itself, which broke new ground in identifying and utilizing counseling and training skills of its own staff.

There are many instances unions have negotiated redeployment–retraining programs with employers. It is a favored adjustment strategy in West Germany. For example, the automotive company Daimler-Benz has a negotiated plan for shifting auto workers to plants with unused capacity when business falls off at any of its other plants. Under this scheme, workers can be redeployed for as long as a year, with not only their salaries kept intact, but living expenses for them and their families provided by the company. In the United States, the Communications Workers of America negotiated a redeployment–retraining program to help its members who were forced to change jobs as a result of the break-up of AT&T. Similarly, the British Communications Workers union has an agreement with British Telecoms, the recently privatized communication arm of the British Post Office.

One of the best examples of a successful in-house retraining program is provided by the Xerox company. For several years, Xerox has operated a program to permit its professional staff, whose particular skills are no longer needed by the company, to undertake training in new careers and jobs in which the company has openings. The program is operated in conjunction with a local university, which in cooperation with Xerox designed a special one-year, full-time curriculum for this purpose. On completion of the program, the graduating trainees move into new pre-defined jobs in the company. Even though the program is relatively expensive (trainees pay no tuition and receive full salary and benefits throughout the training period), the company has found the program to be cost effective. The costs are less than if the employees were dismissed, and new staff recruited and hired to take the company's unfilled jobs.

The defensive strategies mentioned thus far generally depend on private sector initiatives, taken by employers, unions, or both working together. Other strategies, however, are more dependent on government involvement.

First among these are legislatively-mandated *early warning systems*. All European countries as well as Canada have such programs. Varying by size of the company, under these laws employers are required to provide advance notice—six months or less—of impending closures or mass lay-offs. Notice must be given not only to the workers and their union representatives, but also to the government agencies involved in labor market management, usually the employment service. The advance notice requirement typically triggers a range of activities, the fundamental purpose of which is to find an appropriate adjustment solution for every affected worker.

The United States has never had a universal advance notice requirement, although some unions, notably the big industrial unions such as the United Auto Workers, the Steel Workers and the Rubber Workers, have negotiated such programs through collective bargaining. But since they are not linked to a government network of supportive services as is the case in Europe, their effectiveness as an adjustment mechanism is questionable.

In two countries, advance notice requirements set in motion particularly interesting and effective adjustment mechanisms. One is in Canada, where advance notice can bring into play a Canadian government agency, the Industrial Adjustment Service. The other is in Sweden where a prospective layoff of white-collar workers can trigger adjustment prevention activities by the Swedish Employment Security Council, a unique, hybrid organization dedicated to employment security and positive adjustment. Both of these organizations involve themselves in every aspect of adjustment policy and program, applying containment measures and aggressive adjustment strategies as necessary. However, while they do not limit the scope of their activity to defensive measures, generally speaking, the prevention of layoffs and closures is the first strategy considered.

The Canadian Industrial Adjustment Service (IAS) is a small, low-budget government agency within the Department of Employment and Immigration. As the name implies, its objective is to facilitate adjustment of workers facing mass layoffs. Whenever the agency learns of an impending closure or mass layoff, it offers its services—which may or may not be accepted—to the companies and workers involved. The mechanism for provision of the service is a tri-partite committee made up of representatives of the employer, the union (or in non-union companies, representatives selected by the workers), and chaired by an outside expert nominated by IAS. Half the costs of the committee are supported by the IAS; the employer must agree to meet the balance.

While the primary role of the IAS is to act as a catalyst, bringing together employer and employees to work cooperatively to find solutions to the adjustment problems, the IAS also provides a considerable measure of technical assistance to help the committee take advantage of existing support programs, most but not all of them, government support programs. These include training, mobility assistance, and other employment services including job search assistance, labor market information, job placement, and employment counseling. In recent years, the IAS has increased its attention to layoff prevention, encouraging the tri-partite committees to look for ways to correct or ameliorate the situation that led to the company's initial decision to cut back or close down its operations. This can take the form of various restructuring measures and can include suggestions for the introduction of new technology, shifts in marketing strategies, or even the addition or conversion to the production of new and different products. The Canadian approach has been remarkably successful, placing as many as 85% of those asking for help. Although the program has not been fully replicated in other industrial countries, at the present time the U.S. Department of Labor is engaged in an effort to encourage the states to set up their own programs based on the Canadian model.

In response to union concern with adjustment issues, in 1974 the Swedish Employment Security Council was established by collective agreement between the Confederation of Swedish Employers (SAF) and the Federation of Salaried Employees in Industry and Services (PTK), the joint negotiating body for the major Swedish white-collar unions. The objectives of the Council, in the words of its executive director, Hans Ursing, are to repair old jobs and develop new ones. By "repair," the Council means making the kind of adjustments within the particular work situation that are necessary to keep people working despite cyclical ups and downs and structural changes. The development of new jobs, though outside the work situation, sometimes can be an integral part of the repair operation.

To accomplish these objectives, the Council engages in five different areas of activity. These include the administration of various basic unemployment insurance programs which have been negotiated between employers and unions; personnel clearing—a program to help displaced workers find new jobs; assistance to its members to start new businesses; job creation—the encouragement of entrepreneurship; and dismissal prevention. It is this last activity that has received increased attention in recent years. The focus of the activity is to help companies with surplus personnel reduce their staffs without dismissal. Whenever the council hears of an impending reduction of staff—which it does through its link to the early warning system—it sends its professional staff to work with both management and the unions to plan a prevention program. This program will typically include a full range of employment security measures, starting with a carefully calculated program of attrition, and backed up by early retirement for some workers. It certainly will include provision for retraining workers who are affected by the proposed restructuring, and transfer of those workers either to other jobs within the firm or to jobs with other employers.

Funded by a mandatory contribution from member employers (nonmember organizations can also use its service, but must pay a fee), and essentially a private sector organization, the Swedish Employment Security Council operates in conjunction with the Swedish government labor market boards. The Council utilizes the government programs and resources to the fullest extent possible, and considers itself to be a complementary organization, not a substitute for government adjustment policies and programs.

Containment Strategies

Containment strategies are based on the assumption that a plant closure or major restructuring will have to or has already taken place, that employees must be dismissed on a significant scale, and that they will have to find new jobs with other employers, or some other appropriate adjustment outcome will have to be arranged. The containment measures are those that are designed to "contain" or limit, insofar as possible, the negative impact of dislocation on affected individuals and their communities and to facilitate the adjustment process. Among the containment strategies are:

- Job search assistance

- Early retirement plans

- Employee buyouts

- Community action programs

- Compensation programs

Jocelyn F. Gutchess

Job search assistance, the most important and most prevalent of the containment strategies, embraces a wide range of adjustment enhancement measures. These include:

(a) *Provision of labor market information.*
    This is usually the first order of business in helping dislocated workers. It is particularly necessary when long-time employees are laid off; these employees have not had to look for a job for many years, and therefore are apt to be unaware of current labor market developments and requirements. Similarly, when a closure or layoff takes place in a one-industry town, particularly a town in which a single employer dominates the labor market, the affected workers, lacking reliable labor market information, can be crippled in their attempts to adjust, however willing they are to try.

(b) *Individual career counseling.*
    Along with labor market information, most dislocated workers need and can benefit from experienced, professional help in making career choices, especially under the duress of dislocation.

(c) *Family counseling, including financial counseling.*
    Studies have shown that it is not only laid-off workers who are affected by dislocations, but their families as well. Both may very well need expert help in managing family finances during the period of unemployment.

(d) *Basic instruction in job search techniques.*
    These include instruction in how to look for a job, how to prepare a resume, and how to respond to an interview.

(e) *Job development and job placement.*
    Strong efforts must be made to find replacement jobs and to place the dislocated workers in such jobs.

In most European countries, it is the state employment service that provides these adjustment assistance services. In the United States, although job search assistance services are generally available from the state employment service agencies, there are numerous examples where employers—especially employers committed to the principles of employment security—have assumed responsibility for helping their laid-off or displaced employees in this way. Sometimes the employer effort is carried out as a joint endeavor, in cooperation with the union, in conjunction with the employment service, or both.

208

A good example is provided by the Dana Corporation, a manufacturing company associated with the automotive industry and headquartered in Ohio. Like other companies in the industry, Dana found that it had to close some plants in the early 1980s. However, long before the shutdowns, Dana had established a policy and program for handling the situation. The first step was to give workers from the shut-down plants priority for openings in other Dana Corporation plants, and provide these workers with financial assistance in moving to new locations. For those workers who could not be placed in this way, the company established an intensive job search program. All of the affected workers were offered a week-long course designed to build confidence and to give them the skills and knowledge they needed to successfully search of new jobs. The company also opened a job search center, easily accessible to Dana workers, where they could obtain information on job openings, consult counselors (on loan from the local employment service), and make use of a bank of telephones which could be used free of charge to make calls to prospective employers. A critical element of the program was the effort made by Dana staff to locate potential employers. Thousands of letters were written and calls made to all employers in the area, informing them about the skills and qualifications of the Dana workers and requesting their assistance in identifying suitable new employment. Over 3,000 employers were contacted as part of this effort. The program paid off: over 95% of the white-collar workers, and 85% of the blue-collar workers were placed by the time the program ended.

Another kind of job search assistance is provided by the United Automobile Workers and the Ford Motor Company through the UAW-Ford Employee Development Center. This center, established through collective agreement, carries out a wide range of individual development and adjustment programs, one of which is the National Assistance Center for Plant Closings. As closings occur, the center takes the initiative, helping local unions and plant managers establish their own local centers to provide job search assistance, career guidance and retraining to dislocated workers. The centers are locally operated by selected consortiums representing both educational institutions and service providing agencies, but are under the general direction of the UAW-Ford Center. Each local center can develop the programs that best meet its needs, though usually high among the requests are job search assistance programs.

Some French employers have gone to great lengths to provide job search assistance for their displaced workers. For example, one French company, Rhône-Poulenc, not only makes an effort to canvass other local employers to find new jobs for its dismissed employees, but is even willing to pay a premium to the new employers when a displaced worker is hired.

While job search assistance programs are aimed at helping active workers who want to remain in the labor force, *early retirement plans* are designed to encourage some older workers to leave it. The objective is the same in both cases: to limit the negative impact of large-scale restructuring decisions. In many European countries, early retirement is an accepted and favorite "adjustment" strategy adopted by employers to protect the employment security of the remaining work force. This occurs in part because European employers are less free than their American counterparts to adjust their work forces to changing economic conditions—having to comply with a range of government requirements and procedures, including specified mandatory separation payments. In addition, in western Europe a strong sentiment exists that the shortage of jobs is a chronic condition; that the economy cannot and will not in the foreseeable future be able to generate sufficient jobs for all those who might want them. That being the case, there is a feeling that older workers have an obligation to withdraw from the labor force in order to make way for younger workers.

In America, where the trend is to extend the work life of the individual, this reliance on early retirement is hard to understand. However, despite the general belief in the right of the individual to work as long as he or she wants, many employers in the United States who are having to reduce their work forces are using early retirement programs as a means of doing so.

Two important differences separate the American early retirement plans from those implemented in European countries. First, the European plans are generally supported by government, both directly and indirectly, while in the United States the financial burden of supporting such plans is borne entirely by the employer. Indirect support comes from the extensive network of social programs for older people, such as health care, housing, and recreation, which are typically provided by western European governments. With these programs in place, the annuities paid to early retirees can be lower than might otherwise be the case. Direct support is provided in a variety of ways, often by linking financial aid to the companies adopting early retirement to schemes for the employment of the currently unemployed. For a period in the early 1980s, the French government had a program in which employers were subsidized if they hired unemployed youth to replace those who left employment through voluntary early retirement. Relatively popular with French employers, it was dropped when it became too expensive.

The British also subsidize a program that exchanges older workers for the currently unemployed, not necessarily a young worker. The subsidy is in the form of assistance in paying the pension of the retiree. This program is in addition to the regular program of financial aid initiated by the present British government to help companies meet the gap between early retirement at the age of fifty or fifty-five and eligibility for normal social security benefits and/or regular earnings related pensions. Similarly, in West Germany the government normally pays up to 50% of the cost of the pension that an early retiree receives until he or she reaches the normal retirement age and can receive social security. A further subsidy is available to companies that hire a replacement worker from the ranks of the unemployed.

A second difference between early retirement plans in the United States and those in Europe is the penalty that many European workers face if they take another job after "retiring." In France, for example, workers in the coal and steel industries who accept early retirement (unionists say that many do not "accept" the retirement offer but are in effect pushed out) are prohibited from ever working again, or at least from working at a job covered by the social security system. Such an arrangement simply does not occur in the United States. This difference between retirement practices reflects the different attitudes that exist regarding age and retirement. In European countries, retirement seems an honorable solution to an intractable economic adjustment problem. In the United States, such a solution is regarded as discrimination.

Employee buyouts of a faltering company represent a third kind of containment strategy. Instances can be found where employees of a company or plant threatened with closure or elimination by merger have banded together to buy the company and remain in business. The most serious problems relating to buyouts are the huge capital investment required of the new worker-owners and the great, often drastic, changes necessary to correct the conditions that led to the initial decision to close down the enterprise. A buyout, however, does more than shift ownership of a company. It buys much-needed time for adjustment to take place and in this respect should be regarded as a positive action. A buyout can be particularly helpful to older workers who are not quite ready for retirement. On the other hand, if the failure of the enterprise is simply deferred, then the workers will lose not only their jobs but also their life savings, making eventual adjustment even more difficult.

Finally, a word must be said about *community action efforts* to contain the damage of closures and mass dismissals. Frequently, in one-industry, single-employer towns, announcement of closure triggers a broad-based community effort to keep the plant going, or to find or develop alternative employment for the affected workers. In both the United States and Europe,

211

there have been some notable successes with this strategy. One U.S. example is the Downriver Community Conference, a consortium formed by sixteen local governments located "downriver" from the city of Detroit, the capital of America's hard-hit automotive industry. With dynamic leadership and a dedicated and imaginative staff, this organization has become a community catalyst, brokering the development of a new job-creating business, including defense contracts for the companies in the area. Another interesting community-sponsored employment protection initiative, this one the result of joint actions on the part of the unions and the local government, is an informal employment council in Munich, West Germany. The council includes representatives of all of the major institutions concerned with employment and unemployment in the area; employers, unions, educators, and local and federal government. By sharing information and coordinating efforts, the council is finding ways to ensure employment security and promote adjustment for the Munich area labor force.

In no Western country has containment been left entirely to the private sector. All of the industrialized nations have at one time or another carried out government *compensation programs* to assist workers who lose their jobs because of structural economic changes. Perhaps the best example is the U.S. Trade Adjustment Assistance program which provides extended unemployment compensation and training to workers who lose their jobs as a result of shifting international trade patterns, specifically an increase in imports. The rationale for the program is that the financial cost of actions taken by the U.S. government to improve trade which benefit the population as a whole should be shared, insofar as possible, by the whole society and not just by those workers who lose their jobs as a result of those actions. Implementation of the program has passed through several phases since it was first initiated in the early 1970s. In the first seven years, the standards for eligibility of participation were very rigid, with the result that very few workers were ever certified. This was followed by a period when eligibility standards were greatly relaxed and thousands of workers received benefits, many of them even after they were working in new jobs. Under the Reagan administration, eligibility was again tightened, and although training has been given new emphasis, there has been a substantial cutback in the program.

Positive Adjustment

As previously noted, aggressive positive adjustment strategies go beyond containment strategies in that they are aimed at facilitating the entire adjustment process, not just for affected individuals, but for the economy as a whole. In my view, three major strategies can be classified as aggressive positive adjustment. The first, a basic strategy, is government implementation of macro-economic policies which provide a climate favorable to economic growth, and particularly to the development of new employment opportunities. However, it is not within the scope of this chapter (nor the expertise of the author) to discuss those policies. A second strategy is the provision of opportunities for retraining. While the principal instrument for doing so is the public, government-supported educational system, much can be and has been done in this regard by the private sector. A third strategy involves efforts to replace jobs lost because of restructuring, again in most cases a joint public-private effort.

While retraining is accepted as a public responsibility in most countries the problem has been, at least in the United States, to make such training available to those workers who need it, and to make it relevant to the current employment situation. In the United States, some of the most successful efforts in this regard have been set in motion as a result of collective bargaining agreements between the United Auto Workers Union and the big automotive companies, specifically Ford and General Motors.

Under the UAW-Ford agreement, an Employee Development and Training Program has been established to help Ford employees—both active workers and those who have been permanently dismissed because of economic reasons—realize their career potential and fully develop their skills, aptitudes and interests. The principal objectives of the program are to provide training, retraining, and developmental opportunities for both active and displaced employees; support local and national UAW-Ford efforts to more fully involve Ford employees in the operations of the company; and provide opportunities for the cooperative exchange of ideas and innovations with respect to employee development and training needs.

Union-management cooperation is the key to the implementation of the program, which is overseen by a joint board of governors, with equal representation from both sides. Although the program operates as a development program for individuals, it is clear that the impact is not limited to the participants, nor even to the Ford Company community. Emphasis on maximum development of each person's career potential cannot help but increase both the value and the flexibility of the labor force as a whole, thereby making future adjustments much easier.

The retraining goals of the UAW-Ford program are pursued by a variety of measures. For example, for displaced workers there is a prepaid tuition assistance program, which pays for up to four years' training so that workers can prepare themselves for new and perhaps different jobs, even jobs outside the auto industry. Career guidance and counseling are available to help workers decide what it is they want to do, what kind of training they should undertake, and where they can go to get the training. Once workers have decided on and enrolled in an approved program (for the most part the actual training takes place in regular educational institutions), the full tuition costs plus certain fees are paid directly to the educational institution. Literally thousands of Ford workers have availed themselves of this opportunity. Although initially begun as a program designed to serve displaced workers, this same kind of support is now being made available to active workers.

Another interesting program in the automotive industry is one carried out on a joint basis by the United Auto Workers local union and the Buick division of General Motors. This program, designed to win the support of Buick workers for the introduction of new technology essential to improve the company's productivity and competitiveness, protects employees who are displaced as a result of such action. The program is financed by a special fund, itself the result of union-negotiated company contributions. Under the Buick program, workers who are threatened with dismissal resulting from introduction of new technology, can receive up to two years of retraining at institutions in skills or disciplines of their choice, with all costs covered by the special fund. In addition, workers receive full pay and benefits during the training period. Both the union and management credit the program with contributing substantially to the company's improved performance and profitability.

Such programs are not unknown in most European countries. Perhaps the best-known program was the Fiat "reconversion leave" program, which provided Fiat workers made redundant by the company's restructuring with a two-year "leave of absence" at full pay to enable them to undertake retraining for new careers and new employment.

Another positive adjustment strategy, more popular in Europe than in the United States, is a job creation effort in which companies responsible for causing mass dismissals take the lead in encouraging the establishment of new enterprises to provide new employment opportunities for their unemployed workers. The strategy often involves the creation of a subsidiary organization specifically dedicated to identifying and assisting new businesses in areas where the company has closed plants and dismissed a large number of workers. The subsidiary organization is typically staffed by management and technical experts drawn from the parent company and is financed through the corporate budget. Generally, the subsidiary offers a range of technical services useful to fledgling entrepreneurs such as access to financial resources, marketing assistance, legal and accounting help, assistance in taking advantage of government support programs (including training programs), and in some cases, use of abandoned facilities at a minimal cost. This kind of adjustment strategy is quite prevalent in France, where almost every large company that has gone through a major restructuring in recent years has established such a subsidiary. Examples can also be found in the United Kingdom. One such is British Steel Industries, Ltd., a subsidiary organization of British Steel which was established in 1975 to help the communities affected by large-scale closures of British steel plants. The goal that BSC Industries set for itself was the creation of 25,000 jobs in a ten-year period, a goal that has been met. In recent years, BSC has shifted emphasis, merging its activities with the newly developed Enterprise Agencies, essentially a consortia of local businesses encouraging entrepreneurship in their communities. More than 200 local Enterprise Agencies have been established at the present time.

Future Directions for Employment Security and Adjustment Policy

As we have seen, employment security and adjustment are major policy concerns affecting both public and private sector policymakers. Much is being done in the area, and different strategies are being used to resolve the problems. Will these issues continue to demand attention? What directions will policy take? It is not within the purview of this paper to make general predictions of what is going to happen in all of the industrialized nations. However, it is possible to speculate to some degree about the future direction of policy in the United States.

1. There can be no doubt that the problems of employment security and adjustment will continue and indeed may become even more acute, primarily because the pace of change will remain high and even accelerate. Even if U.S. markets and U.S. industries become more protected—itself a possibility—the advance of technology will continue to force radical shifts in employment security and adjustment policy.

2. Whereas today, the principal focus of attention is with the employment security problems of blue-collar workers, in the very near future, it will be white-collar workers, and particularly pink-collar employees, who will have to face the need to adjust. The U.S. economy is already dominated by service industries, providing white-collar jobs, especially office and sales jobs, to millions of workers. Indeed, the majority of new jobs created in the last year are in these fields and have been taken by women. However, technology is rapidly changing the way this kind of work is performed, so that it may very well be women in clerical jobs who are the dislocated workers of the future. Adjustment strategies to meet their special needs may have to

be different from current strategies; for example, providing different kinds of training, developing more part-time jobs, and finding ways to move jobs to people, rather than people to jobs.

3. The continuing need for employment security and adjustment will certainly affect the conduct of labor relations as well as the strength (or lack of it) of the labor movement. At the present time, union negotiators are apt to put a premium on employment security for their members, asking for guarantees of continuing employment or, at least, compensation for dismissal. Frequently these demands are a trade-off for union acceptance of a reduction in wages and/or other benefits. However, U.S. unions—losing members as they are—must find ways to attract new members, and that means younger workers and women. Historically, neither of these groups have shown as much interest in employment security as older workers, generally having more confidence in their ability to make adjustments on their own. Whether these perceptions will change as the technological revolution begins to affect them as well as older, blue-collar workers, remains to be seen. To the extent that they do, that is if women and younger workers become as concerned with adjustment as for example "rust belt" workers are today, the adjustment issue could very well turn out to be a strong stimulus to union growth.

4. Employers' concern with employment security and adjustment will probably increase, particularly in highly competitive industries, dependent on skills currently in short supply. The link between employment security and productivity has been well established. There is no question that a well developed human resource policy that provides a reasonable degree of security to a company's employees will give that company a strong foundation for on-going productivity improvements. Employers who have such policies will be better equipped to develop and apply new technology as it becomes available, and hence, will be able to maintain or improve their ability to compete.

5. The question of who will be responsible for employment security and adjustment remains murky. Much depends on the general political and economic situation at any one time. Under a Republican administration, and with a continuing high federal budget deficit, it is clear that most of the burden of adjustment policy will be borne by the private sector. A Democratic administration would look more favorably on direct government intervention both to accelerate the general process of adjustment, and to assist those individuals hurt by the need to make adjustments. However, even a Democratic administration will face the federal budget problem, thus limiting effective intervention on any large scale.

Finally, while it is clear that employment security and adjustment policies will remain priority issues for the industrialized nations, it is also clear that the countries which learn how to deal with these problems equitably and effectively will be better able to compete on a global basis, and better able to serve their own citizens.

References

Blanpain, Roger, ed. (1980). *Job Security and Industrial Relations*, Bulletin of Comparative Labour Relations, Bulletin 11, 1980; Deventer, The Netherlands.

Daniel, W. W., and Elizabeth Stilgoe (1978). *The Impact of Employment Protection Laws*, Policy Studies Institute, Vol. XLIV No. 577, London.

Gutchess, Jocelyn F. (1985). *Employment Security in Action: Strategies that Work*, New York.

Lall, Betty D., ed. (1985). *Economic Dislocation and Job Loss*, New York.

Rosow, Jerome M. and Robert Zager (1984). *Employment Security in a Free Economy*, A Work in America Institute Policy Study, New York.

Work in America Institute, Inc. (1987). *Training for New Technology*, A Work in America Institute National Policy Study, New York.

Oliver Clarke

9
Employment Adjustment: An International Perspective

I. Introduction

Employment adjustment is concerned with providing labor quickly and easily to meet society's changing needs for an efficient human contribution to producing goods and providing services. It relates to adjusting the numbers of workers, the hours they work, and their mix of skills and abilities. It also necessarily concerns the movement of workers to where they are needed, be it to another job in the same enterprise, a job elsewhere in the same industry or occupation, or a job in a different industry or occupation. But pursuit of economic efficiency is not the only criterion. Account must also be taken of human and social objectives, even when these may not easily be compatible with economic efficiency. Sound adjustment policies are concerned with finding the best balance between the pursuit of economic and social goals.

But what is the nature and size of present needs for adjustment? What is new? Adjustment has, of course, always been with us. The machinery of the industrial revolution, the harnessing of steam and electricity, the invention of the gasoline engine, all necessitated substantial adjustment—

and, at least in the nineteenth century, with little help from the state or employers to affected workers. The answer would seem to be, first, that OECD countries are currently passing through a period marked by changed trading patterns, volatile energy prices, a noteworthy shift from manufacturing to services, more extensive product differentiation, and a new international division of labor that, together with other things, has had damaging effects on some of the long-established industries of the old industrialized countries, notably steel, textiles, shipbuilding, motor vehicles, and coal mining. Second, countries are having to accommodate a particularly rapid and pervasive wave of technological change. Third, the changes are taking place against a background of generally modest economic growth and, for many countries, unemployment levels far beyond those usual before the late 1970s. (Adjustment is clearly easier in times of high growth and low unemployment).

There is nothing to suggest that the kinds of changes that have been taking place are temporary, or transitory. Nor are they, overall, undesirable. Structural change has been a necessary feature of the historical growth in real output and improved living standards, and reallocation of labor is essential if economic growth and new job creation are to result in a significant reduction in unemployment. Lastly, our societies have evolved to a point at which the state is expected to facilitate industrial activity and at which it is simply unacceptable that people should be left to struggle unaided against adversities resulting from the play of markets. Effective and equitable adjustment raises a whole range of issues for the employing enterprise, the state, and for trade unions. The policies and procedures followed are, and should be, complementary but the mix varies appreciably between countries. Here, I shall deal first with what happens in the enterprise and then with the range of possible policies.

II. Employment Adjustment: Three Models

Whenever people work together at a common task, be it in a private company, a publicly owned enterprise, or a service of the state, it is a managerial responsibility to ensure that the nature, quantity, and quality of labor is such as may best help to achieve the goals of the organization. However, labor is not a mere commodity: the conditions for its employment are restricted and many of them must be negotiated, the skill mix of the labor force cannot be varied very much at short notice, and both for human reasons and because the skills and experience acquired over time are, in the great majority of cases, of continuing value to the employer,

Oliver Clarke

employment is normally regarded as being for an indefinite term. Obviously, the optimal labor requirement will vary according to the nature of the product or service the enterprise provides. Within these parameters there is scope for a considerable variety of personnel policies, including policies for adjustment, and certainly there is appreciable variation in the policies followed in different industries and enterprises within countries. However, what are noteworthy and significant for the purposes of this paper are the differences in practice between countries. Three markedly different models may be distinguished, the American, the Japanese, and the European—though there are, as will be seen, substantial variations among European countries.

The main characteristics of the *American* model are as follows. People cannot count on having a job for life. The United States is a land of opportunities; people should seize them whenever they present themselves. The employer is free to dismiss workers who no longer meet his/her needs, often with as little as a week's notice.[1] Employers can and do transfer their operations from one part of the country to another as the principle of net advantage suggests. The external labor market is valued at least as highly as the internal labor market. The law offers little protection from dismissals and states that enact protection might face a falling off of investment. The greatest formal job security, outside public service, has been in the long-established unionized industries—though it is this very sector, or at least much of it, that has borne the brunt of the large-scale labor force reductions of recent years.

There are, of course, many variations in what actually happens in the United States in respect to job security. A number of federal and state laws afford workers some help when they lose their jobs, the most important being the Trade Adjustment Assistance Program established under the Trade Act of 1974. There are enterprises like IBM that pride themselves on not dismissing workers for economic reasons and so far have been largely successful in doing so. There is continuing debate about how to deal with plant closures and the Labor Department encourages avoidance of dismissals and promotes a code of good practice when dismissals are unavoidable.[2] The emphasis of public policy is on helping workers who are displaced, rather than protecting them from dismissal. Lest it be thought that the tenure of American jobs is always brief it is worthwhile mentioning that, to cite 1983 figures, average job tenure for all persons in the United States was 7.2 years (for comparison the corresponding figure for Japan was 11.7 years [1982 figures], whereas the figures for seven European countries ranged from 7.1 to 9.9 years [some of which statistics related to years earlier than 1983]) (OECD, 1984a, p. 56).

The characteristics of *Japanese* enterprise manpower practices I take to be as follows. Large enterprises, and smaller ones insofar as they can, seek to offer employment with the expectation that once engaged the male worker—though not the female—is likely to stay indefinitely, even to retirement. Second, though individual ability will be reflected in opportunities for promotion and increasing pay, as a general rule, workers can expect their earnings to progress with years of service in the enterprise. Third, the necessary flexibility to meet changes in required output is obtained partly by control of recruitment, overtime work, and retirement but largely by use of subcontractors who themselves are commonly unable to assure long-term employment. Fourth, the extent to which women workers commonly leave the enterprise on marriage, after relatively few years service, presents another aid to adjustment. Fifth, half-yearly bonus payments, at least in part related to profitability, form a substantial element of overall earnings. Last, the highly developed consultative practices of Japanese enterprises delay decisions on employment adjustment, as they do other decisions, but at the same time ensure more considered and generally acceptable decisions, which then can be implemented rapidly.

There are some useful concomitants to this pattern. First, recruitment tends to be much more careful than would be the case if workers were being sought on a short-term basis. Second, reliance on the internal labor market presupposes training and retraining to satisfy the need of the enterprise for different skills, as opposed to recruiting workers who have nationally recognized qualifications. Third, insofar as organizational or technological change is not likely to have adverse effects on employment or wage, workers willingly accept it. Fourth, workers' futures being so directly linked with the success of the enterprise has a motivating effect. Advantages of Japanese practice lie in the high level of development of the internal labor market, making for greater versatility, readiness to accept change, and commitment to the objectives of the enterprise on the part of the workforce. The main disadvantages are the difficulty of adjusting numbers and types of workers to meet changing requirements and the necessity of retaining an accumulation of less competent workers.

European practice in employment adjustment, while differing considerably between countries, lies between American and Japanese practices. Insofar as one can generalize, European countries have increasingly, over the postwar years, made dismissal more costly, and provided income, job search support, and sometimes training, for laid-off workers. Special arrangements are now frequently made in conjunction with governments where the decline of an industry or a major enterprise has resulted in numerous dismissals. To summarize, European practice may broadly be characterized

Oliver Clarke

as humane but cumbersome, giving neither the flexibility of deployment of Japanese practice nor the easy and inexpensive (to the employer) adjustment of American practice.

III. Employment Adjustment and the Enterprise

Turning now to the enterprise, there are basically three responses to changing needs for labor: numerical flexibility, functional flexibility, and distancing.[3] *Numerical flexibility* refers to the volume of labor input; that is, the number of workers employed by the enterprise and the hours that they work. Changes in products or product functions are met by engaging or shedding labor, including replacing people whose skills are no longer required by other workers. *Functional flexibility* refers to the mix of skills required and the utilization of workers. It is basically an internal labor market approach. The emphasis is on making the best use of an existing labor force, training and retraining to meet changing skill requirements, and requiring considerable versatility and interchange of functions on the part of workers. *Distancing* refers to the practice of meeting fluctuating labor requirements by having work done outside the enterprise, either by a subcontractor or by self-employed workers, including workers working from their homes. It is essentially a device for putting much of the burden of fluctuations onto someone else.

Numerical Flexibility: Job Security

Adjusting the size of the labor force raises the issue of job security. Nearly all workers are dependent on work for income, to a considerable extent for standing in society, and to some extent for satisfaction and self-esteem. To have to change what they do for their employer, unless it results from promotion or desired transfer, is at least disturbing; it is worse if they have to seek new employment, lose seniority of service and fringe benefits, and perhaps have to move out of the area. With unemployment as high as it is now in most OECD countries, and current needs for structural and technological change, it becomes even more important to ask the questions: do we have too much, not enough, or the wrong type of security?

While discussion in the United State centers on doing more to help workers who are laid off, or who are likely to be laid off, notably when workplaces close, in Europe the debate is rather about whether job security has been taken too far, to the point of having adverse economic effects. Job security and help to those displaced have indeed been extended considerably in most European countries since the Second World War. Most of the improvements made have taken one or more of the following forms:

(a) Extended notice of dismissal, the length being commonly related to length of service;

(b) lump-sum payments to dismissed workers, the amount commonly being related to length of service;

(c) improved state unemployment benefits and continuing payments made under collective agreements to supplement them;

(d) requirement of the employer to consult with a works council or other workers' representatives when it seems that dismissals are likely to be necessary;

(e) requirement of the employer to secure authorization from a public agency before dismissals can take place;

(f) provisions to protect the employment of special groups, such as workers' representatives, disabled persons, and pregnant women; and

(g) rights to appeal against dismissal to an independent tribunal.

From the worker's point of view the benefits are clear. Lengthy notice gives time to find another job (and also gives public agencies more time to help). Lump sum payments (and continuing payments) help to make loss of a job more acceptable and to bridge the difficult time without a job, as well as recognizing the seriousness of the loss as measured by length of service. The requirement to consult enables workers both to suggest alternative courses of action that may have been overlooked by management and to consider with management how consequential social problems can be eased. The desirability of administrative authorization can be argued not only on the ground that the community has an interest in dismissals, particularly when a large number of workers are in danger of losing their jobs at the same time, but also on the ground of protection against arbitrary decisions. And the continued employment of vulnerable groups can be considered to deserve special protection. In such an important matter as loss of one's job it can be argued that a right of appeal to an impartial agency should be available as a matter of justice.

But valued as it is socially, the greater job protection built up over the postwar period can also be said to harm the competitiveness of enterprises by increasing operating costs. Labor costs become more of a fixed

Oliver Clarke

cost, reducing the flexibility of operation of the enterprise. Long periods of notice usually mean that the workers concerned are paid even if there is no work for them—and they have little incentive to work with enthusiasm during the period of notice. Severance payments and supplementary unemployment payments discourage the employer from dismissing workers for whom there is insufficient work, thereby reducing mobility. Insofar as some workers move directly into good jobs while others spend a long time without one, higher unemployment pay is arguably a more desirable option than lump sum payments. The requirement to consult a works council is not cost free; nor is the need to obtain authorization from a public agency. The protection of special groups may lead to the employment of a suboptimal labor force. So may application of the fairly commonly applied principle of selecting the workers with the least service for dismissal. Machinery for dealing with disputed dismissals is also, directly or indirectly, at least in part a charge on industry. The direct and administrative costs of dismissing people encourage employers to use temporary or self-employed workers rather than regular employees, thereby increasing segmentation of the labor market, and inclines employers to turn to capital-intensive as opposed to labor-intensive methods of production, which may increase unemployment. Job security for existing employees makes it more difficult for would-be entrants to the labor market to find jobs. The costs of job security, it can be argued, might have been bearable when there was little need to reduce employment, but are too heavy when large-scale reductions have to be made. Small firms may be particularly adversely affected by the costs, to the point that special dispensations should be granted to them. Last, a case can be made that if workforces were closer to the optimum, with a fluid labor market, competitiveness and hence ability to employ would be strengthened.

Apart from responding to a profound human need, however, job protection is widely considered to have benefits as well as costs to the employer. It is generally considered to be more efficient to work with a stable, integrated labor force than with a constantly changing labor force. If many workers stay only a short time the costs of recruitment, induction, and training become disproportionately large. Workers who feel secure—and that if their jobs are lost they will be fairly and generously treated—are likely to accept change more readily and to be more motivated and cooperative than workers who feel insecure. The various procedures intended to ensure that any dismissals are justified, by adding to workers' confidence that they will be fairly treated, also aid cooperativeness and decrease the likelihood of strikes.

224

It can also be argued that the real costs of job security to the employer are not as great as is sometimes claimed. If dismissal is costly, the employer will be more careful in recruitment, planning manpower policies on a long-term basis, and keeping and making better use of the existing labor force, retraining workers to meet new needs rather than seeking trained workers from outside. Established procedures discourage over-hasty decision making. Administrative authorization for dismissing workers is not often withheld if the dismissals are justified and, again, any delays give an opportunity for second thoughts.

The issue can perhaps be best addressed in terms of what combinations of arrangements can best satisfy four criteria:

(a) workers' natural desire to feel secure in their jobs;

(b) necessary provisions to minimize workers' fears of losing their jobs;

(c) the need for enterprises to decrease, as well as increase, their labor force to meet changing requirements; and

(d) the need for optimal labor mobility between and within enterprises.

These criteria are to some extent dependent on external factors. For example, if there is a ready supply of vacant and acceptable jobs, less fear is attached to the possibility of losing a job. If industry is expanding the costs of job security fall, because employers are less likely to reduce their labor force. The criteria are also to some extent interdependent. Thus, if there is a high degree of internal mobility within enterprises, there is likely to be less need for interenterprise mobility. If enterprises try to avoid dismissing workers, as is commonly the case in Japan, there may be less demand for measures to provide job protection or compensation for loss of job.

But how should job security be regulated? What combination of law and collective bargaining is desirable, and what should be left unregulated? The main advantage of legislation is its universality compared with the partial coverage afforded by collective bargaining. The disadvantage is its relative inflexibility compared with the sensitivity of collective bargaining to the particular needs of different industries and enterprises. A further, to some extent related, problem area is "who pays"—how the costs of adjustment are to be shared between employers, workers, and the community. Views will vary on this, but there would be widespread agreement that the desired structural change should not be achieved at the sole expense of the workers concerned.

Oliver Clarke

Numerical Flexibility: Working Time

A second way of adjusting the volume of employment in an enterprise is through the changing duration of work. There has been a fairly steady decline in weekly and annual hours worked over more than a century. The usual rationale for reduction has been workers' desire for more leisure. The recent reductions (which have largely been confined to Europe—there has been little change in North America) have, to some extent, been a reaction to high unemployment, with trade unions arguing that shorter hours would create more jobs. Annual working hours do, of course, vary across countries, as table 1 demonstrates.

One of the most interesting recent developments in Europe is a loosening up of traditional restrictions on working time. A degree of flexibility of individual working hours, "flexitime," is not new. Where the requirements of the work permitted, it was quite widely developed in the early 1970s on the basis of a core time observed by all workers in the plant

TABLE 1
STANDARD ANNUAL HOURS OF WORK AS PROVIDED
BY COLLECTIVE AGREEMENTS, AS OF NOVEMBER 1986

Country	Annual Hours
United States	1,912
Japan	2,156
Germany	1,708
France	1,771
Great Britain	1,778
Italy	1,776
Sweden	1,792
Belgium	1,748
Netherlands	1,740
Switzerland	1,913

Source: German Employers' Confederation: Internationale sozialpolitik, 18 November 1986. For statistical qualifications see the original.

Note: Since this table was prepared there have been further movements in working time. In Germany, important agreements were reached in the metal industry in the Spring of 1990, providing a phased reduction toward a 35-hour week, and in the British engineering industry the unions gained reductions in some major firms. In Japan the Labor Standard Law was amended in April 1988, setting a 46-hour working week and extending paid vacations to a minimum of ten days (previously six days). The Law also envisaged adaptation of a 40-hour week by 1993. Average yearly hours worked in all industries in Japan fell to 2,088 hours in 1989 and the government has decided that the figure should be reduced to 1,800 hours by the year 2000.

with a measure of freedom outside the core, all within a framework requiring the agreed working hours to be attained over a fixed settlement period such as a month. More recently, however, there has been a liberalization of traditional constraints. Faced with calls for reduced hours, employers have responded that if competitiveness is not to suffer they must be paid for. One way of affording reduced working hours is to ensure that working time fits the needs of production more closely and makes better use of plant and equipment. Thus, an enterprise that always has a heavy work load at the end of the week could work longer hours at that time without paying overtime premiums, provided that shorter hours were worked at another time. Or weekly hours could be varied between different departments of an enterprise, according to the work load, provided that the hours worked over a fixed period of settlement conformed to the agreed standard. Yet another form of flexibility could be where an enterprise is permitted to work one shift of four weekdays and another of two weekend days plus a weekday, the shifts, say, being remunerated equally. All of these ideas have gained currency in the last few years. At the same time, an increasing distinction is being made between employee working hours and plant utilization or production hours, using part-time workers to ensure more intensive use of plant and equipment. Where new methods of arranging working time have come into conflict with legal restrictions, governments have shown themselves willing to ease the restrictions, within certain limits, at least if employers and unions agree on so doing. Thus the Belgian government, originally using a special powers provision, specifically authorized experiments in working time, provided that the conditions were agreed between management and unions. In another field, the restrictions commonly placed on night work by women, in accordance with ILO Convention No. 89, are also being reconsidered in some countries.

The Belgians had already used reduction of working time as a means of attacking their high unemployment (Tuchszirer 1986) on the basis of what became known as the 5:3:3 formula; that is to say, a 5% reduction in working time accompanied by the engagement of 3% new labor, with the cost to be partly funded by offsetting 3% from wage increases. If the employer could not meet the requirement for new engagements he was required to pay his savings, due to the wage offset, into a national fund for employment.

France, too, has moved toward greater flexibility in working time. The Ordonnance of January 1982, reducing the statutory working week from forty to thirty-nine hours also introduced a measure of flexibility concerning variations in the agreed weekly working hours and overtime and Sunday

227

working. A law of 1987 provided further flexibility, largely based on the terms of an agreement reached in the engineering industry in July 1986.

In *Germany*, the chief example of flexibility resulted from the agreements made in the metals industry in 1984, after the greatest strike in postwar German history (Bosch 1986). These agreements transferred responsibility for deciding the modalities of working time from the regional-industry level to the enterprise level. They authorized considerable flexibility over time and between sections provided that the new working week, of 38 1/2 hours, was met over a fairly lengthy period of settlement.

A central agreement of 1982 in the *Netherlands*, associated a return to profitability and a reduction of working time and additional flexibility. As in Belgium, wage increases were waived by workers in consideration of the reduction in working hours. A feature of the Dutch discussion of working time has been an insistence that reduction should be coupled with better utilization of productive facilities.

Overtime Working

Overtime working has, of course, always been used as a means of varying working time to meet peak needs, as well as for effecting necessary maintenance and dealing with breakdowns. Its systematic use for general production purposes has always been deprecated but, even with high unemployment, considerable overtime is by no means unusual since workers are commonly glad to have the opportunity to earn extra money while employers, even with premiums to be paid, often find overtime cheaper than engaging new workers. Overtime working is, however, limited by law or collective agreement in most European countries and in some, for instance Greece, Italy, and the Netherlands, administrative authorization is required for it.

Temporary Lay-Offs and Short-Time Working

Another form of employment adjustment is to reduce working time either by laying off workers for a period or by operating a working week of, say, four days, with a corresponding adjustment of pay. The term layoff, incidentally, needs to be used carefully since without the adjective "temporary" it is often interpreted in British usage as dismissal while in American usage it is likely to signify a cessation of work but without severing the contract of employment and probably retaining seniority rights.

Temporary layoff and short-time working are "a means of reducing the level of labor input in the short term without necessarily affecting the size or capabilities of the workforce available to the firm when economic conditions improve" (Grais 1983, p. 7). From the employer's point of view both avoid the cost of dismissals and subsequent recruitment, and they enable the enterprise to keep together a trained labor force, familiar with the work and representing a considerable investment. The inattraction depends on whether the cut back of activity is expected to be brief or long term, which cannot always, of course, be known in advance. If the external labor market is tight, the employer may wish to keep his labor force together as far as possible (though in this case good workers may leave anyway rather than take a cut in earnings); if unemployment is high, so that new labor is easy to come by, the employer may prefer to dismiss workers. Another factor influencing a decision between temporary layoff and different forms of short time working is the incidence of unemployment or other social security benefits. Provided they get the working time input they need, employers are likely to adopt the form of reduced time that ensures the highest benefit from public funds for their employees.

The short-time alternative is open to considerable variation. Thus Hansen reports a case in Colorado of rotating layoffs, whereby job slots on maintenance work were filled every two months, over a continuing period of eight months, by a different set of employees, with the remainder receiving unemployment benefits (Hansen 1986, p. 19). In France, in the autumn of 1986, the Minister of Labor suggested that enterprises experiencing reduced demand might split their present labor force into two half-time shifts, each group receiving half of their normal wage from the employer and an additional 20% of that wage from the national unemployment fund.

An interesting form of public support for laid-off workers is the Italian Earnings Supplement Fund (Cassa Integrazione Guadagni). Its objectives have been to give time for restructuring and to avoid dismissals by permitting derogation, in specific cases, from the basic requirement in Italian law that the employer should pay normal wages when workers are laid off or put on short time, and instead to provide a high level of compensation—in some cases indefinitely—to laid-off workers. The number of hours paid by the fund has increased steadily, reaching some 800 million in 1984. In the Federal Republic of Germany fairly high payments (Kurzarbeitgeld) are made to workers on short-time, subject to certain conditions.

Flexible Retirement

To a small extent employment adjustment can be effected by adjusting retirement age or by providing partial retirement. In the early days of industry, automatic retirement was rare. It was the introduction of national state pension schemes, usually, until recently, with a single standard age for entitlement (or one for men and a lesser one for women), later supported by occupational pension schemes adopting the same age, that led to a particular birthday ending most people's working life. This age was

Oliver Clarke

commonly sixty-five but until recently it was more in Scandinavia (it is still sixty-seven in Norway and sixty-six in Ireland) and less in a few (it is sixty in France, Italy [for males], and New Zealand). But the fixed retirement age has discouraged both the employment of people who reach the stated age with undiminished ability, vigor, and desire to continue working, and those who, for whatever reason, would like to leave paid employment early.

But the arbitrariness of fixed retirement ages has been breaking up in recent years, under the dual pressures of workers' desire for early retirement and the massive reduction of workforces, which has frequently led to help being given to workers so that they can afford to take early retirement and thereby lessen the burden of unemployment. The increasing propensity toward early retirement in the sixty to sixty-four year-old groups is shown in table 2. Note that the reduction in percentage points in the activity rates for these groups from 1970 to 1983 is over 16%—and as high as 34.5%—for eight of the twelve OECD countries covered.

Although in Europe standard retiring age is still tending to come down, in the United States, Congress has abolished compulsory retirement

TABLE 2
PARTICIPATION RATES OF MEN AGED 60–64
IN TWELVE OECD COUNTRIES, 1970–1983
(IN PERCENTAGES)

	1970	1975	1983	State pensionable age
Australia	77.4	68.6	42.9	65
Finland	65.0	53.1	44.3	65
France	68.0	56.7	33.6	60
Germany (Fed. Republic)	74.9	56.2	41.3	65
Italy[a]	85.2	85.7	82.0	60
Japan[b]	91.2	92.2	91.3	60
Netherlands	73.9[c]	64.9	42.3	65
Norway	70.9	66.9	60.2	67
Spain	77.7[d]	71.5	58.8	65
Sweden	78.7[e]	74.0	68.4[f]	65
United Kingdom	87.0	82.5	66.0	65
United States	71.7	64.5	55.5	65

Source: OECD "Labour Force Statistics."
[a] 50–59
[b] 55–59
[c] 1971
[d] 1972
[e] 1971
[f] 1982

230

on grounds of age for nearly everyone. Also, a variety of arrangements are now available in European countries to facilitate early retirement[4] or partial retirement (i.e., working a reduced working week for some time before final retirement). Early retirement programs have certainly eased situations where alternative employment opportunities for redundant older workers are limited, but they have usually proved a somewhat expensive form of adjustment, despite the offsetting savings on unemployment benefit payments.

Part-Time, Temporary, and Fixed-Term Employment

Another approach, offering considerable possibilities for varying labor input, is employing workers on other than full time and indefinite contracts. The extent of such forms of employment has increased widely in recent years, particularly part-time working, crudely defined for the present purpose simply as distinctly shorter hours compared with standard hours. Though statistics present some problems on account of differing national bases (OECD 1983a, pp. 101–3; 1987a, p. 29), table 3 gives an indication of the rise in the share of part-time in total employment for eight OECD countries.

The main reasons for the growth of part-time work are first the shift in the structure of the economy toward the service sector (many service occupations lending themselves to part-time working) and, second, the growth of the proportion of women in the labor force (many women being attracted by the possibility of part-time work). (Indeed, in eighteen OECD countries in 1981 the proportion of women part-time workers ranged between 63% and 94.3%) (OECD, 1983a, p. 44). Third, many employers have no doubt been influenced by the lower labor costs commonly associated with part-time workers, since frequently they do not have the same job protection or fringe benefits as full-time workers.[5] Lastly, a small but growing number of workers are involved in job sharing, commonly on systems of morning/afternoon, Monday–Wednesday/Wednesday–Friday, or alternate week working.[6] Interestingly, despite the lack of formal job security that part-time workers have, part-time employment in the aggregate seems to be more stable than full-time employment, though this is partly a compositional effect since the service sector is less affected by cyclical fluctuations than the goods-producing sector (OECD, 1983a, p. 45).

Statistics relating to temporary and fixed-term working are not advanced enough to permit full international comparison but it would seem that these forms too are growing (see OECD 1987a, p. 36 concerning temporary workers). They have been inhibited in some countries by legislation but some of the restrictions on them have recently been softened; for

TABLE 3
SHARE OF PART-TIME EMPLOYMENT IN TOTAL EMPLOYMENT 1973–83
(IN PERCENTAGES)

Year	Canada	France	Germany (Fed. Rep.)	Japan	Netherlands	Sweden	United Kingdom	United States
1973	12.4	5.1	7.7	13.6	4.4	16.2	15.3	14.3
1975	10.6	6.6	9.0	15.2	5.6	16.8	16.9	14.3
1977	11.7	7.3	9.6	14.2	5.9	18.6	16.9	14.5
1979	12.5	7.1	9.5	15.0	7.5	19.5	15.4	14.3
1981	13.5	7.4	10.2	15.3	19.4	20.2	15.4	14.3
1983	15.4	9.7	12.6	15.8	22.0	24.8	19.1	14.1
1986	15.6	11.7	12.3	—	24.0	23.5	21.2	—

Sources: de Neuburg, op. cit., and OECD, 1987a, p. 29 (qualifications given in originals).
Note: For Japan and Sweden part-time workers are shown as a percentage of employed persons actually at work during the reference week; for other countries, as a percentage of total employment.

example, in France a Decree of August 1986 lifted certain restrictions on the use of both forms and facilitated part-time and intermittent employment. On the other hand, a danger with part-time and temporary and fixed-term workers is that they may be employed under less favorable conditions than regular employees. Some countries have legislated to prevent this.

Functional Flexibility

Functional flexibility, the ability of enterprises to organize the deployment of workers to meet changing needs, has increased in importance in recent years. The most important reasons appear to be the increasing pressure on enterprises to provide a greater variety of products or services and to make changes in them more rapidly. Today's labor force must be able to deal with greater uncertainty. Second, skill boundaries are becoming increasingly blurred as a result of technological change, affecting both products and processes, and workers are deployed over a wider and less clearly defined range of tasks than in the past.

There are substantial differences between labor utilization practices in different countries. Probably no other OECD country can match Japan in the flexibility that it enjoys in its internal labor market. In the United States, it is still common to allot work on the basis of occupational categories, and within categories seniority of service often plays a substantial role. However, as U.S. Secretary of Labor Brock reported to a meeting of Labor Ministers in OECD countries in November 1986, there is a recent trend in the United States for companies "to shift away from rigidly defined occupational structures towards a broader skilled-defined genre of employment status and the modification of restrictive work rules. Employers are striving for fewer discrete job classifications in order to increase flexibility, decrease inefficiencies in coordinating work functions and improve overall job satisfaction."

In the United Kingdom and Ireland, there are still many parts of industry where particular work is regarded as "belonging" to a particular craft, occupation, or trade union, and it is not unusual for work to be held up because an operation is required that is the responsibility of someone other than the worker engaged on the job (who is probably perfectly capable of performing that operation), and nothing more is done on that job until the operation is performed. Manning levels are sometimes negotiated more according to the balance of bargaining power than as a function of efficient working.

In continental European countries, again the efficiency of adjustment within the enterprise varies, but it is still common for workers to be trained for specific nationally recognized trades or occupations, with a measure of

233

Oliver Clarke

variation of skills within a trade according to the work done in the enterprise. In Germany, apprenticeship and occupation are still highly structured but there is nevertheless considerable cooperation within the workplace to ensure efficient working. In Sweden the Codetermination at Work Act 1976 makes virtually all aspects of working life negotiable, in principle, but in practice employers have considerable freedom to deploy labor as efficiency may require.

Distancing

A further way in which enterprises make employment adjustment is by "distancing"—in effect having a contract for a product, operation, or service instead of a contract of employment. The objectives of distancing may be summarized as

- to meet peak production needs;

- to get work done more cheaply than it could be done in the enterprise;

- to avoid the cost of engaging additional labor;

- to concentrate effort on those tasks for which the enterprise has the greatest expertise or cost advantage;

- to restrain the size of the enterprise; and

- to reduce uncertainty about labor needs.

The most common form of distancing is, of course, subcontracting to other firms, but another quite old form is homeworking, which traditionally has mainly been used for making simple articles. Now it is increasingly being used, at least judging by British experience, for white-collar, service, and professional activities. The use of home computer terminals has facilitated "telework" (Empirica, in European Foundation 1986, pp. 89–99), with arrangements like Rank Xerox' "Networking" (Clutterbuck 1985, p. 53) and F International's computer operation, which employs more than 1,000 homeworkers, (Shirley 1986, pp. 127–36). Partly for tax reasons in some countries, there has been a growth in the use of independent workers who contract to do work for a fixed hourly payment or price per unit but who enjoy few of the rights and fringe benefits of normal employees.

Segmentation

The traditional enterprise in Western countries was commonly stratified, with its white-collar and blue-collar workers of various types and

234

degrees of skill and sometimes rigid demarcations concerned with who does what. Such classifications are still fairly common in Western countries but the divisions between them are blurring under the pressure of competition, rapid product changes, and technological change. The more skilled workers, notably, are being required to exercise a broad range of skills. Maintenance and inspection functions are increasingly built into job designs. Increasingly too, tasks are being allotted to groups of workers, to divide as the group thinks fit. And many jobs can no longer clearly be characterized as blue- or white-collar work.

But as old distinctions are fading there are signs of a new grouping, though it is still vague, is rarely overt, and has not yet been effectively measured. The concept of the dual labor market, of a class of relatively secure and well-paid, mostly skilled workers, and another of workers less skilled, on poorer pay and tending to move from job to job, is not new (Doeringer and Piore 1971). But now, under pressure of change and uncertainty, a tendency seems to be emerging for enterprises to build a stable "core" labor force of multiskilled, versatile workers enjoying good pay and relatively secure employment, with the rest of the work being done by a "periphery" of workers on jobs needing skills that are readily available in the external labor market and affording little autonomy, or being put outside the enterprise.[7] Core workers stay, the number of peripheral workers varies according to demand. Core workers are expected to be motivated and to feel commitment to the enterprise, which may not be the case with the peripheral workers. Core workers receive training as needed within the enterprise; peripheral workers get little attention. Peripheral workers' chances of achieving core status are often slim. Some people prefer peripheral work because their main life-interests lie outside employment but many ar engaged in it because they could find no other work. Such arrangements respond to some present and likely future needs for efficient operation. They seem likely to grow but their present extent should not be exaggerated. Should they grow, consideration may have to be given to softening distinctions at the workplace and providing ladders of promotion. The implications for trade union membership and policies also deserve attention.

IV. Policies for Adjustment

A century ago the role of the state in relation to employment adjustment was minimal. Governments might ban or tax imports to protect industries or firms that were no longer competitive, but there were few attempts to influence adjustment or to help workers who lost their jobs. During the twentieth century, however, the role of the state has steadily increased (even without considering the special case of wartime). Particularly with the extensive job losses of recent years, it has come to be considered that since society as a whole expects to profit from structural change, society should bear its share of the costs and that workers who are disadvantaged through no fault of their own should be compensated. The tests for aid programs are that they should seek to assure rapid re-employment and that, while maintaining equity vis-à-vis all workers in need, they should be targeted to help those worst affected. A whole range of policies has come into play. Some of these policies belong mainly to the domains of economic, industrial, fiscal, and social policies. More narrowly, the relevant policies may be summarized as being concerned with

(a) *Maintenance and Creation of Jobs*
- General subsidies or loans to help continued operation of an enterprise.
- Selective employment subsidies.
- Direct job creation policies—both general and targeted to help particular groups.

(b) *Regulation of Dismissal*
- Requirement for advance warning or notice.
- Requirement for a social plan.
- Early retirement.

(c) *Help to Workers Dismissed or Laid Off*
- Job search services.
- Relocation assistance.
- Redundancy payments.
- Unemployment benefits.
- Training and retraining facilities.

The following discussion concentrates on the relevance of such policies to the kind of major displacement that has been a feature of recent shifts in industrial structure.

Of policies concerned with the *maintenance of jobs* it is sufficient to say that opinion in the West has moved against the direct propping up of industries and enterprises of doubtful viability, though it is still done where it is deemed particularly important from the point of view of national interest, or, on a short-term basis, to provide time to deal with the social problems involved. Given time, internal restructuring can be carried out to some extent. The problem with many recent run-downs is that the enterprises affected have not had the capability to restructure. There are a few cases where enterprises in difficulty have been bought out by management or have become worker cooperatives, but the success rate of such endeavors does not appear to have been high.

Selective employment subsidies and public job creation programs belong to the more general domain of responses to unemployment and cannot be discussed here, except to mention the particularly interesting development whereby some, mainly large, industries and enterprises have established facilities for helping their redundant employees to set up their own businesses, and the equally interesting case where communities have set about creating enterprises and jobs for their unemployed citizens (OECD 1985a, 1986e).

The *regulation of dismissal* starts with requirements for *advance warning or notice*, already discussed above. Of relevance here are the internationally applicable OECD Guidelines, International Investment and Multi-national Enterprises (Revised edition, Paris, OECD, 1984) which state:

> In considering changes in their operations which would have major effects upon the livelihood of their employees, in particular in the case of the closure of an entity involving collective lay-offs or dismissals, (enterprises should) provide reasonable notice of such changes to representatives of their employees, and where appropriate to the relevant government authorities, and cooperate with the employee representatives and appropriate governmental authorities so as to mitigate to the maximum extent practicable adverse effects.

Public policy since the war, at least in Europe, has been to lengthen periods of notice (OECD 1986c, pp. 91–114). In the United States a number of congressional and state measures have been promoted to this end, without much success.[8] There are provisions concerning notice in a number of collective agreements (Harrison 1984). In European countries having statutory works councils, duties have commonly been laid on the employer to consult about the handling of dismissals and what can be done to help displaced workers. (There is usually no duty to negotiate the decision to dismiss.) There are, of course, many collectively bargained provisions concerning dismissals. In France and Germany, as in Japan, enterprises are required to work out a "social plan" with workers' representatives, dealing with how displaced workers can be helped. While the postwar trend was toward strengthening job protection, there has recently been a small movement the other way, with France, Germany, Italy, and Spain, for instance, all relaxing their earlier provisions, in ways such as excluding small enterprises or short-service workers.

Early retirement has already been discussed above. *Job search services* and to some extent *relocation assistance* are standard forms of aid to anyone seeking employment. They are often strengthened in cases of major dismissals, with efforts being made to plan with each worker how new employment can be secured. Arrangements made may involve opening a temporary office of public employment services at the workplace and giving workers time off to attend job interviews. Relocation assistance may extend to finance sale and purchase of houses.

Redundancy payments—lump sum payments by employers to workers no longer needed—are found in some European countries (EIRR 1980). Some collective agreements provide such benefits on top of statutory benefits. Payments are sometimes related to length of service, and age may also be a factor, on the ground that it is more difficult for older workers to find work. In the United States, a number of major collective agreements provide lump sum and/or continuing payments to redundant workers. The intentions of such payments are first to help the displaced workers and, second, to make it easier for the employer to reduce his/her labor force when there is not enough work. Redundancy payments have been effective in both respects but they do not take account, as continuing unemployment benefits do, of the different time needed by different workers to find work. A variant on declared redundancy payment is to offer lump sum cash inducements to anyone—or anyone in specified categories—who will volunteer to leave. A parallel to redundancy payments as an aid to reducing the labor force is to be found in the payments made available, at least in France and Germany, to immigrant workers to encourage them, in a time of high unemployment, to go back to their own countries.

Unemployment benefits have a social justification in themselves but from the point of view of adjustment they can be regarded as providing income support during job search and during *training or retraining courses*—though where courses are followed the allowances paid may be higher and paid for longer. OECD work on training programs in relation to employment suggests that there is often a lack of knowledge of such programs among potential beneficiaries. Counseling is needed from local labor market officials who know about the likely availability of jobs. Provision of training programs is not very flexible, given the time and investment needed to set them up: in this connection the utilization of idle facilities in local firms has proved useful. Workers' preference has tended to be for on-the-job rather than classroom training. Selection of workers for retraining programs at public expense does raise questions of equity vis-à-vis other unemployed workers.

V. Comparison of Approaches

As stated earlier, in OECD countries there are basically three different approaches to—one might better say three different philosophies about—employment adjustment; the American, the Japanese, and the European. We are fortunate in having a careful comparison of American and Japanese practice (Orr, Shimada, and Seike 1985). In the United States, this study (ibid. pp. 9–10) noted that adjustment relies on layoffs, some in conjunction with plant shutdowns. The authors found limited communication and information sharing on future plans of employment adjustment and restructuring of corporate activities. There were quick and large-scale shifts of capital resources in the form of shutting down unprofitable plants, building new plants, acquiring new firms, and the like. Income maintenance was found to be well developed. Japanese experience, on the other hand, was characterized, at least for large firms in major industries, by minimum resort to layoffs or dismissals; reduction of employment was carried out only sluggishly, when unavoidable. Reducing overtime and part-time and temporary workers; halting recruitment; and moderating wage increases were used to lower labor costs. There were extensive transfers of workers within and between the company's plants and even between companies. Employers attempted to maintain employees on the payroll as much as possible, even though they might be temporarily idle, and sought to prepare them for other work by retraining. Government policies supported these efforts, including assistance to employers to facilitate the conversion of their business to new lines of operation (ibid. p. 18).

Orr, Shimada, and Seike (1985) found differences between the two countries in how the costs of adjustment were shared, but no great difference in terms of efficiency associated with resource allocation. On the impact on workers they considered that in the United States the burden tended to be concentrated on youths and newcomers to the labor market, while in Japan it was shared relatively by older workers and female secondary workers. Lastly, they saw the greater participation and information sharing in the adjustment process in Japan as making for slower but smoother adjustment than in the United States. The study also noted that the Japanese system of communication and information sharing was well developed for the core labor force of large firms in major industries but that part-time and subcontract workers were not integrated into this system and that the system was less developed for small firms and for peripheral industries.

To add a European element to this comparison, insofar as it is possible to generalize from so many diverse countries, it appears that European workers have much greater apparent job protection than American workers—though what they have is not a great deal of help to them if their enterprise collapses. They have less real security than Japanese workers in large enterprises. A large variety of publicly funded assistance programs are available to them. The costs of adjustments are shared between workers, employers, and the state but core workers, as a whole, bear less of the cost than other workers. European workers, at least in the countries that have works councils or other institutional forms of participation, generally enjoy more information and consultation than is usual in American enterprises and probably something like as much as Japanese workers. The adjustment process is slower and more expensive to the employer than in the United States but probably quicker than in Japan. The barriers to rapid action in Europe are such that enterprises are typically much less able than American enterprises to react quickly to needs for change.

Which system is best? What can profitably be learned from one country by another concerning employment adjustment? There is certainly no single "best" system. Each has its merits and drawbacks, and each is deeply rooted in a set of national traditions and values. It is well known that institutions and practices do not transplant easily. However, examination of other countries' practices certainly helps to provide a perspective on one's own. Comparison with the United States has been a potent factor in promoting new thinking about the adequacy of adjustment processes in Europe, and European protection for workers is widely cited by advocates of greater job security in the United States. Japanese practice, nowadays, is regarded elsewhere as having much to teach.

Insofar as trends are concerned, it seems clear that the countries considered are not exactly moving in the same direction. In the United States there is a slight movement toward doing more to alleviate the human costs of adjustment. In Europe there is a tendency toward re-examining existing obstacles to ready adjustment but, at the same time, at least in some countries, a readier recognition is emerging of the human problems caused by major job losses in industries or enterprises, and how to respond to them. For Japan, one wonders how much "lifetime employment" owes to the almost continuous economic growth over the last thirty-five years, during which large-scale dismissals were rarely necessary, and whether that practice can hold with the new level of the yen,[9] higher domestic costs relative to some competitor countries, and the worldwide decline in several industries. But countries also differ in the speed and care with which they face and adapt to new or enlarged problems. And in these respects, too, Japan seems likely to be in the forefront of progress.

240

Notes

1. A recent General Accounting Office survey found that 34% of larger establishments gave individual notice to blue-collar workers of two weeks or less. A section of the Trade Bill proposed, in 1987, more ample periods of notice.
2. See Hansen, 1986; and U.S. Department of Labor, 1982 and 1983.
3. This categorization has been developed in the Institute of Manpower Studies in the University of Sussex, England. See, for their elaboration, John Atkinson, "The Changing Corporation," in Clutterbuck, (1985) and John Atkinson, "Employment Flexibility in Internal and External Labour Markets," in European Foundation (1986). For a forceful criticism see A. Pollert, "The 'Flexible Firm': A Model in Search of Reality or a Policy in Search of a Practice?" Warwick Papers in Industrial Relations, no. 190, Industrial Relations Research Unit, Warwick, December 1987.
4. For a five-country international comparison see European Industrial Relations Review (1985).
5. For a review of conditions see "Part-time work in 15 countries," in European Industrial Relations Review (1985).
6. See J. Epstein, "Issues in Job Sharing," in European Foundation (1986).
7. For a fuller review of segmentation see John Atkinson, "Employment Flexibility in Internal and External Labour Markets," in European Foundation (1986).
8. A difficult debate on layoffs in the context of the mammoth Trade Bill of 1987–88 ended in the passage of a stand-alone bill in 1988, though the effects of this measure are hardly substantial.
9. See Koshiro (1990).

References

Addison, John (1986). "Job Security in the United States: Law, Collective Bargaining, Policy and Practice," *British Journal of Industrial Relations*, November.

Blanpain, R., ed. (1980). "Job Security and Industrial Relations," *Bulletin of Comparative Labour Relations No. 11*, Kluwer, Deventer, Netherlands.

Blyton, Paul. "Changes in Working Time"; Croom Helm, London, 1985.

Bosch, Gerhard (1986). "The Dispute over the Reduction of the Working Week in West Germany," *Cambridge Journal of Economics*, p. 10.

Clutterbuck, R., ed. (1985). *New Patterns of Work*; London: Gower.

Clutterbuck, R., and Hill (1981). *The Re-making of Work*, London: Grant McIntyre.

Cross, Michael., ed. (1985). *Managing Workforce Reduction; an International Survey*, London: Croom Helm.

Doeringer, Peter B., and Michael J. Piore (1971). *Internal Labour Markets and Manpower Analysis*, Lexington, Mass.: Heath.

Oliver Clarke

European Foundation for the Improvement of Living and Working Conditions (1986). "New Forms of Work and Activity," Dublin: The Foundation.

European Industrial Relations Review (1980). "Dismissals and Redundancy Pay in 10 Countries," *EIRR*, no. 75, April.

——— (1985a). "Early Retirement: An International Comparison," *EIRR*, December.

——— (1985b). "Part-time Work in 15 Countries," *EIRR*, June.

Gennard, John (1979). *Job Security and Industrial Relations*, Paris: OECD.

Grais, B. (1983). *Lay-Offs and Short-Time Working in Selected OECD Countries*, Paris: OECD.

Gray, H. P., T. Putel, and I. Walter (1986). *International Trade, Employment and Structural Adjustment*, Geneva: ILO.

Gutchess, J. F. (1985). *Employment Security in Action: Strategies that Work*, New York: Pergamon.

Hakim, C. (1984a). "Employers' Use of Homework, Outwork and Freelancers, *Employment Gazette*, April.

——— (1984b). "Homework and Outwork: National Estimates from Two Surveys;" *Employment Gazette*, January.

Handy, C. (1984). *The Future of Work*, Oxford: Blackwell.

Hansen, Gary B. (1986). *Preventing Layoffs: Developing an Effective Job Security and Economic Adjustment Program*, Washington, D.C.: U.S. Department of Labor.

Harrison, Bennet (1984). "The International Movement for Prenotification of Plant Closures," *Industrial Relations*, vol. 23, n. 3.

Hooks, Gregory (1984). "The Policy Response to Factory Closings: a Comparison of the United States, Sweden and France." *Annals of the American Academy of Political and Social Science*, vol. 475, September.

Koshiro, K. (1985). "Job Security: Redundancy Arrangements and Practices in Japan," mimeo, Yokohama: Yokohama National University. January 1985.

——— (1990). "Labor Market Flexibility and Work Organization—Expert's Report on Japan," Paris: OECD, Conference of Experts, 17–19 September.

McKersie, R. B., and W. Sengenberger (1983). *Job Losses in Major Industries: Manpower Strategy Responses*, Paris: OECD.

Meyers, Frederic (1964). *Ownership of Jobs: A Comparative Study*, Los Angeles: University of California Press.

National Economic Development Office (NEDO) *Changing Working Patterns: How Companies Achieve Flexibility to Meet New Needs*; London: NEDO.

de Neubourg, Chris (1985). "Part-time Work: an International Quantitative Comparison," *International Labour Review*, September–October.

OECD (1977). *Structural Determinants of Employment and Unemployment*, vol. 1, Paris: OECD.

——— (1979a). *The Case for Positive Adjustment Policies*, a compendium of OECD documents, 1978–79, Paris: OECD.

——— (1979b). *Structural Determinants of Employment and Unemployment*, vol. 2, Paris: OECD.

——— (1983a). *Employment Outlook*, September, Paris.

——— (1983b). *Positive Adjustment Policies: Managing Structural Change*, Paris: OECD.

——— (1984a). *Employment Outlook*, September, Paris.

——— (1984b). *Positive Adjustment in Manpower and Social Policies*, Paris: OECD.

——— (1985a). *Creating Jobs at the Local Level*, Paris: OECD.

——— (1985b). *Employment Growth and Structural Change*, Paris: OECD.

——— (1985c). *Employment Outlook*, September, Paris.

——— (1986a). *Employment Outlook*, September, Paris.

——— (1986b). Centre for Educational Research and Innovation (CERI), "The Evolution of New Technology, Work and Skills in the Service Sector," mimeo, general distribution, Paris: OECD.

——— (1986c). *Flexibility in the Labour Market: The Current Debate*, Paris: OECD.

——— (1986d). Centre for Educational Research and Innovation (CERI), "New Technology and Human Resource Development in the Automobile Industry," mimeo, general distribution, Paris: OECD.

——— (1986e). *The Role of Towns and Cities in Job Creation*, Paris: OECD.

——— (1987). *Employment Outlook*, September, Paris.

Orr, J. A., H. Shimada, and A. Seike (1985). *United States-Japan Comparative Study of Employment Adjustment*, Washington, D.C.: Department of Labor.

Piore, M. (1986). "Perspectives on Labor Market Flexibility," *Industrial Relations*, vol. 25, no. 2, Spring.

Renshaw, G. T. (1986). *Adjustment and Economic Performance in Industrialized Countries: A Synthesis*, Geneva: ILO.

Robertson, James (1985). *Future Work: Jobs, Self-Employment and Leisure after the Industrial Age*, New York: Universe Books.

Schatz, K. W., and F. Wolter (1987). *Structural Adjustment in the Federal Republic of Germany*, Geneva: ILO.

Sharp, M., and G. Shepherd (1987). *Managing Change in British Industry*, Geneva: ILO.

Shirley, Steve (1986). "A Company without Offices," *Harvard Business Review*, January–February.

Strath, Bo (1986). "Redundancy and Solidarity: Tripartite Politics and Contraction of the West European Shipbuilding Industry," *Cambridge Journal of Economics*, 10:147–63.

Summers, Gene F., ed. (1985). "Deindustrialization: Restructuring the Economy," *Annals of the American Academy of Political and Social Science*, vol. 475, September.

Tuchszirer, Carole (1986). "L'Amenagement du Temps de Travail en Belgique," *Travail et Emploi*, June.

Oliver Clarke

U.S. Department of Labor (1983) *Plant Closing Checklist: a Guide to Best Practice*, Washington, D.C.: Department of Labor.
—— (1982). *Plant Closings: What can be learned from Best Practice*, Washington, D.C.: Department of Labor.
Wilkes, John (1981). *The Future of Work*, Sydney: George Allen and Unwin.
Work in America Institute (1984). *Employment Security in a Free Economy*, New York: Pergamon.
Yemin, E., ed. (1982). *Workforce Reductions in Undertakings: Policies and Measures for the Protection of Redundant Workers in Seven Industrialized Market Economy Countries*, Geneva: International Labour Office.

Atsushi Seike

10

The Employment Adjustment Patterns of Japan and the United States

I. Introduction

The aim of this paper is to compare and evaluate the employment adjustment patterns of Japan and the United States. The economies of both Japan and the United States have undergone substantial structural changes in recent years as a result of the expansion and liberalization of international trade, the oil crisis, the introduction of new technologies, and various other changes affecting a broad spectrum of products and industries. Naturally, these structural changes have been accompanied by the need to reallocate human resources; that is, the need for employment adjustments.

Although Japan and the United States have had to wrestle with the same basic employment adjustment problems, they appear to differ in the methods they used and the success they achieved in coping with such adjustments. Figure 1 illustrates the relationship between economic growth and unemployment in the United States and Japan between 1961 and 1983. It can be seen that fluctuations in the annual rate of economic growth in the United States have been transmitted to the unemployment rate relatively quickly. Also, the unemployment rate in the United States, regardless of the prevailing growth rate, has been considerably higher than that in Japan. These differences in the aggregate relationship between unemployment and

FIGURE 1
THE RELATIONSHIPS BETWEEN ECONOMIC GROWTH AND UNEMPLOYMENT

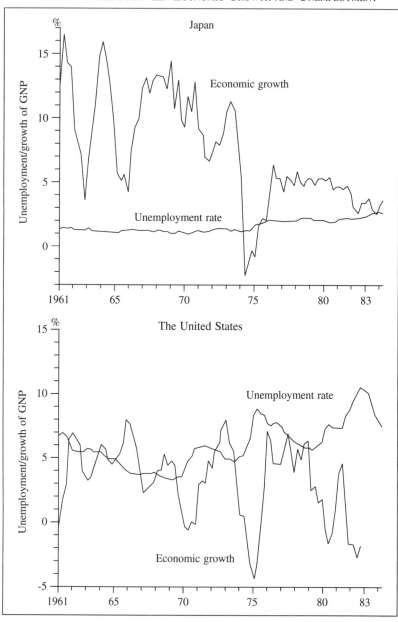

economic growth seem to suggest that firms in Japan differ from those in the United States in the way they adjust employment in response to changes in production.

Since labor is employed only to produce output, our goal when analyzing employment adjustment is to find the relationship between output and employment. The comparative analysis of employment adjustment attempted below is restricted to manufacturing industries because they are the only industries for which we are able to observe an employment-output relationship that is stable enough to permit rigorous analysis.

The organization of this paper is as follows. Section II illustrates the basic pattern of employment adjustment in the two countries and discusses the various costs of employment adjustment that may help to explain differences in the pattern. In section III, an econometric analysis is presented that attempts to measure employment adjustment costs in Japan and the United States. Section IV discusses the employment adjustment practices that lie behind differences in the employment/output relationship observed between Japan and the United States. Finally, by comparing the different employment adjustment measures used, an attempt is made to evaluate the employment adjustment performance of the two countries in terms of their efficiency in reallocating human resources.

The main arguments relate to the different employment adjustments experienced in Japan and the United States. Basically, employment adjustment takes place at a slower rate in Japan than in the United States and overtime hours are also more sensitive to production changes in Japan than in the United States.

Further, firms cannot clear excess labor instantly and only a certain proportion of the excess labor can be made redundant. The relatively low labor "shake out" in Japan is related to the ideas of reallocation and transfer to subsidiaries. In addition, the role of the state in labor subsidies will be investigated and an assessment will be made of the merits of an unemployment *prevention* system such as Japan's in relation to a system such as that prevailing in the United States, which is designed to cope with unemployment *after* it occurs.

II. Fluctuations in Employment and Output

1. Trends in Japan and the United State

Over the past two decades, production in manufacturing industries in both Japan and the United State has fluctuated considerably, with manufacturing employment being naturally affected as a consequence. Figures 2

Atsushi Seike

FIGURE 2
FLUCTUATIONS IN EMPLOYMENT AND PRODUCTION*
(JAPAN)

*Quarterly figures

and 3 show changes in the aggregate indices of production (the solid lines) and employment (the dotted lines) for the manufacturing sectors of Japan and the United States.[1] Both the indices are based on quarterly data, seasonally adjusted, using the Bureau of Census method. The base year taken is 1980 and the period covered lies between the first quarter of 1964 and the fourth quarter of 1984.

It can be seen that, in both countries, the level of manufacturing production has fluctuated substantially. The first sharp increase peaked around the end of 1973, followed by a drastic decline in 1974 and 1975 after the

248

FIGURE 3
FLUCTUATIONS IN EMPLOYMENT AND PRODUCTION*
(UNITED STATES)

Index of employment and production (1980 = 100)

*Quarterly figures

oil crisis, and then a subsequent recovery. The level of employment did respond to fluctuations in production, but, in both countries, employment fluctuations tended to lag behind fluctuations in production and to be less severe. One interesting contrast between the two countries is that the severity of employment adjustment is much less conspicuous in Japanese manufacturing industry than in the United States. In the United States, the timing of increases and decreases in production and employment is similar, and the elasticity of employment with respect to production is high. In Japan, there is a fairly long lag between any given production fluctuation and the

249

Atsushi Seike

employment fluctuation associated with it; the corresponding elasticity is quite low.

The cause of the longer lagged response and the smaller employment elasticity in Japan appears to be linked to the greater flexibility in hours worked per worker in Japanese manufacturing industry. Figures 4 and 5 show indices of production and per capita overtime hours worked in the manufacturing sector of each country between January 1973 and December 1983. Both indices are, as before, seasonally adjusted monthly data with

FIGURE 4
FLUCTUATIONS IN OVERTIME HOURS AND PRODUCTION
(JAPAN)

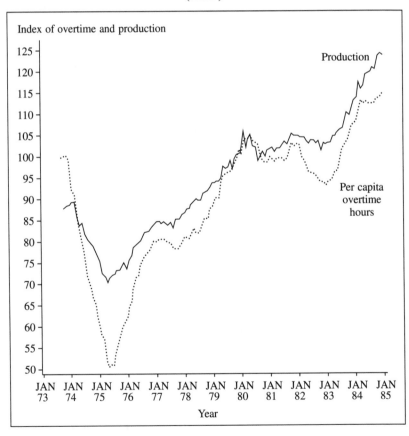

1980 as the base year. It can be seen in figure 4 that overtime hours in Japan were very sensitive to movements in production, but figure 5 shows that this was not so in the United States.

2. The Costs of Employment Adjustment

Given that a technological relationship exists between production and employment, the level of production will determine the optimal level of

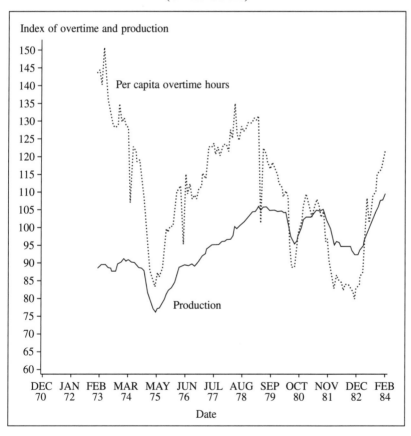

FIGURE 5
FLUCTUATIONS IN OVERTIME HOURS AND PRODUCTION
(UNITED STATES)

Atsushi Seike

employment. Employment adjustment can be regarded as the process by which a firm strives to adjust its employment toward this optimal level. But, because of "frictional" problems, employment adjustment cannot be carried out immediately, and hence the lags noted above.

Although there are many factors that contribute to the total cost of employment adjustment, it is convenient to discuss them under four headings.[2] First, whether explicit or not, long-term employment contracts often prohibit employers who reduce output from dismissing their employees immediately. On the other hand, long-term contracts also make employers cautious and therefore hesitant about recruiting new workers, even when production increases, because they want to minimize the costs of hoarding surplus labor in the future (i.e., costs of long-term contracts). Second, in cases where some necessary skills can be acquired only within a firm, employers will have invested in "firm-specific" human capital for their current employees and thus stand to lose some of the return on these investments if they dismiss these employees before the payback period for this human capital is complete. In these cases, it is also difficult to recruit human resources from outside the firm even when production is increased (i.e., costs of firm-specific human capital).

Third, employment adjustment also involves transaction costs that must be incurred when recruiting and dismissing employees and implementing the organizational reforms that often accompany this process (i.e., transaction costs). Fourth, frequent employment adjustments tend to engender worse labor-management relations and to lower the morale of workers. This may result not only in lower productivity but also in restrictions of a firm's business activities and recruiting power because of its lower image in the community (i.e., costs of morale and reputation).

Differences in the employment adjustment patterns between Japan and the United States may reflect differences in these various employment adjustment costs. Although it is hard to observe these costs directly, they can be estimated by observing the magnitude of the "frictions" in employment adjustment that result from their presence. In order to do this, I have estimated an econometric model in which these frictions can be observed.

III. An Econometric Analysis of Employment Adjustment

1. The Model

The econometric analysis of employment adjustment in Japanese and U.S. manufacturing industries that is presented in this section is based on the short-run labor demand model developed by Fair (1969). The model has the form

$$\ln M_t - \ln M_t^d = v(\ln M_{t-1} - \ln M_{t-1}^d) + \sum_{i=0}^{n} bi(\ln X_{t+i} - \ln X_{t+i-1}^e)$$

$$+ \sum_{j=1}^{m} cj(\ln X_{t-j} - \ln X_{t-j-1}), \qquad (1)$$

where M_t is the actual employment level; M_t^d is the optimal employment level; X_{t+i}^e is the expected output level; the subscript t denotes the month to which a variable pertains; and v, b, and c are parameters.

The optimal employment, M_t^d, is obtained by dividing nonidle man-hours necessary to output, $M_t^* \cdot H_t^*$, by the cost-minimizing hours of work per worker H_t^d. That is,

$$M_t^d = M_t^* \cdot \frac{H_t^*}{H_t^d}. \qquad (2)$$

The variable denoting nonidle man-hours necessary for a given output is derived from a putty-clay production function as

$$X_t = \alpha_t M_t^* \cdot H_t^*. \qquad (3)$$

Estimating the parameter, α_t, of the production function by the interpolation method, $M_t^* H_t^*$ is obtained as

$$M_t^* \cdot H_t^* = \frac{X_t}{\hat{\alpha}_t} \qquad (4)$$

where $\hat{\alpha}_t$ is the estimated parameter of the production function by the interpolation method. The cost minimizing number of hours per worker is assumed to be proportional to standard hours of work, HS_t. That is,

$$H_t^d = \beta HS_t. \qquad (5)$$

By putting equations (4) and (5) into equation (2), the optimal level of employment can be determined. The expected output, X_{t+i}^e, is estimated under the assumption of adaptive expectations as

$$\ln X_{t+i}^e = \ln X_{t+i-12} + \lambda_i(\ln X_{t-1} - \ln X_{t-13}). \qquad (6)$$

This short-run labor demand function shows that the employment adjustment of a firm over a certain period, namely from month $t-1$ to month t, depends on the amount of excess labor at hand (the first term on the right-hand side of eq. [1]), expected future output fluctuations forecast in month $t - 1$ (the second term on the right-hand side of eq. [1]), and output fluctuations in the past period, where the last factor is regarded as a proxy for excess labor in the past (the third term on the right-hand side of eq. [1]). The restrictions on the signs of the parameters in equation (1) are as follows. First, the parameter v, of the excess labor term, must be negative because, ceteris paribus, if a firm has positive excess labor (a labor surplus) it would try to reduce its work force and, if it had negative excess labor (a labor shortage) it would try to recruit new employees. Second, the parameter b must be positive because, ceteris paribus, a firm would try to increase employment if it expected its output might increase in the future. Finally, the parameter c must also be positive since a positive change in output in the past means there was negative excess labor and vice versa.

The parameter v, of equation (1), generally has an absolute value of less than unity because adjustment costs prevent a firm from being able to clear all of its excess labor immediately; rather it can only clear $100 \cdot V$ percent of it. Thus adjustment costs can be represented by the absolute value of the parameter v, which will be referred to as an employment adjustment ratio.

2. Data

In order to control the technological relations between output and employment, the manufacturing industry is broken down to the two-digit level for estimation. The subindustries can be seen below Figure 6.

For employment levels and the number of hours worked, data pertaining to Japanese manufacturing industries have been taken from the *Maigetsu Kinro Tokei* (*Monthly Employment and Earnings Survey*) published by the Japanese Ministry of Labor and data pertaining to U.S. manufacturing industries have been obtained from the employment and earnings statistics published by the U.S. Department of Labor. For indices of manufacturing output, data pertaining to Japanese manufacturing industries originate from the *Tsusan Tokei* (*The Industrial Statistic Monthly*) published by the Japanese Ministry of International Trade and Industry, and data pertaining to U.S. manufacturing industries from the industrial production statistics published by the U.S. Federal Reserve Board.

3. Empirical Results

Figure 6 and 7 show the employment adjustment ratios (i.e., v), for Japanese and U.S. manufacturing industries, for the periods 1969–1979

254

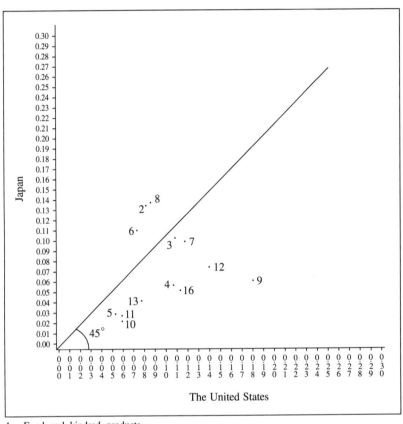

FIGURE 6
COMPARISON OF EMPLOYMENT ADJUSTMENT RATIOS
BETWEEN JAPAN AND THE UNITED STATES (1969–1979)

1. Food and kindred products.
2. Textile mill products.
3. Lumber and wood products.
4. Paper and allied products.
5. Chemicals and allied products.
6. Petroleum and coal products.
7. Rubber and misc. plastic products.
8. Leather and leather products.
9. Stone, clay and glass products.
10. Steel industries.
11. Nonferrous metal industries
    (in the U.S: 10–11. Primary metal industries).
12. Fabricated metal products.
13. Machinery, except electrical.
14. Electric and electronic equipment.
15. Transportation equipment.
16. Instruments and related products.

Atsushi Seike

and 1974–1979, respectively.[3] In both figures, the vertical axes represent the employment ratios of Japanese industries, and the horizontal axes represent those of the United States. In figures 6 and 7 only those industries for which a significantly negative estimate of v existed for both Japan and the United States were plotted.

Since the employment adjustment ratio indicates the proportion of excess labor on hand that can be eliminated, it can be said that a larger employment adjustment ratio corresponds to smoother employment adjustment,

FIGURE 7

COMPARISON OF EMPLOYMENT ADJUSTMENT RATIOS
BETWEEN JAPAN AND THE UNITED STATES (1974–1979)

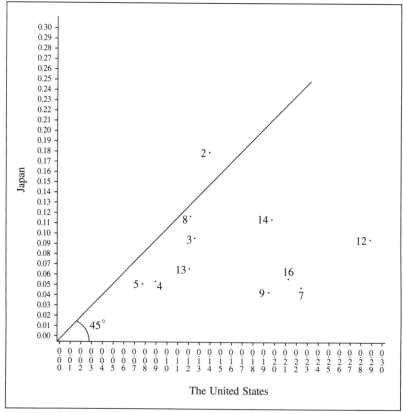

Note: Figures indicate the same industries as in Figure 6.

256

or, in other words, a larger ratio corresponds to a smaller cost of employment adjustment for the firm.

Before comparing the employment adjustment ratios of Japan and the United States, let us look briefly at the technologically determined relationship between these ratios and some industry types. Figures 6 and 7 indicate that those industries with larger employment adjustment ratios tend to be light, labor-intensive industries, and those with smaller employment adjustment ratios tend to be heavy, capital-intensive industries. Most machinery industries tend to lie between these two types. This pattern suggests that there may be a systematic relationship between employment, adjustment costs, and the type of industry.

The influence of the cost of long-term contracts may be larger in heavy industries that have a larger average firm size and a larger proportion of regular male workers. Firm-specific human capital investments may also be of greater importance in heavy industries than in light industries.

Since the vertical axes of figures 6 and 7 represent employment adjustment costs of Japanese manufacturing industries, and the horizontal axes represent those of the United States, the industries for which the plot lies below the 45° line are those for which the employment adjustment ratio is smaller in Japan than in the United States. Figure 6 suggests that, for most manufacturing industries (except textile mill products [#2], petroleum and coal [#6] and leather and leather products [#8]), the employment adjustment ratios of Japan were smaller than those of the United States throughout the 1970s. Figure 7 shows that this tendency became much more conspicuous in the period just after the oil crisis, when manufacturing firms in both countries had to reduce their workforce. The employment adjustment ratios of all manufacturing industries, except textile mill products, were smaller in Japan than in the United States. Thus, for each of these industries in this period, the proportion of excess labor that was eliminated in an average month in Japan was smaller than in the United States. This suggests that employment adjustment was more costly for Japanese firms.

The costs of long-term contracts and in-house firm-specific human capital investments seem to be larger for Japanese firms. Looked at in terms of its impact on the cost of long-term contracts, the lack of a lay-off system in Japan seems to increase the cost of employment adjustment for Japanese firms. This is consistent with the fact that the employment adjustment ratios in Japanese manufacturing industries were much smaller after the oil crisis period, when employment in the manufacturing industries of both countries was reduced.

IV. Efficient Resource Reallocation and Employment Adjustment Measures

1. Resource Reallocation and the Pattern of Employment Adjustment

The discussion above has shown that employment adjustment costs for Japanese manufacturing firms are relatively large and the pattern of employment adjustment in Japan is characterized by a long response lag and low elasticity with respect to production fluctuations. In contrast, the pattern of employment adjustment in manufacturing industries of the United States shows that employment responds to production fluctuations much more quickly and with a higher elasticity. This observation seems to imply that human resources are reallocated more efficiently in the United States than in Japan. Despite this fact, it is not so easy to decide which country's pattern is more efficient because the overall efficiency of employment adjustment depends not only on the speed and magnitude of adjustment, but also on the method used.

In view of this, a field survey was conducted to investigate the methods of employment adjustment that are used by selected manufacturing industries in Japan and the United States (Shimada, Orr, and Seike 1985). In terms of resource reallocation, some interesting differences in the employment adjustment practices of Japan and the United States were observed in the survey.

Japanese employment adjustment practices have been characterized by the following features, which differ from U.S. practices particularly in terms of resource reallocation.[4] Japanese firms transfer their workers within a plant, between plants, and even between companies in order to make the most efficient use of the existing workforce. This practice is especially utilized in the process of employment adjustment. Firms also attempt to maintain employees on the payroll as long as possible, even though they may be temporarily idle, and then retrain them so that they develop skills appropriate to other jobs. In order to make this process as smooth as possible, firms constantly strive, by utilizing formal and informal communication channels, to promote communication and information sharing between labor and management on current and future business conditions, including strategies for the restructuring of corporate activities. In contrast, employment adjustment practices in the United States are characterized by quick and large-scale shifts of capital resources involving shutting down unprofitable plants, building new plants, and acquiring new firms. In this process, firms rely heavily on quick, massive layoffs in conjunction with plant closures and also on the recruitment of new workers when opening new plants in new locations. In this situation, there seems limited communication and information sharing between labor and management.

It may be true that resource reallocation takes relatively longer in Japan because it requires a lot of retraining, restructuring of organizations, and extensive sharing of information across relevant members of the firm. This sluggish process appears on the surface to be a deterrent to resource reallocation. However, this process minimizes frictions that arise from abrupt actions such as massive layoffs or plant shutdowns, and the unemployment resulting from transferring human resources from declining sectors to growing sectors. In the United States, resource reallocation by means of massive layoffs and plant shutdowns, on the one hand, and the opening of new plants and large-scale recruitment, on the other, may indeed facilitate quick shifts of resources across different regions or industries. However, such shifts may involve large costs in terms of unemployed labor resources and high transaction costs of recruiting and training new labor forces.

Although the employment adjustment pattern of each country has both merits and demerits, it seems that the Japanese method is more efficient in the sense that it tends to minimize the resources made idle in the process of adjustment. Its advantage is more pronounced the greater are the frictional costs associated with the reallocation of resources. This point will be considered more extensively in the following sections.

2. The Employment Adjustment Measures of Japan and the United States

The most important measure that has been introduced by the Japanese government to support employment adjustment is the Employment Adjustment Subsidy (hereafter called EAS), which was put into effect in 1975. Under this measure, eligible employers whose industry is experiencing a recession are entitled to receive subsidies equal to half (for large firms with more than three hundred employees) or two thirds (for medium- and small-sized firms with less than three hundred employees) of the wages paid to idle workers who are participating in intrafirm training programs or who are on temporary leave. This subsidy is paid out from the Employment Stabilization Fund, which is funded by the contributions of employers (0.35% of their wage bill).

The Employment Creation Subsidy for Designated Structurally Depressed Industries (hereafter called ECS-DI) and the Employment Creation Subsidy for Designated Structurally Depressed Areas (hereafter called ECS-DA) were also established, in 1978 and 1979, respectively, as links in the

259

Atsushi Seike

chains of ad-hoc measures for job leavers in selected depressed industries and areas. Employers who are able to recruit job leavers from these designated industries or areas as regular employees through Public Employment Service Offices, are entitled to receive subsidies. These subsidies amount to half the wages paid to recruits taken on by large firms, or two thirds of the wages paid by medium- and small-sized firms.

In the United States, the most important special measure for assisting employment adjustment is Trade Adjustment Assistance (hereafter called TAA) established by the Trade Act of 1974. The TAA provides special assistance for workers who are laid off as a result of increases in imports penetration. Under this measure, eligible workers are entitled to receive monetary compensation in addition to the unemployment benefit, and to receive other support such as retraining assistance, job search assistance, and relocation assistance.

3. The Performance and Evaluation of Employment Adjustment Measures in Japan and the United States

Japanese expenditures on employment adjustment measures are listed in table 1. The most obvious feature of the data is that, in the employment

TABLE 1
EXPENDITURES ON EMPLOYMENT ADJUSTMENT MEASURES IN JAPAN
(IN MILLION YEN)

Year	EAS (Training subsidies)	ECS-DI	ECS-DA
1975	55,220	—	
1976	5,430	—	
1977	3,290		
	(131)		
1978	6,800	200	
	(2,505)		
1979	2,430	270	60
	(1,263)		
1980	2,750	230	150
	(282)		
1981	9,330	190	90
	(623)		
1982	9,890		20
	(2,040)		

Source: Data compiled by the Employment Policy Division, the Ministry of Labor.

260

adjustment period due to the first and the second oil crisis, the EAS was utilized much more than the ECS-DI or the ECS-DA. The main reason for this may be that the EAS is well suited to the job of complementing employment adjustment practices that are used by Japanese manufacturing firm. Japanese manufacturing employers tried to confine the reduction of their labor force to that which could be achieved by natural attrition and the slowing down or stopping of recruitment. They attached a high priority to avoiding layoffs, even if it meant maintaining idle employees for a while. Employees who had been made idle were reassigned to very different workshops within their firms in order to minimize the costs of this policy. In a large shipbuilding firm that we surveyed, hundreds of redundant workers who had been severely affected by the oil crisis were transferred to a machinery factory that was not lined to shipbuilding and had reasonable prospects for growth. Some shipyard workers were even transferred, as automobile salesmen, to a motor company that was connected to the shipbuilding firm. Considerable intrafirm retraining was needed to execute these transfers. Some other firms attempted to diversify or change their business activities, maintaining idle workers while initiating various intrafirm retraining programs. It seems that the EAS, and its training subsidies in particular, facilitated these adjustments and was fairly effective in minimizing unemployment and promoting the efficient reallocation of human resources through internal labor markets adjustments.

Of course, it would have been impossible to implement such an intrafirm reallocation of human resources if there had been no scope for idle workers to be shifted within the firm or the corporate group. It is thus not surprising to find that, in medium- and small-sized firms, the employment adjustment was in fact more frictional, with layoffs or dismissals used more often. The process of internal reallocation is easier in the deep and extensive internal labor markets of large firms who often have both declining and growing sectors in their portfolio of business activities. Therefore, it is probably safe to say that the EAS is effective mainly when this type of firm is involved. The fact that human resources are most efficiently reallocated through internal labor markets means that reallocation by the process of firing and rehiring in the external labor market is relatively inefficient in Japan since it is hard to find adequate new jobs for job leavers who have departed from under the umbrella of an internal labor market. This may be one reason for the low utilization of the ECS-DI and the EXS-DA.

Table 2 lists expenditures on TAA in the United States. It can be seen that these expenditures increased in the latter half of the 1970s and reached $1,652 million in 1980. The expenditures are more than ten times greater than the Japanese expenditures on the EAS when calculated at the exchange

261

TABLE 2
EXPENDITURES ON TRADE ADJUSTMENT ASSISTANCE IN
THE UNITED STATES
(IN MILLION DOLLARS)

Year	Weekly payments	Relocation	Job search	Training
1976	69.9	0.05	0.01	0.47
1977	150.8	0.25	0.03	0.84
1978	258.3	0.60	0.16	4.04
1979	258.1	1.17	0.31	6.36
1980	1,644.9	0.61	0.11	6.41

Source: Data compiled by the Office of Trade Adjustment Assistance,
U.S. Department of Labor.

rates that prevailed in those years. Another interesting point emerges from the items of expenditure in the table. The expenditures are disproportionately concentrated in weekly payments (i.e., income maintenance) because the TAA was designed not to prevent unemployment but to support workers who were made unemployed by industries that were adversely affected by increasing imports. On the other hand, since most workers who were eligible for TAA were dismissed from firms in industries such as automobiles and steel, whose wage level was far higher than the average, the TAA benefit (about 70% of their former wages) was even higher than the wage they could make in the alternative job opportunities open to them. Thus there was little incentive for them to move to other industries or areas while they could receive the benefit. Nonetheless it must be acknowledged that it was difficult for them to find new jobs because, in most cases, there were very few job opportunities available to them. In other words, the cost of reallocating labor under this system was so high that the measures taken to promote reallocation were simply insufficient to help much. This suggests that, even in the United States where the system of reallocating labor through the external labor market seemed to be much better developed than in Japan, using external labor markets to reallocate labor in response to structural changes is very costly.

Notes

1. For figures describing the pattern of employment adjustment in particular industries, see Shimada, Orr, and Seike (1985).
2. For a detailed discussion of factors affecting the costs of employment adjustment, see Fair (1969) or Soligo (1966).
3. For references to other empirical studies of employment in Japan, see Muramatsu (1981), Shinotsuka and Ishihara (1977), and Yamamoto (1982).
4. For detailed discussions of employment adjustment practices in selected industries in Japan and the United States, see Shimada, Orr, and Seike (1985).

References

Fair, Ray C. (1969). *The Short-Run Demand for Workers and Hours*, New York, London, Amsterdam: North-Holland.

Muramatsu, Kuramitsu (1981). "Determinants of Employment Adjustment- Comparison between Japanese and U.S. Manufacturing Industries," *Monthly Journal of The Japan Institute of Labor*, vol. 23, no. 1 (January) (in Japanese).

Shimada, Haruo, James Orr, and Atsushi Seike (1985). *U.S.-Japan Comparative Study of Employment Adjustment*, Washington D.C. and Tokyo: U.S. Department of Labor and Japanese Ministry of Labor.

Shinotsuka, Eiko, and Mieko Ishihara (1977). "Employment Adjustment after the Oil Crisis," *Japan Economic Study*, no. 6 (August) (in Japanese).

Soligo, Ronald (1966). "The Short-Run Relationship between Employment and Output," *Yale Economic Essays*, vol. 6, no. 1 (Spring).

Yamamoto, Taku (1982). "Empirical Analysis of Employment Adjustment in Terms of Workers Employed and Hours Worked," *Mita Journal of Economics*, vol. 75, no. 1 (February) (in Japanese).

Index

Index

—Japan, 33, 42, 92; and "lifetime employment," 240; oil crisis and, 34, 102, 192; and unemployment rates, 245–47; and wage flexibility, 103, 107, 109–11, 112–13, 115, 124
—United States, 131–32, 133; and unemployment rates, 245–47
Economic recessions: management responses to, 27; and unemployment rates, 12, 38; United States, 135
—Japan, 33; and employment adjustment, 89, 94, 113; and wages, 49, 94, 100n.9, 102–3
Education levels, 90, 92
Elderly workers, 35, 38–39, 41
Electric power industry, Japan, 50, 54, 55, 57
Employee buyouts, 207, 211
Employee Relations Act (West Germany), 178
Employers (companies): advance notice of layoffs, 205; and employment adjustment, 22, 197, 199, 202, 216, 223, 224, 225, 228–29, 231, 252; and employment security, 22, 151–53, 154, 155-56, 159, 201, 202; and labor costs, 11, 29; and labor flexibility, 14, 24, 26, 166; West Germany, 161, 176
—Japan: in collective bargaining, 46, 47, 53; diversification, 27–29; employment adjustment premiums, 39, 259, 260; and employment relationship, 79–80, 105, 106; and employment security, 33, 186; handicapped employment, 39; restrictions on dismissal of employees, 21, 183–85, 186–94; and retirement age, 41; segmentation, 65–67; unemployment taxes, 99-100n.7; and wages, 49, 53, 59, 105, 106, 119–20, 122
—United States: and employment adjustment, 133, 210, 233; and employment relationship, 129, 130; and employment security, 19, 128, 134, 139–40, 145, 146, 208; and labor costs, 135, 139; and plant closure, 143; right to hire

replacement workers, 147n.9; right to terminate employment, 129, 130, 200, 220
Employment Act (U.S., 1946), 142
Employment adjustment, 218–20; distancing, 222, 234; and employment security, 162–72, 196–98, 151–52; flexible retirement, 229–31; functional flexibility, 166–72, 222, 233–34; government nonintervention, 198; government policies, 235–38; hours of work, 226–28; in labor flexibility, 13, 16; media attention, 198–99; numerical flexibility, 163–66, 169, 222–25, 226–33; output changes and, 20; part-time and temporary work, 231-33; redundancy payments, 238; segmentation, 234–35; statistical analysis, 14, 15; temporary layoffs, 228–29; unions and, 198
—containment measures, 21–22, 201; community action plans, 207, 211–12; compensation programs, 207, 212; early retirement, 29, 207, 210–11; employee buyouts, 207, 211; job search assistance, 207, 208–10, 238
—defensive strategies, 21, 201; advance notice, 202, 205–6, 237; buffering, 202–3; redeployment and retraining, 202, 204–5, 238; unemployment insurance, 203–4, 206–7, 238; work sharing, 202, 203–4
—Europe, 220, 221–22, 238, 239; government involvement, 22, 198, 200, 201, 203, 208, 211–12, 237; management and, 27, 205; training, 214, 233–34; working hours, 226–28
—Japan, 20, 22, 96, 167, 220, 221; costs of adjustment, 251–52; econometric analysis, 252–57; economic growth and unemployment, 245–47; government policies, 39, 200, 215–17, 259–61; layoffs, 29, 33, 92, 96, 155–56, 239; manufacturing employment and output, 247–51; resource reallocation, 258–59; segmentation of labor, 24;

Index

Employment adjustment (cont.)
unemployment prevention, 23, 26,
225, 239, 240; wage flexibility and,
18, 79, 96, 104; working hours, 164,
166, 250–51
—positive adjustment, 21–22, 201,
212–13; government policies, 213;
job replacement, 213, 214–15;
retraining, 213–14
—United States, 18, 20, 22, 79, 196, 220,
240; advance notice, 143–44, 155,
205; automobile industry, 163–64;
collective bargaining, 171; costs of
adjustment, 251–52; econometric
analysis, 252–57; economic growth
and unemployment, 245–47;
government policies, 22, 26, 200,
215–17, 260, 261–62; layoffs, 21,
23, 27, 96, 222, 239; manufacturing
employment and output, 23, 247–51;
resource reallocation, 258–59;
vocational training, 200, 201
—West Germany: automobile industry,
163–64; employment protection
and, 172; short-time work, 166;
vocational training, 158–59, 173–74,
175, 200–201
Employment Adjustment Subsidy (EAS,
Japan), 259, 260–62
Employment conditions, 158
Employment Creation Subsidy for
Designated Structurally Depressed
Areas (ECS-DA, Japan), 259–61
Employment Creation Subsidy for
Designated Structurally Depressed
Industries (ECS-DI, Japan), 259–61
Employment Insurance Law (Japan, 1975),
39, 92
Employment levels: labor market flexibility
and, 13; stability, 12, 14–15, 16,
20, 23. See also Employment
adjustment; Employment security
—Japan: economic growth and, 33–34;
elderly workers, 35–39, 41;
government policy, 35–38;
manufacturing, 247–48, 249–50,
251–52; oil crisis and, 102;
productivity and, 87, 88, 92–94;
stability, 33, 79, 96, 102–3, 107,

111–12; wage flexibility and, 46,
111–12; wages and GNP and,
103–5, 109–13, 115, 124; women,
41–42
—United States: fluctuation, 79, 94, 96,
107; import restraints and, 131;
manufacturing, 247–48, 249–50,
251–52; productivity and, 87, 88, 89
Employment Measures Law (Japan, 1965),
35
Employment Opportunities Review System
(EORS), 137
Employment Promotion Act (West
Germany, 1985), 177–78
Employment relationship, 166; Japan,
79–80, 105, 106; United States, 19,
78, 129, 130, 131, 146n.2
Employment security, 13–14, 29, 150–51;
employment adjustment and,
162–72, 196–97, 202–3, 222–25;
exchange strategies, 159–62,
179–80; government policies, 22;
job demarcation and jurisdiction,
153, 154; labor flexibility and,
15; labor mobility and, 157–59,
179, 180; labor segmentation
and, 20, 172, 174–76; labor
substitutability restrictions, 152–57,
179; layoff protection, 155–57, 180;
management policies, 151–52, 199,
201; seniority systems, 153–54,
159; unemployment effects, 172–73;
unions and, 150; vocational training
and, 157–59, 173–74, 200–201
—Europe, 150, 156–57, 222–23, 239–40;
government involvement, 22, 198,
200, 201, 203, 208; legislation, 20,
155
—Japan, 33, 46–47, 240; abusive exercise
of dismissal rights, 190–94;
contracts, 21, 183, 186–87, 252;
labor segmentation and, 175;
legislation, 17, 20, 155, 187–88,
191–92; management policies, 27,
41; restrictions on dismissal rights,
20–21, 155–56, 183–90; Supreme
Court cases, 184–85, 189, 193–94;
unions and, 175, 186–87; working
hours and, 166

268

Index

Governments (cont.)
227–28; employment security
policies, 22, 200, 201, 203; labor
market intervention, 26, 198;
unemployment insurance, 203–4
—Japan: employment adjustment policies,
259–60; employment security
policies, 186; labor market
intervention, 26
—United States: employment security
policies, 20, 22, 127, 128, 142–45,
146, 200; labor market intervention,
130–31, 198, 216; unemployment
assistance, 26, 212
Grais, B., 228
Great Depression, 132
Greece, 228
Gross national product (GNP), 103–5, 109,
112, 113–15, 124
Grubb, Dennis, 45
Gutchess, Jocelyn F., 21–22, 26, 29

Hahn, F. H., 15
Hall, R. H., 104
Hall, Robert E., 97
Hanami, Tadashi, 80
Handicapped, employment of, 34, 39
Handicapped Person's Employment
Promotion Law (Japan), 39
Hansen, Gary B., 229
Harrison, Bennet, 237
Hart, Robert, 16, 80
Hashimoto, Masanori, 18, 24, 45, 46, 49,
50, 62, 71–72n.9, 78, 80, 81, 96, 97,
107
Hewlett-Packard Company, 19, 27, 140
Home work, 234
Hours of work, 218; Europe, 226–28;
Japan, 23, 84, 87, 88, 94, 113, 166,
250; United States, 84, 87, 88–89,
163, 164; West Germany, 163, 164,
228
Human capital investment, 82, 94; bonus
payments and, 18, 49, 80; and
employment adjustment, 23, 26,
252, 257; transaction costs and, 18,
79, 96; wage flexibility and, 80–81,
90

Individualism, 129
Industrialization, 34, 197, 218
Industrialized countries, 12–14, 113, 119,
197, 198, 219
Industrial relations, 16, 196; Japan, 53–54,
59, 78, 79–80, 106, 160; United
States, 78, 171; West Germany, 161,
175
Industrial revolution, 218
Inflation: Japan, 21, 45, 56, 188, 189;
United States, 142; and wage
rigidity, 62–63
Information networks, 29
Information technology, 12, 39
Inoue, S., 48
Integrated circuits, 40
Interest rates, 63
International Business Machines
Corporation (IBM), 19, 27, 140–41,
202–3, 220
International Labor Organization, 16;
Convention No. 89, 227
Investment, 33, 35, 53, 81–82, 107
Ireland, 230, 233
Ishida, H., 48
Ishikawajima Harima Industries, 29
Italian Earnings Supplement Fund, 229
Italy: employment adjustment in, 20, 164,
167, 237; employment security
regulations, 156–57; overtime work
in, 228; profits in, 63; retirement
age, 230; seniority rights, 154

Jackman, Rilchard, 45
Japan: Basic Employment Measure Plan,
35, 39; Basic Training Plan, 38;
diversification, 27–29; economic
growth, 33, 34–35, 42, 92, 102,
103, 107, 109–11, 112–13, 115,
245–47; economic recessions, 102-3,
113; employment relationship,
79–80, 105, 106; "hollowing" of
production, 41; human capital
investment, 18, 23, 79, 80–82, 90,
94, 96; "Income Doubling Plan,"
33; industrial relations, 16, 53–54,
59, 78, 79–80, 106; job training,
174; labor contracts, 87, 96–97;

270

Index

Job demarcation, 26, 27, 153, 154, 156, 233
Job maintenance, 236–37
Job Opportunity Bank Security Program, 136–37
Job search assistance, 207, 208–10, 238
Job sharing, 202, 203–4, 231
Job Training and Partnership Act (U.S., 1982), 144–45

Kahn, G. A., 45, 107
Katz, Harry C., 171
Keynes, John Maynard, 15–16
Kobrin, C., 16
Kochan, Thomas A., 171
Kochi Hoso (Broadcasting) Company Case (Japan, 1977), 184–85
Koike, Kazuo, 27, 48
Korean War, 33
Koshiro Kazutoshi, 17, 24, 48, 89, 104, 166, 175
Kyushu, Japan, 48

Labor costs, 11; Japan, 12; job protection and, 223–24; part-time work and, 231; Sweden, 158; United States, 131, 135, 136; West Germany, 175–76, 177
Labor demand, 100n.9, 115–17, 158, 252–54
Labor-force participation rates, 109
Labor legislation: employment protection, 20, 155, 225; Japan, 17, 20–21, 34, 36, 187–88; United States, 20, 142, 143–44, 155, 220; West Germany, 176–78
Labor market information, 208
Labor markets, 16, 22; convergence toward Japanese model, 15, 27, 29; cost control and, 11; economic conditions and, 20; employment security and, 19, 20, 150, 151, 172; government policies and, 26; international competition and, 13; mobility and, 157–58; privatization and, 13; technology and, 12; United Kingdom, 26; West Germany, 176–79

—flexibility, 11–12, 13–14, 15, 16, 23, 29, 180; functional, 14, 24, 26, 166–72, 222, 233–34; Japan, 15, 24, 30, 45–46, 221, 233; numerical, 14, 24, 163–66, 169, 222–25, 226–33; unions and, 198; United States, 18, 45, 80, 96, 233; West Germany, 176–79, 228. *See also* Wage flexibility
—Japan, 23, 26, 38–39, 40–42, 79, 83–84, 96, 103, 107, 113–15, 221; duality in, 48, 105–6; oil crisis and, 102; transaction costs and, 80; and wage changes, 119, 124
—segmentation, 20, 24–26, 27, 172, 174, 224, 234–35; Japan, 46, 65–67, 105, 175, 176; United States, 19, 24, 175; West Germany, 175–76
—United States, 79, 83–84, 96, 220; government nonintervention, 130–31, 142, 144, 200; mobility and, 132; transaction costs and, 80
Labor shortages, 48
Labor Standards Law (Japan), 183, 184, 186, 188, 191–92
Labor unions: and employment security, 150, 153, 154, 226; and labor flexibility, 15; public sector, 13, 71n.4; redeployment and retraining schemes, 204; unemployment rates and, 12; unionization densities, 198
—Japan, 50; discharge clauses, 183–84, 186–87; and economic growth, 33; and employment security, 39, 41, 175; unionization density, 48, 65, 71n.4; and wage flexibility, 120; wage negotiations, 35, 38, 46, 47, 55, 59, 69, 106, 113
—United States: and employment adjustment, 208, 213; and employment guarantees, 19, 145; and employment security, 132–33, 134, 135–36, 160, 171, 175, 216, 220; and plant closure, 138, 143, 205; seniority systems, 138–39, 145, 171, 203; unionization density, 147n.7, 198; wage concessions, 19, 135–36, 160
Layard, Richard, 45

272

Index

Organization (cont.)
47, 49, 63, 167, 173, 219, 222,
230, 231, 239; and labor market
flexibility, 45, 49, 62, 63; surveys,
24, 99n.5; and training programs,
238
Orr, J. A., 239, 258
Otis Elevator Company, 134
Overtime work: and employment
adjustment, 202, 203, 221, 228;
Japan, 67, 166, 221, 250, 251;
United States, 140, 203, 251

Panel Study of Income Dynamics (PSID),
95, 97–98
Part-time work: Japan, 24, 190, 192–93;
numerical flexibility, 14, 227, 231;
United States, 19–20, 88–89, 141;
West Germany, 177, 178
Pensions, 210–11, 229
Perlman, Selig, 132
Petroleum industry, 257
Phelps Dodge, 147n.9
Pilkington Glass, Ltd., 201
Piore, Michael J., 171, 175, 235
Placement services, 157, 208
Plant closure: advance notice, 20, 138,
143–44, 149n.38, 205, 237;
containment strategies, 207, 209,
211–12; Japan, 33, 160; United
States, 19, 138, 220, 239, 258–59
Politicians, 199
Private property, 129–30
Private sector: and employment adjustment,
198, 203, 205, 213, 216; and
employment security, 127, 201
Privatization, 13, 71n.4
Production technology, 12
Production workers, 90–92, 94
Productivity, labor, 11; employment
security and, 199; employment
sensitivity, 87, 88; Japan, 68, 69,
70, 78; technology and, 169; United
States, 78; wage sensitivity, 24,
63–64, 117
Profits, Japan: and bonus wages, 17, 19, 47,
49, 50, 53–56, 59–62, 69, 74nn.22
and 23, 119, 120; "ordinary,"

73n.12; and regular wages, 56, 57,
69; and wage flexibility, 17, 46, 50;
wage rigidity and profit squeeze,
63–65, 67–68, 70, 71n.1
Profit sharing, 49, 50, 80, 106, 136
Property rights, 19, 26–27, 129–30
Protectionist legislation, 180
Public Employment Service Offices (Japan),
260
Public policy: employment adjustment,
235–38; Japan, 35–38, 42, 186;
labor mobility, 157; United States,
220. See also Governments; Labor
legislation
Public sector unions, 13, 71n.4

Railway industry, Japan, 50, 54, 57
Raisian, John, 18, 24, 78, 80, 81, 97
Raw materials management, 12
Reagan, Ronald, 212
Recruitment, 221, 225, 252, 258–59
Redeployment, 202, 204
Redundancy payments, 238
Reich, Michael, 175
Relocation assistance, 238
Replacement workers, 147n.9
Republic Airlines, 143
Resource reallocation, 258–59
Retirement: compulsory, 193, 230–31; early
retirement programs, 29, 140, 141,
207, 210–11, 230, 231, 238; flexible,
229–31; Japan, 38, 39, 41, 193, 221
Rhône-Poulenc, 201, 209–10
Richardson, S., 104
Robotics, 12, 38, 42
Rosenberg, Sam, 175
Rotemberg, Julio J., 45

Sabel, Charles F., 171
Sachs, Jeffrey D., 45, 46, 47, 63, 68, 71n.1,
107
Sano, Yoko, 48, 54
Sarfati, H., 16
Scientific management, 171
Seasonal workers, 192
Seike, Atsushi, 23, 24, 26, 239, 258
Self-employment, 222, 224

274

Index